Themes and Issues in Hinduism

WORLD RELIGIONS: THEMES AND ISSUES

Written for students of comparative religion and the general reader, and drawing on the chapters originally edited by Jean Holm and John Bowker in the *Themes in Religious Studies* series, the volumes in *World Religions: Themes and Issues* explore core themes from the perspective of the particular religious tradition under study.

Already published:

Themes and Issues in Christianity

Other volumes in preparation:

Themes and Issues in Buddhism
Themes and Issues in Judaism

Themes and Issues in Hinduism

Edited by

Paul Bowen

CASSELL

London and Washington

Cassell
Wellington House, 125 Strand, London WC2R 0BB, England
PO Box 605, Herndon, VA 20172, USA

First published 1998

British Library Cataloguing in Publication Data
A catalogue record for this book is available from the British Library.

ISBN 0-304-33850-8 hardback
0-304-33851-6 paperback

Library of Congress Cataloging-in-Publication Data
Themes and issues in Hinduism / edited by Paul Bowen.
p. cm.
Includes bibliographical references and index.
ISBN 0-304-33850-8 (hardcover). – ISBN 0-304-33851-6 (pbk.)
1. Hinduism. I. Bowen, Paul.
BL 1210.T49 1997
294.5–dc21 97–15235
CIP

Earlier versions of chapters appeared in the following books in the *Themes in Religious Studies* series, edited by Jean Holm with John Bowker and published 1994 by Pinter Publishers: *Human Nature and Destiny*; *Making Moral Decisions*; *Women in Religion*; *Attitudes to Nature*; *Myth and History*; *Sacred Writings*; *Picturing God*; *Worship*; *Sacred Place*; *Rites of Passage*.

The illustrations on pp. 181–92 are used by permission of the artists and Westhill RE Resource Centre.

Typeset by York House Typographic Ltd
Printed and bound in Great Britain by
Biddles Ltd, Guildford and King's Lynn

Contents

The contributors

Anantanand Rambachan is Professor of Religion and Asian Studies at St Olaf College in Northfield, Minnesota, USA. Dr Rambachan has been working on the interplay between scripture and personal experience as sources of valid knowledge and is the author of *Accomplishing the Accomplished: The Vedas As a Valid Source of Knowledge in Śaṅkara* (University of Hawaii Press, 1991), *The Hindu Vision* (Motilal Banarsidass, 1992) and *The Limits of Scripture: A Critical Study of Vivekananda's Reinterpretation of the Authority of the Vedas* (University of Hawaii Press, 1994). His writing has also appeared in various scholarly journals, including *Philosophy East and West*, *Religion*, *Religious Studies* and *Journal of Dharma*.

Anuradha Roma Choudhury is a librarian working with the South Glamorgan County Library Service and is responsible for its Asian language collection. She is also a part-time tutor with the Department of Continuing Education at the University of Wales, Cardiff. She studied Sanskrit literature at the University of Calcutta, India, and taught in schools for a number of years. She holds the Gitabharati diploma in Indian music from Calcutta and is an accomplished singer. She lectures extensively on topics related to Indian music, customs, family life and Hinduism. She is the author of a book on Indian music called *Bilati-gan-blanga Rabindra-sangeet* (influence of British music on Rabindranath Tagore's songs) written in Bengali and published in Calcutta (1987). She is also one of the contributors to *The Essential Teachings of Hinduism* (ed. Kerry Brown; Rider, 1988). She is actively involved with the multicultural arts and with inter-faith groups.

Gavin D. Flood is a Lecturer in Religious Studies at the University of Wales, Lampeter, where he teaches courses on Hinduism and Sikhism.

His research interests include Śaivism and Hindu Tantra, ritual, the understandings of the self in Indian religions and issues of methodology in the study of religion. He has published articles on Kashmir Śaivism and is the author of *Body and Cosmology in Kashmir Śaivism* (Mellen Research University Press, 1993) and *An Introduction to Hinduism* (Cambridge University Press, 1996).

Jacqueline Suthren Hirst is a Lecturer in Comparative Religion at the University of Manchester, where she teaches Indian religions. Prior to this, she was Senior Lecturer in Religious Studies at Homerton College, Cambridge, training primary and secondary teachers. Dr Hirst's research is in the Vedāntin traditions, specializing in the thought of Śamkara, the famous Advaitin commentator. She is also interested in attitudes to religious education among Hindus in Britain. She has written on Śaṃkara's thought for the *Journal of Indian Philosophy* and for a collection edited by Karel Werner entitled *Love Divine: Studies in Bhakti and Devotional Mysticism* (Curzon Press, 1993). She has also written books and articles for pupils and teachers on teaching about Hindu traditions, including *Growing Up in Hinduism* (Longman, 1990) with Geeta Pandey, and *Sita's Story* (Bayeux Arts, 1997).

Paul Bowen is undertaking doctoral research at Cheltenham and Gloucester College of Higher Education. His research interests include the relationship between religion and gender in (post)modernity, feminist theology and ethics, the religious body and the goddesses of India. He has spoken on issues relating to religion, gender, human rights and the goddesses of India, and is working on a thesis concerning the concept of Goddess in the feminist spirituality movement.

Sharada Sugirtharajah lectures on Hinduism at Westhill College in Birmingham. She has led sessions on topics ranging from Hindu spirituality to women's issues for clergy, nurses, social workers, counsellors and multi-faith groups. She has co-authored the text for a photo learning pack on Hinduism (a resource for primary and secondary religious education) and also contributed articles to journals.

Abbreviations

BSB	*Brahma-sūtra-bhāṣya*
BSBS	*Brahma-sūtra-bhāṣya of Śaṃkara*
ISKCON	International Society for Krishna Consciousness
KT	*Kulārṇava-tantra*
Manu	*Manusmṛti*
MS	*Mīmāṃsā-sūtra*
PH	*Pratyabhijñāhṛdaya*
RV	*Ṛg-veda*
SK	*Spanda-kārikā*
SN	*Spanda-nirṇaya*
SSV	*Śiva-sūtra-vimarśinī*
TA	*Tantrāloka*
TAV	*Tantrāloka-vivaraṇa*
VC	*Vivekacūḍāmaṇi*
VCR	*The Vedantā-sūtras with the Commentary of Rāmānuja*

Introduction: raising the issues

Paul Bowen

It has become customary, in recent years, to begin any enquiry into Hinduism with a consideration of the issue of religious definition and, more specifically, an evaluation of the problem of how to adequately define Hinduism. This trend normally begins with the tracing of the word 'Hindu' to its Persian roots, as a term referring to the people who lived beyond the Indus river (Sanskrit *Sindhu*), before proceeding to focus upon how the term developed, during the nineteenth century, so as to exclude the religious and cultural groups of Muslims, Sikhs, Jains and Christians living in the same geographical area. The remaining population, today representing 80 per cent of nearly 900 million people living in India, is said to constitute both the Hindu people and, perhaps more properly, the people who practise the religion of Hinduism. However, the important question remains, what is Hinduism? Has Hinduism been adequately defined by tracing the term Hindu to the people dwelling in the geographical location of India who are not Muslim, Sikh, Jain etc.? Is Hinduism simply to be understood as the religion of the Hindus? Such a definition assumes a unified religious system but tells us nothing of the content or structure of that system. Can the religious practices and beliefs of the Hindus be satisfactorily defined as a unified system? There is considerable evidence that they cannot.

Raising the issue of definition, with regard to Hinduism, tends to trigger considerable academic disagreement and debate. While it is a relatively uncontentious fact, amongst religionists and Indologists, that the term Hinduism, as the signifier for a unified religious system, is misleading and misplaced, there is no consensus about what exactly it is that Hinduism does encompass. As an umbrella term Hinduism can be shown to encompass a vast array of traditions, beliefs and practices, the breadth and diversity of which make the differences between Christianity, Islam and Judaism appear small by comparison. How, if at all, is one to reconcile these differences? Hinduism has no founder and is neither a prophetic nor a credal faith; it has authoritative texts – such as the Veda and the *Purāṇa*s – but none are exclusively accepted; it has no unifying structure, doctrine or dogma; and furthermore its understanding of the divine/absolute encompasses polytheism, henotheism, monotheism, monism and atheism. Is there an essence to Hinduism that lies beneath this diversity? Are there areas of coherence and convergence that are sufficiently widespread as to be accepted as normative and typical of Hinduism as a whole? This is uncertain; the heterogeneous character of Hinduism is a recurrent source of academic discourse and confusion, and it is with Hinduism, perhaps more so than with any other religion, that the issue of definition is most forcefully thrust upon us. The religionist Heinrich von Stietencron addresses the issue as follows:

> Why is 'Hinduism' so difficult to define? It is because we always try to see it as *one* 'religion'. Our problems would vanish if we took 'Hinduism' to denote a socio-cultural unit or civilization which contains a plurality of distinct religions.[1]

This is a useful point and one that is closely paralleled and supported by E. J. Sharpe's assessment of the word Hinduism:

> Its connection with the land and life of India must be our starting point, but we must on no account use the word as though it indicated one fixed system of religious beliefs and practices.[2]

Both Stietencron and Sharpe make the important point that Hinduism cannot be understood to represent one fixed homogeneous religious system, but both fail to engage fully with the Hindu appropriation of the word Hinduism. Neither Stietencron's notion of Hinduism as a socio-cultural unit, nor Sharpe's comment on the connection with the land and life of India, completely captures the use of the word in contemporary Hindu self-understanding. Although in the nineteenth century the term Hinduism was, in a sense, imposed as a category by Western colonialism, it was later adopted as an instrument of national identity and empowerment. Today Hinduism is constructed by the national consciousness of a shared history, a sense of connection with the land of India, and issues of political, religious and self-identity. Despite the fact that Hinduism may resist a comprehensive definition from the outside, the Hindu appropriation of the word has resulted in the creation and consolidation of a world religion from within. Hinduism is defined by the intersubjective consensus, the mutual acceptance and assent, despite differences, of its individual members. Unfortunately, this does not help the religionist approach Hinduism; the diversity remains.

Studies of Hinduism tend either to descend into gross religio-cultural generalizations, which are often misleading because of their generality, or to be restricted to those specific systems, beliefs and practices that can be understood to exist somewhere within the abstract environment of Hinduism as a whole. Although much of value can be learnt by attempting to work with and define Hinduism in broad terms, such endeavours tend to lack qualitative depth, and when they do not, are truly monumental undertakings. How then can one approach Hinduism? One can focus upon particular traditions and religious systems within Hinduism, which range from the pan-Indian traditions of Vaiṣṇavism, Śaivism and Śākta or Devī worship, at one extreme, to the local village religions at the other; or, alternatively, one can adopt a more thematic approach. The former approach permits many research methodologies and academic disciplines to be brought to bear upon a single thread of religiosity, often resulting in the production of a detailed and qualitatively rich corpus of information. The latter approach, the approach of this book, can, in contrast, encompass and penetrate a diverse range of traditions and systems. A thematic approach to religion can illuminate multiple areas of coherence and difference, both within and between religious traditions and systems; it is, therefore, particularly well suited to the study of a heterogeneous, abstract religion such as Hinduism. If one decides to adopt a thematic approach to the study of religion, the question that next arises is one of selection. Which themes should be focused upon, which themes and issues will prove to be the most illuminating and fertile? Although Hinduism as a 'world religion' is comparatively recent, the origins of Hindu traditions and religious systems are very ancient, going back over 3000 years to the time of the Indus valley civilization (*c.* 2000 BCE). It is likely that the emergence of recurrent and significant themes can be located within that ancient history.

The contemporary, abstract, religio-cultural construct of Hinduism is often conceived as being founded upon the collision and/or unification of two very different cultural entities. Beginning *c.* 1500 BCE, the Indian subcontinent encountered an ongoing migration from the steppes of Asia Minor. Large numbers of nomadic, militaristic tribes, collectively labelled Aryan, began to push into the subcontinent's interior and impose their rule upon the indigenous Dravidian population (and the probable descendants of the Indus valley civilization). It has been argued that over a period spanning many centuries the religio-cultural identities of these two populations became closely entwined and formed the foundations and context of later Hindu society. Although the degree of contribution from each religio-cultural group remains a matter of considerable academic debate, it is almost unanimously agreed that the Aryan invasion did not completely overwhelm or erase the Dravidian identity. There was, rather, a process of interpenetration and assimilation that resulted in the formation of a new religio-cultural order. However, what the Aryan invaders did bring with them was their language, Sanskrit, and it is this language which forms the earliest layer of Hindu revelation and makes accessible some of the religious thought of the past.

The foundational religious texts of Aryan society are collectively referred to as the Veda. The texts comprising the Veda, literally translatable as knowledge, divide into four (the *Ṛg-veda*, *Sāma-veda*, *Yajur-veda* and *Atharva-veda*), can be dated to between 1500 and 1000 BCE and constitute revelation or *śruti* (that which is heard). They are the product of semi-divine sages (*ṛṣi*) and consist primarily of rituals, hymns and the complex sacrificial rites of the Aryan religion. As the religiosity of India developed in the centuries following the Vedas, the Aryan- and Brahman-controlled writing of Sanskrit became the authoritative stamp upon religious texts. *Brāhmaṇa*s, *Upaniṣad*s and *Āraṇyaka*s were followed by the texts of the epic period (300 BCE – 300 CE) and later the *Purāṇa*s (500 CE – 1500 CE). The forms of Hindu religiosity changed dramatically, and diversified immensely, over the space of three millennia but Sanskrit continued to carry both epistemic and ontological weight, perhaps going someway towards justifying its status as the language of eternity (*apauruṣeyatva*). The Veda and Sanskrit appear to be dominant themes in the development of Hinduism. Indeed, the legitimizing authority of the Veda can be understood to be of primary religious importance. The Veda as revelation has been used as a criterion for distinguishing 'orthodox' systems of theology (*āstika darśana*) from heterodox teachings (*nāstika darśana*) such as Buddhism and Jainism (even though these 'orthodox' systems might be as widely divergent with each other as with the *nāstika* systems). Are the primary revelations of the Veda and the religious medium of Sanskrit themes that should be focused upon?

The Veda is a vast body of 'texts' passed through the generations of Brahmans, the highest Hindu caste, by recitation and ritual use. Indeed, the Veda is not a credal system of propositions to be believed, but is above all else a text used in ritual which legitimates brahmanical socio-ritual traditions. Vedic mantras are used to this day in initiation rites, weddings, funerals and for private or personal devotion. As Anuradha Roma Choudhury observes in the present volume (p. 207), the mantra 'should be learnt by ear from the oral chanting of a teacher (*guru*)'. While the meaning of the mantra repetition has been disputed,[3] the repetition of the vedic verses has been an important factor in the transmission of the brahmanical tradition. These ritual traditions can be shown to give an important sense of coherence to Hinduism, although there have been frequent challenges to the Veda and some Hindu traditions have rejected its authority entirely.

Is the Veda and its development through Hindu religious history a theme to be pursued? Are the vedic traditions and the medium of Sanskrit primary themes in the evolution and/or construction of Hinduism? I believe that these are important questions but also questions that can prove distracting and ultimately damaging to the academic study of religion. The search for a singularly privileged theme, issue or aspect of religion can become entangled with various forms of reductionism as well as the methodological search for an epistemologically privileged position, an Archimedean point or an objective view from nowhere. Although these positions are not *a priori* wrong, they are open to a variety of cogent and well developed critiques and I advocate a more open, reflexive and methodologically pluralistic approach to the study of religion. The approach of this volume is similarly pluralistic and is promoted by a number of religionists, above all, perhaps, by Ninian Smart and his dimensional analysis of religion.[4] The approach can be usefully labelled polythematic.

With the intention of achieving some level of phenomenological balance in the academic study of religion, Ninian Smart has argued that religions should be studied on a number of different levels. Or, more specifically, he has noted that religions possess many dimensions and one should not focus exclusively upon a single dimension to the detriment of others. To do so is to risk a distorted understanding of a particular religious tradition or system. Unfortunately, if one examines the academic discipline of religious studies it is relatively easy to identify a certain bias towards a particular dimension of religion. Religious studies possesses a definite bias in favour of the textual dimension of religion. Whether or not this bias is grounded in the relative ease of access to textual sources, or the educational and academic media bias towards writing, is not relevant; what matters is the fact that religious phenomena are being neglected or completely ignored because of this bias. This same point is made by John Hinnells when he notes that 'if the study of religions focuses on textual sources then it is "plugging in" to a level of religion which most of the practitioners are not, or have not been, engaged in'.[5] A more thematic approach to religious studies, such as Smart's dimensional analysis of religion, can go some way towards correcting this bias. Smart currently suggests that religions can be divided into nine dimensions: (1) ritual and practice; (2) doctrine and philosophy; (3) myth and narrative; (4) experience and emotion; (5) ethics and law; (6) organization and society; (7) material and art; (8) politics; (9) economics. There are certainly other possible ways of dividing a religion but the framework is useful in so far as it emphasizes the multiple nature of religious systems (or any social/cultural system; Smart further argues that 'it is important that we study religions and ideologies together'[6] and that we should indulge 'not so much [in] religious studies as world-view analysis and evaluation'[7]).

The following chapters provide a thematic survey of Hindu attitudes to issues of concern to all the major religious traditions and systems of the world. The chapters begin with Hindu understandings of human existence and their relation to the universe; these are followed by Hindu attitudes to myth, texts and time, and then by Hindu attitudes to the divine, in terms of representation, worship and location. The final chapter, on rites of passage, brings the survey full circle and returns to a consideration of Hindu understandings of a person's place in the universe and the journey from birth to death. Each chapter takes a particular theme and reveals something of the abstract nature of Hinduism as a whole.

We begin with 'Human nature and destiny' by Anantanand Rambachan, which discusses the legitimate ends (*puruṣārthas*) of Hindu life. From a Hindu perspective the four goals of *dharma*, *kāma* (pleasure), *artha* (profit) and *mokṣa* (liberation) give meaning to, and order, human existence. *Dharma*, which can be understood to constitute both a micro- and macrocosmic moral law, defines the nature of society (*Varṇāśrāmasdharma*) and, in combination with *kāma* and *artha*, forms the basis of a worldly and pragmatic religion for the Hindus. *Mokṣa*, in contrast, provides a soteriological dimension to human existence and is the goal that allows escape from the cycle of life and death (*saṃsāra*). Rambachan examines these issues and the related topics of the human relationship to *brahman* (the absolute/infinite) and the question of free will and determinism.

In Chapter 2 Gavin Flood develops several of these issues when he considers ethics to be the semantic equivalent of *dharma*, and examines the idea that '*[d]harma* provides the resources for the making of moral decisions in Hinduism' (see p. 54). He assesses the relation of ethics to revelation (*śruti*) and the apparent sensitivity to context that is present in many aspects of Hindu moral law. This is followed by Sharada Sugirtharajah's account of the role of women in Hinduism. In a volume that focuses upon different themes and issues in Hinduism, Sugirtharajah's chapter is itself polythematic, focusing as it does upon texts, myths, society and philosophy. The chapter uses both gender and women as categories of analysis and examines the representation and role of women in history and myth. Marina Warner once observed that '[t]here is no logical equivalence in any society between exalted female objects of worship and a high position for women',[8] and nowhere is this more forcefully emphasized than in Hinduism. Sugirtharajah's chapter identifies the different attitudes to women in Hinduism, in both history and worship, and concludes with an overview of the contemporary situation.

Connected with attitudes to human beings and gender roles are Hindu attitudes to the natural world. Much recent environmental feminist literature has focused upon the invidious consequences of conceptual and metaphorical associations between women and nature, and the inclusion of Anuradha Roma Choudhury's chapter on Hindu attitudes to nature, in conjunction with Sharada Sugirtharajah's chapter on women, allows the reader to reflect on how religious systems participate in the construction of both the natural world and gender roles. Anuradha Roma Choudhury's chapter on nature identifies a range of Hindu responses to the natural world, from the emotional to the philosophically sophisticated, and traces various concepts of creation through the six *darśanas* (systems of theology).

The chapter closes with a consideration of Hindu attitudes to the plant and animal kingdoms and the issue of vegetarianism.

Although the first four chapters draw heavily upon Hindu narratives and texts as their source material, they none the less engage with distinctive themes and issues. Chapter 5 continues this trend by examining the issue of time and the notion that India is changeless and ahistorical. Jacqueline Suthren Hirst discusses the distinction between history (*itihāsa*) and myth (*purāṇa*) and the problem of their conflation into *itihāsapurāṇa*. By giving separate textual consideration to myth and history, Dr Hirst is able to address the puzzling issue of a changeless India and also illuminate the central place of story in Hinduism. In Chapter 6 Gavin Flood focuses upon the place of sacred texts in Hinduism and considers the relationship between primary revelation and texts of human authorship, or secondary revelation. Commenting on the vast amount of material involved, the 3000-year history of texts in India, and the absence of a singular authoritative text, Dr Flood notes that the 'category of "sacred writings" . . . tends to have more fluid boundaries within Hinduism than in most other traditions' (p. 132).

In Chapter 7 we depart from textuality and move on to consider conceptions and representations of the divine in Hinduism. Sharada Sugirtharajah discusses the central role of images in Hinduism by considering the iconography and symbolism of some of the major deities of the Hindu religious traditions. She moves from a consideration of masculine images of the divine, such as Viṣṇu (and his *avatāra*s), Śiva, Gaṇeśa and Skanda, to feminine portrayals as represented by Śakti, Sarasvatī, Pārvatī, Durgā and Kālī; and in Chapters 8 and 9 Anuradha Roma Choudhury explains how and where these images are worshipped.

Chapter 8 examines the relationship of the worshipper to the worshipped, and the uses of *mantra*s, *yantra*s, *yoga* and images of the divine are considered. In Hinduism, proper conduct and ritual performance are probably more important than what one believes (orthopraxy rather than orthodoxy is dominant), and Anuradha Roma Choudhury discusses these issues in addition to the much neglected, although religiously significant, topics of music, dance and the visual arts. In Chapter 9 Hindu attitudes to nature are revisited when the theme of sacred space is addressed. The idea that places such as rivers, mountains and lakes are perceived as sacred by many Hindus is linked with the widespread practice of pilgrimage. Sacred places may act as *tīrthas* (crossing points), 'the intersection of two realms, the mundane and the spiritual' (p. 235), and confer benefits upon the pilgrim. These issues and Hindu attitudes to temples and shrines are considered before the final theme of this volume is raised.

The last chapter focuses upon rites of passage and the orthoprax Hindu's life journey from birth to death. As noted earlier, this chapter brings us full circle and returns us to the themes of human nature and destiny. These are questions and issues that all religions seek to answer and it may be useful to conclude with a definition of religion formulated by John Bowker. In his book *The Sense of God* Bowker argues that

> religions should be conceived as route-finding activities, mapping the general paths along which human beings can trace their way from birth to death and through death, and that the peculiarly 'religious' quality is evoked by a focus on limitations which circumscribe the continuity of human life-ways, of a particularly intransigent kind.[9]

The issue of definition is always close to the surface when one considers Hinduism, and attempts to define religion, such as Bowker's, can usefully inform one's understanding of the themes in this book. It is acutely apparent how the Hindu religious concepts of *dharma*, *kāma*, *artha* and *mokṣa* can be understood to be tools, or route-finding aids, to guide Hindu praxis from birth to death and beyond.

Notes

1 H. von Stietencron, 'Hinduism: on the proper use of a deceptive term' in G. Sontheimer and H. Kulke (eds) (1991) *Hinduism Reconsidered*. Delhi: Manohar, p. 11.
2 J. R. Hinnells and E. J. Sharpe (eds) (1973) *Hinduism*. Newcastle upon Tyne: Oriel Press, p. 6.
3 See H. Alper (ed.) (1987) *Understanding Mantras*. Albany: SUNY Press.
4 N. Smart (1996) *Dimensions of the Sacred: An Anatomy of the World's Beliefs*. London: HarperCollins.
5 J. R. Hinnells, 'Religion and the arts' in U. King (ed.) (1990) *Turning Points in Religious Studies: Essays in Honour of Geoffrey Parrinder*. Edinburgh: T. & T. Clark, p. 257.
6 N. Smart, 'Buddhism, Christianity and the critique of ideology' in L. S.

Rouner (ed.) *Religious Pluralism*. Notre Dame, IN: University of Notre Dame Press, p. 146.

7 Ibid., p. 145.

8 M. Warner, cited in J. J. Preston (ed.) (1982) *Mother Worship*. Chapel Hill, NC: University of North Carolina Press, p. 327.

9 J. Bowker (1973) *The Sense of God: Sociological, Anthropological and Psychological Approaches to the Origin of the Sense of God*. Oxford: Oxford University Press, p. 82.

1. Human nature and destiny

Anantanand Rambachan

The value of human existence

Birth as a human being is considered to be a rare privilege in the Hindu understanding. Among the various species of life, the human being exhibits an unrivalled capacity for choice in action and the ability for acquiring knowledge. The human being is capable, not only of gathering empirical information about the world, but also of speculating and wondering about the ultimate meaning and purpose, if any, of existence. The concern and quest for meaning is, as far as we know, unique to the human species. Because of this potential for ascertaining life's meaning and achieving fullness of existence, Hindu scriptural texts repeatedly remind us of the opportunities of human existence.

The Hindi poet Tulasidas (*c.* 1532–1623), in the extremely influential text, the *Rāmacaritamānas* (commonly referred to as the *Rāmāyaṇa*), extols the significance of human existence.

> It is a great and good fortune that you have secured a human body, which – as all the scriptures declare – is difficult even for heavenly beings to attain. It is a tabernacle suitable for spiritual discipline and the gateway to liberation.
>
> (pp. 720–1)

While praising the possibility offered by human existence for the attainment of liberation (*mokṣa*), the Hindu scriptures also lament the fact that few avail themselves of this opportunity. 'Those born as human beings', says Tulasidas, 'who indulge only in the limited delights of the senses, are fools who would choose poison in exchange for nectar.' In *Bhagavadgītā* 7.3, Kṛṣṇa similarly laments that only one person, among many thousands, strives for liberation. The philosopher and theologian Śaṃkara, in his famous poem *Vivekacūḍāmaṇi* (4–5), contends that one who is fortunate to be born as a human being and who does not make appropriate efforts for liberation commits suicide by clinging on to things that have no ultimate value. 'What greater fool is there', asks Śaṃkara, 'than the person who having obtained a human body, neglects to achieve the real end of this life?'

The four goals

While the Hindu tradition upholds liberation (*mokṣa*) as life's ultimate end and, in one sense, only goal, it has also accepted the legitimacy of other subsidiary goals in the scheme of human existence. In most cases, according to the Hindu viewpoint, the necessity and desire for *mokṣa* are appreciated only after the experience of these subsidiary goals and their limitations. What are these auxiliary ends and how are they limited?

The various legitimate ends (*puruṣārthas*) which a human being is capable of pursuing and achieving have been classified by Hinduism under four headings. The first of these is *kāma*, or pleasure. *Kāma* includes sensual as well as aesthetic enjoyment. Sculpture, music and dance flourished with the blessings of Hinduism, and Hindus love to celebrate life through these forms. The Hindu recognition of *kāma* as a valid human pursuit challenges the common characterization of this tradition as being life-negating and other-worldly. While it is indeed true that Hinduism does not uphold *kāma* as life's highest value, it has not been condemned as intrinsically evil. As long as the individual has the maturity and good sense to be moderate in indulgence and to observe standard rules of morality (*dharma*), he or she has the approval of Hinduism to fulfil the urge for pleasure. The fundamental role of *dharma* to be observed is the avoidance of injury, distress and suffering to others.

Kāma, however, is dependent for its realization and expression on the gaining of *artha* (worldly success). The term *artha* is very broad in its application and, while including wealth, it also encompasses success, power and prestige. By acknowledging *artha*, Hinduism recognizes the need of every human being for access to those material necessities which make life possible and comfortable, and which enable one to fulfil social obligations and duties. While historically approving the voluntary renunciation of material possessions in order to seek liberation, Hinduism has never given its blessing to involuntary poverty and material deprivation. T. W. Organ was correct when he wrote that the 'impoverished state of both the private and public sectors of the Indian economy should not be interpreted to mean that Hinduism has blessed poverty, in spite of the words and actions of no less honored leaders than Mahatma Gandhi and Vinoba Bhave' (Organ, 1970: 125).

While freely giving their approval to the pursuit of *kāma* and *artha*, the Hindu scriptures continually call our attention to the limitations of these twin ends. We are told that these, although valid, will never fully satisfy our deepest needs, and their attainment will still leave us incomplete. The reasons afforded are many. The gains of pleasure and worldly success are transient, leaving us hopelessly addicted to their momentary gratifications. This is the insight of *Bhagavadgītā* 5.22:

> Whatever pleasures are born out of contact [between the mind, senses and objects], are sources of sorrow, since they have a beginning and an end. O son of Kuntī [Arjuna], a wise person does not indulge in these.

Ultimately, in death, we leave wealth and worldly success behind.

There are other reasons, however, why *kāma* and *artha* leave us unsatisfied. Wealth, fame and power are exclusive and, therefore, competitive and risky (Smith, 1958: 19–20). These are assets which diminish when they are shared. One lives in uncertainty as to whether one's rivals will soon gain the advantage, and hence one suffers from inadequacy and uncertainty. 'The idea of a nation', writes Smith,

> in which everyone is famous is a contradiction in terms; if power were distributed equally no one would be powerful in the sense in which we customarily use the word. Fame consists in standing out from one's fellows and power is control over them. From the competitiveness of these values to their riskiness is one short step.

The pursuit of *kāma* and *artha* does not distinguish us as a unique species of living beings. Other forms of life, in different degrees, have material needs and reflect the capacity for pleasure. It is the third end of human existence, *dharma*, which, in the first instance, distinguishes us as human begins.

Dharma is a very rich and multi-faceted concept, and therefore difficult to define. It is derived from the Sanskrit root *dhṛ*, meaning to support or to sustain, and can be partly equated with duty, morality and virtue. The goal of *dharma* emphasizes the social context in which we exist and in which we strive for *artha* and *kāma*, and the need to regulate these pursuits in the interests of the whole. *Dharma*, in other words, establishes the boundaries for *kāma* and *artha*. The personal attainment of worldly success and enjoyment by inflicting pain and suffering on others, or by denying them the right freely to pursue these ends, is opposed to *dharma*. *Dharma* is the goal in Hinduism which presupposes the special human capacity for concern and responsiveness to the needs and interests of others. We are the only animal species with the ability to make conscious moral choices in relation to our wealth- and pleasure-oriented activities. Being human requires that we continually exercise this choice.

The concept of *dharma* also includes particular duties and obligations to be followed by members of the four Hindu *varṇa*s (social groups) and by persons in the four stages (*āśrama*s) of life. The term *varṇāśrāmadharma* refers to duties related to caste and stage in life.[1] In the *Bhagavadgītā* 2.31–37, Kṛṣṇa points out to Arjuna the necessity of being faithful to his duty as a member of the warrior (*kṣatriya*) caste, in order to convince him to engage in battle against his unjust cousins. Failure to engage in battle will be an abnegation of duty (*svadharma*), with a consequent loss of honour.

High value, therefore, is placed on *dharma*, and on meeting the difficulties of living up to its demands. But, as with *kāma* and *artha*, it is not considered to be the highest end of human existence. In other words, a life which consisted of the search for pleasure and worldly success within the boundaries of *dharma* would still not exhaust the human potential. Even society, the object of *dharma*, is, after all, limited. 'Even when extended through history', writes Huston Smith, 'the human community, as long as it stands alone remains both finite and tragic; tragic not only in the sense that it must eventually come to an end, but also in its inflexible resistance to perfection. The final want of man must lie elsewhere' (Smith, 1958: 24–5). The term, *mokṣa*, is the fulfilment of human want and, in the Hindu view, our highest goal.

We do not, however, come to the discovery of our need for *mokṣa* very easily. It is the rarest of all human desires and is discovered only when we have experienced or reflected on the frustrations and limitations of *kāma* and *artha*, and long for a fullness which is not transient. It is the close examination and analysis of the limitations of our many pursuits and their inability to lead us to fullness which bring us to the *mokṣa*-quest.

Mokṣa liberates us not only from the sense of want, but also from the repetitive cycle of birth and death (*saṃsāra*) to which we are subject. So long as we remain content with the finite gains and results of *artha* and *kāma*, we will continue to be caught in the chain of births and deaths. This cycle is seen as being perpetuated entirely by the forces of our desires, and the actions and results which they entail. The meaning of *mokṣa* will not be appreciated unless the realities of rebirth and *karma* are understood: for Hindus, it is ignorance (*avidyā*) at least as much as fault or sin which impedes progress towards *mokṣa*. What, then, do rebirth and *karma* mean?

Rebirth and *karma*

All the traditions of Hinduism hold the doctrine of the rebirth of the individual after death. The term used to describe this process is *punarjanma*, which literally means 'birth after death'. The basic belief is that we do not cease to exist at the end of this current life, but that we are born again, in this or some other world (*loka*), with a new physical body. Like the universe itself, which is viewed in Hinduism as always existing, but which goes through cycles of manifestation and dissolution, individual beings also have an existence that is without beginning. Under the impulse of desires (*kāma*) of various kinds, a variety of actions (*karma*) are performed and these produce results (*karmaphala*) which must be experienced by the performer of the action. The necessity to experience the consequences of one's actions requires embodiment in some form or another, during which result-producing actions continue to be performed – and so the cycle of birth and death, referred to as *saṃsāra*, endures.

For the purpose of appreciating the doctrine of *punarjanma*, we must understand that the true being or identity of the human person, in the Hindu view, is the self (*ātman*). It is the changeless basis and unifying reality of all other changing components of the human personality. It is described in *Bhagavadgītā* 2.20 as being free from birth and death, changeless and eternal. The *ātman* is clothed with, though not limited by, the psychophysical components of the individual personality, and these are described as consisting of three bodies, constituting, as it were, the vehicle of the self (VC 87–109).

The outermost body or sheath is the physical body, referred to as the gross body (*sthūla śarīra*). It is so called because it is composed of matter in the same form as the visible universe and can be perceived and experienced through the sense organs. *Bhagavadgītā* 5.13 likens the physical body to a city of nine gates (*navadvāre pure*) in which dwells the master or *ātman*. The nine gates referred to are the two eyes, the two ears, the two nostrils, the mouth, and the organs of excretion. The gross body is regarded as being different from the self, for whom it is an object of knowledge and an instrument of action.

Different from the gross body is the subtle body (*sūkṣma śarīra*), so called because it is composed of matter in a subtle or uncompounded form.[2] Its components include all thinking and decision-making faculties.[3] The subtle body is also different from the self, for whom it is an object and instrument of knowledge. It is considered to be the repository of all our tendencies (*vāsanās*), good and evil.

The third body, or sheath, is the causal body (*kārana śarīra*). It expresses itself most prominently in the state of deep sleep, when all mental, emotional and intellectual activities become dormant and unmanifest. From this latent or causal condition, they again emerge to express themselves in experiences of waking and dreaming. The term 'causal' is justified since the gross and subtle bodies are absorbed, as it were, into the causal body at the time of deep sleep, and from it they again emerge (VC 120–121). The causal body is regarded as being other than the *ātman*, to whom it is also related as an object. Even as one is aware of one's physical body and mental states, one is also aware of the ignorance of the deep sleep state, and this direct knowledge is expressed in the waking affirmation, 'I slept happily; I did not know anything'. I know, in other words, that I did not know anything.

The event of death marks the disintegration of the gross body. The individual being (*jīva*), clothed with the subtle and causal bodies, seeks a new physical form to express its peculiar inclinations and to experience the results of previous actions. The self is associated with its gross and causal bodies until the attainment of *mokṣa*, when, freed from these, it is no longer subject to *saṃsāra* (BSBS IV.ii.8–11).

The movement from death to rebirth has been strikingly compared in the *Bhagavadgītā* (2.26) to a change of clothing:

> Just as a person casts off worn-out garments and puts on others that are new, even so does the embodied soul cast off worn-out bodies and take on others that are new.

This suggestive analogy makes a number of important points about the rebirth process. First, even as a suit of clothing is not identical with the wearer, similarly the gross body, likened here to worn-out garments, is not the true being or identity of the human person. Secondly, there is a similarity of continuity. When a worn-out suit of clothing is cast off, the wearer continues to be. Similarly, with the disintegration of the gross body in death, the indweller – that is, the *ātman* – continues to be. The third point brings us to the relationship between the cycle of birth and death and the doctrine of *karma*. A suit of clothing is cast off when it no longer serves the purpose for which it was worn. Similarly, the gross body is dropped when it has fulfilled the purpose for which it came into existence. Each life-experience is conditioned by those that preceded it. The gross body, as a vital and necessary component in any particular birth, is also conditioned by prior births. It is the instrument through which diverse experience of pleasure (*sukha*) and pain (*duḥkha*), consistent with past attitudes and actions, is gained. Its reason or justification for existence is attained when these experiences are realized and, like a suit of worn clothing, it is shed.

Saṃsāra, therefore, is by no means conceived by Hindus to be a haphazard process, but one governed by the law of action and reaction (*karma*). Hinduism envisages the universe as a moral stage where 'all living beings get the dress and part that befit them and are to act well to deserve well in the future' (Chatterjee and Datta, 1968: 18). The term *karma* literally means action, but it also includes the subtle forces which are understood to be generated by all voluntary actions, and which are seen as capable of producing results in the future. The doctrine, or law, of *karma* is basically an extension into the moral sphere of the physical law of causation. It implies that all moral actions are as potent as physical ones and are capable of producing appropriate results in the future.

Every action – physical, verbal or mental – has an immediate effect, but it also creates an impression on the subtle body which bears appropriate fruit in due course. The result depends, of course, on the nature and quality of the action. The *Bṛhadāraṇyaka Upaniṣad* (4.4.5) succinctly expresses this point:

> According as one acts, according as one conducts oneself, so does one become. The doer of good becomes good. The doer of evil becomes evil. One becomes virtuous by virtuous action, bad by bad action.

It will not, of course, surprise the reader to note that Hindus resist the equation of the doctrine of *karma* with fatalism and predestination. The doctrine is sometimes understood to be denying freedom of will and choice to the human being. It is argued that we lose all initiative and responsibility for actions if our experiences in the present life are determined by our actions in the past.

From the Hindu standpoint, however, the law of *karma* emphasizes free will and insists upon moral responsibility. If in my present life I am experiencing the results and consequences of past actions, this is only because I was responsible for those actions. The important point, of course, is that if I have influenced my present condition by my past behaviour, there is no reason why I should not be able to shape my future through my present conduct. The law of *karma* stipulates that certain kinds of actions will produce certain results, but this does not necessarily paralyse the human will. On the contrary, it places responsibility squarely on my shoulders, since it does not propose a power outside myself which is responsible for my individual and collective destiny (Chatterjee, 1970: 82–100).

From the Hindu standpoint, the basic urge of all human beings is the desire for fullness (*ānanda*). There is an inner inadequacy and incompleteness which yearns for fulfilment and which expresses itself in multifarious desires. Smith wrote of it as a desire for joy, 'a resolution of feelings in which the basic themes are the opposite of frustration, futility and boredom' (Smith, 1958: 26). In the *Chāndogya Upaniṣad* (VII.1.2–3), we are given the example of Nārada, who comes to his teacher enumerating all the branches of knowledge which he has mastered. Among these are the Veda, grammar, mathematics, ethics, logic, philosophy, physical science and the science of war. Yet, declares Nārada, 'I am in sorrow, please make me pass beyond sorrow'. Nārada's sorrow is the pain of an inward incompleteness which all these forms of learning could not resolve.

This basic human desire for fullness expresses itself outwardly in changing desires for objects of pleasure (*kāma*) and various forms of worldly success (*artha*). The fulfilment of any one of these desires allows one temporarily to own oneself to be a full person, but, very soon, that insufficiency is experienced once more and new desires are entertained. Like a person fighting a raging fire by pouring fresh fuel into the flames, the satisfaction of any number of limited desires does not lead to freedom from desire. Like Naciketas in the *Kaṭha Upani-*

ṣad, we will discover that the human being cannot be satisfied with material gains and accomplishments.

The Non-dualist view: Śaṃkara

In the vision of Hinduism, and particularly according to the tradition of *Advaita Vedānta* (Non-dualism) systematized by Śaṃkara (*c.* 788–820), we fail to accomplish the fullness we seek because the very seeking itself is based on an acceptance of the false premise that we are, in reality, incomplete and insufficient. We search for fullness without, in the first place, asking the question 'Who am I?' If we enquired properly into this question we would indeed discover that we are already the full beings we seek to be.

The reason we do not enquire, according to most of the traditions of Hinduism, is that we are all the victims of a beginningless ignorance (*avidyā*). This ignorance, though not limited to, is precisely about, ourselves. It is regarded as basic because our conduct and responses to others and to our environment are, in large measure, determined by our understanding and image of ourselves. Hinduism has a generally optimistic view about the goodness of human nature. The *Aitareya Upaniṣad* (1.2.3), for example, declares the human being to be well-formed and truly fit for righteous action. Attitudes and patterns of conduct which are harmful to oneself and to others are seen as having their causes not in any intrinsic defect in human nature but in false knowledge. The gain of valid knowledge not only removes ignorance, but is expected also to correct erroneous values and conduct.

A popular story is employed by Hindu teachers of the *Advaita Vedānta* tradition to explain the nature of our ignorance and the overcoming of it by knowledge. Ten disciples were on their way to a pilgrimage site when they encountered a river in flood. In the absence of a boat, they decided to swim across the river. On reaching the opposite shore, the leader took a count to ensure that everyone was safe. To his dismay, one seemed to be missing. Every other member of the group did likewise, but ended up with the same result. They were all in deep grief after concluding that the tenth person had drowned. A passer-by, attracted by their loud lamentations, inquired about their problem. After patiently listening and observing, he assured them that the tenth person was indeed available and requested the leader to count again. When the disciple stopped at nine and looked bewildered, the stranger smilingly said 'You are the tenth person!' The error was immediately appreciated. Each had left himself out from his count.

As a consequence of ignorance, according to Śaṃkara, we identify ourselves with the qualities of our limited gross and subtle bodies and superimpose upon the true self the characteristics of these.

> For instance, a man superimposes the attributes of external things on his self, if he thinks himself as sound or unsound when his wife, son, etc., are sound or unsound; similarly, he superimposes the attributes of his body on his self, if he thinks himself fat, lean, fair, standing, going or jumping; similarly he superimposes the attributes of the senses on the self when he regards himself as dumb or one-eyed, impotent, deaf or blind; similarly he superimposes on his own self the attributes of the internal organ like desire, resolve, doubt and determination, etc. In this way, after superimposing the denotations of the concept of 'I' on the inner self that is the witness of its entire activities, and vice-versa, one superimposes that inner self, the witness of all, on the internal organ etc.
>
> (BSBS intro.)

The *ātman*, which is different from all psychophysical processes, is wrongly identified with the limited characteristics of these, and regarded as subject to birth and death, change and incompleteness. One of Śaṃkara's principal arguments for the distinction of the *ātman* from the body and mind is that, even as one is aware of external objects, one is aware of bodily and mental processes. The relationship with these is that of knower and known. The *ātman*, which witnesses all bodily and mental changes, is itself free from all change. It remains the same in all periods of time and is regarded, therefore, as *sat* (eternal). Awareness or consciousness is intrinsic to the *ātman*, whereas everything else is inert. For this reason, the *ātman* is said to be self-luminous. Śaṃkara argues that everyone immediately knows that he or she *is*, and one does not require proof of one's existence (BSBS intro.). Every other object, however, including the body and mind, is illumined and revealed by the self-luminous *ātman*. The nature of the *ātman* as awareness and indeed, according to Śaṃkara, as the only conscious principle in the whole of existence, is indicated by the word *cit*. Finally, the *ātman* is said to be *ananta* or *ānanda*, which indicates its fullness and freedom from limitations of all kinds as well as its nature as the basis and source of all joy.

The Sanskrit expression *sat–cit–ānanda* (reality–awareness–joy) describes the nature of the *ātman*.[4] Because the *ātman* is free from all limitations, therefore, it is identical, for Śaṃkara, with *brahman* – the infinite. In fact, for Śaṃkara, the terms *ātman* and *brahman* are interchangeable. The word *ātman* is used to describe the limitless self from an individual standpoint, while the word *brahman* is used for the self in its cosmic and universal nature as the reality of all existence. *Ātman* and *brahman*, in other words, are not two different realities, but rather terms describing one and the same reality.

For Śaṃkara, the great sentence (*mahāvākya*) of the *Chāndogya Upaniṣad*, '*Tat Tvam Asi*' (That Thou Art), teaches the unequivocal identity of *ātman* and *brahman*.[5] This sentence, contends Śaṃkara, does not ask us to look upon the *ātman* as if it were *brahman*, but asserts a definite identity. It is also not to be conceived figuratively (*gauṇa*) as in the sentence 'You are a lion', nor as a mere praise of the student, Śvetaketu. The latter is not an object of worship in the discussion and it is no praise to *brahman* to be identified with Śvetaketu.

Subject to ignorance, like the tenth person, we do not realize that we are the fullness which we seek in erroneous ways. For Śaṃkara, the *Upaniṣads* (the last section of the Veda, also referred to as the *Vedānta*) constitute a valid means of knowledge in the form of words (*śabda-pramāṇa*) for eliminating ignorance and correcting our knowledge of the self (Rambachan, 1991). The teacher (*guru*) has an indispensable function as someone who has mastered the wisdom of the scripture and who is established in the knowledge of the self. By listening carefully to the words of the texts as unfolded by the teacher (*śravaṇa*), by the application of reason and analysis to remove doubts (*manana*), and by a continuous contemplation (*nididhyāsana*) on the nature of the *ātman* to eliminate false values and attitudes, one becomes established in the knowledge of the self. Spiritual disciplines, including the practical methods of *yoga*, are helpful to the extent that they steady and purify the mind. These serve, therefore, only as indirect aids for the attainment of *mokṣa*. Since the self is always available, but misunderstood, knowledge is the direct means to liberation.

For Śaṃkara, *mokṣa* is synonymous with the gain of self-knowledge, since the fundamental problem is one of ignorance. He subscribes, therefore, to the doctrine of liberation in life (*jīvanmukti*), and not as a post-mortem accomplishment. The liberated person continues in mortal existence only as long as the *karma*, which has brought the particular body into being, endures. Such *karma* may be compared to an arrow which is released from a bow. Even if the archer changes his or her mind, the released arrow must travel to its destination. The exhaustion of *karma* results in liberation from the body (*videha mukti*) and freedom from *saṃsāra*.

Such liberation, it must be emphasized, is not the attainment of immortal existence in some other world. Being identical with the infinite self, it defies definition.

> Sankara declares in many passages that the nature of liberation is a state of oneness with *brahman*, and even as the latter is lifted above all categories of experience, so the state of *mokṣa* cannot be described in terms of our knowledge. Since the latter deals with distinctions of space and time, cause and effect, persons and things, action and suffering, it is said that none of these distinctions applies to the state of freedom. It cannot be said that the liberated live in the geographical area called *svarga* or *brahmaloka*; nor can it be said that they last for endless time.
>
> (Radhakrishnan, 1977, vol. 2: 639–40)

For Śaṃkara, then, the attainment of *brahman* through knowledge (*jñāna*) is identical with liberation. *Brahman*, as we have seen, is not different from one's own self. It has the highest value because it is that which is ultimately real. Śaṃkara, however, does not equate *brahman* with the world, since *brahman* in its transcendental nature far exceeds the universe, and the universe has characteristics of change, insentience and limitations which are opposed to the nature of *brahman* (Rambachan, 1989: 287–97). As *brahman* is the efficient cause and the material basis of the universe, the latter does not exist apart from *brahman*. The infinite *brahman* underlies and runs through all finite effects and these cannot be considered as standing outside of *brahman*.

Śaṃkara neither equates *brahman* with the world, nor asserts that the world possesses a reality which is independent of *brahman*. Avoiding both positions, the *Advaita* tradition asserts that the world, in its relationship to *brahman*, is a mystery and is indefinable (*anirvacanīya*). Without undergoing any change or losing anything of itself, *brahman* is both cause and source of the world. We may view the world as the mysterious manifestation of *brahman*. It is not the infinite plus something else, but the infinite mysteriously appearing as the finite. The nature of *brahman*, it must be remembered, is non-dual.

The Qualified Non-dualist view: Rāmānuja

Śaṃkara's understanding of human nature and destiny has had a deep and wide influence on Hinduism, but there are other influential interpretations. Prominent among these is the *Viśiṣṭadvaita* (Qualified Non-dualism) system promulgated by the South Indian theologian Rāmānuja (traditionally 1017–1137).

Rāmānuja's differences with Śaṃkara on human nature and destiny are all fundamentally related to their different understandings of the nature of *brahman*. Rāmānuja shares with Śaṃkara the view that *brahman* is the only reality. There is, in other words, no other reality outside or independent of *brahman*. However, for Rāmānuja, *brahman*, or God, is internally diverse and complex (*viśiṣṭa*). The all-inclusive *brahman* contains within itself a real diversity, consisting of unconscious matter (*acit*) and conscious selves (*cit*). The term *viśiṣṭādvaita* becomes justified, since the one (*advaita*) *brahman* is qualified (*viśiṣṭa*) by an internal diversity consisting of matter and souls.

Unlike Śaṃkara, who argues for the identity of the self in all beings, Rāmānuja admits that there is a plurality of selves distinct from each other. A central concern of Rāmānuja is the clarification of the relationship existing between God, matter and souls. He attempts his clarification by employing the body–soul analogy. Matter and souls are described by him as constituting the body of God. While our souls are souls in relation to our body, in relation to God our soul becomes part of God's body, and God ought to be seen as the soul of all souls and of matter. The relation between God and the matter and souls which make up God's body, is not identity but inseparability (*apṛthak-siddhi*). In Rāmānuja's view, a body is that which is utilized and supported by a conscious entity for its own purpose, and which is under the control of that entity.

> Any substance which a sentient soul is capable of completely controlling and supporting for its own purposes, and which stands to the soul in an entirely subordinate relation, is the body of that soul . . . In that sense, then, all sentient and non-sentient beings together constitute the body of the Supreme Person, for they are completely controlled and supported by him for his own ends, and are absolutely subordinate to him.
>
> (VCR II.1.9)

Brahman is the support (*ādhāra*), controller (*niyantā*) and principal (*śeṣin*), while the individual souls and matter are supported (*dhārya*), controlled (*niyāmya*) and the means (*śeṣa*). Though dependent and inseparable from *brahman*, souls and matter are real.

For Rāmānuja, unlike Śaṃkara, *brahman* is not an indeterminate (*nirguṇa*) and indefinable reality, but possessed of infinitely good qualities. Among these are limitless knowledge and bliss. God is the creator, sustainer and destroyer of the world, which is brought forth from the matter that is co-existent with and within God. Even when the world is withdrawn into God, there remains within God undifferentiated matter as well as souls, since both are eternal.

The bondage of the soul, for Rāmānuja, is due to ignorance and *karma*. Ignorant of its true nature as a spiritual substance related to God as part, the soul identifies itself with the body and mind, from which it is different, and becomes subject to desires of various kinds. Liberation is attained through a harmonious combination of work (*karma*), knowledge (*jñāna*) and devotion (*bhakti*). By work, Rāmānuja means the diligent performance of rituals which are enjoined in the first sections of the Veda. The performance of these rituals with the motive only of pleasing God and without a desire for reward of any kind destroys the accumulated effects of past actions. One also realizes, however, that rituals of this kind cannot lead directly to *mokṣa*. The aspirant then moves on to the study of the last sections of the Veda, that is, the *Upaniṣads*. From this study, one comes to an understanding of the nature of the soul and its true relationship to God. One learns that the soul is not identical with the body and mind, but is related to God as part to whole and entirely dependent on God.

This understanding of one's dependence on God leads to an acknowledgement of God, as the only object worthy of adoration, and to a loving and unbroken remembrance of God (*dhruvā smṛtiḥ*). This attitude of intense love and self-surrender (*prapatti*) towards God, when combined with the performance of obligatory rituals, pleases God whose grace (*prasāda*) brings about the final liberation of the soul (VCR I.1.1). Through grace, ignorance and *karma* are destroyed and the soul comes into immediate knowledge of God. While Śaṃkara acknowledges the significance of divine grace, Rāmānuja obviously attributes to it a central and indispensable role for liberation.

For Rāmānuja, unlike Śaṃkara, liberation is not the discovery by the soul of its identity with *brahman*. The soul realizes its nature as a part of God's body, but retains its individuality and distinctiveness from God and other souls.

> For scriptural and *smṛti* texts alike declare that the released soul stands to the highest Self in relation of fellowship, equality, equality of attributes, and all this implies a consciousness of separation.
>
> (VCR IV.4.4)

Unlike God, who is all-pervasive, the soul is atomic in size; also it does not share rulership of the world with God.

The most visible inheritors, in the Western world, of the theology of Rāmānuja are the members of ISKCON (the International Society for Krishna Consciousness), an organization founded in the United States in 1966 by A. C. Bhaktivedanta Swami Prabhupada. Drawing generally from the tradition of Vaiṣṇavism, and more specifically from the disciplic succession initiated by the Bengali devotee Caitanya (1485–1533), the movement emphasizes that the goal of human existence is the discovery of oneself as part and parcel of God, and to be engaged in the loving service of God. The proponents of *Advaita* were continually censured by Prabhupada for their characterization of ultimate reality as impersonal and for denying all distinctions in the liberated state. Since the name of God is not different from God, the recommended technique for cultivating devotion and expressing devotional service is the chanting of the sacred mantra, '*Hare Kṛṣṇa, Hare Kṛṣṇa, Kṛṣṇa Kṛṣṇa, Hare Hare / Hare Rāma, Hare Rāma, Rāma Rāma, Hare Hare*'.[6]

The Dualist view: Madhva

Śaṃkara, as we have seen, spoke of the relationship between the self and ultimate reality as one of identity. Rāmānuja, on the other hand, rejected identity and described the relationship as one of inseparability. Madhvāchārya (*c.* 1238–1317), a bitter opponent of Śaṃkara's views, went a step further and argued for an unqualified dualism (*dvaita*).

For Madhva, like Rāmānuja, there are three real and eternal entities. These are God, souls and matter. These three are distinct and different, and Madhva qualifies these differences as being fivefold:

1. God is distinct from souls

2. God is distinct from non-living matter
3. Each soul is distinct from another
4. Souls are distinct from matter
5. Matter particles, when separated, are distinct from one another.

God, according to Madhva, is the only independent reality. Souls and matter are subordinate to, and dependent on, God. God, whose nature is existence, knowledge and bliss, possesses a perfect nature and infinitely good qualities. God creates, sustains and destroys the world. Endowed with a supernatural body, God is transcendent. As the inner controller of all souls (*antaryāmin*), however, God is also immanent. God can incarnate at will, without becoming in any way limited. Madhva identifies God with Viṣṇu and describes him as having the goddess Lakṣmī as his eternal companion. Like God, Lakṣmī is free from ignorance and bondage. She is the personification of his creative power and, through her, he creates, sustains and destroys the universe.

Unlike matter, which is inert, souls are conscious and blissful by nature. Like Rāmānuja, Madhva describes the souls as being atomic in size. Due to the force of past *karma*, souls are entangled with material bodies and subject to the cycle of births and deaths. Madhva classifies souls into those that are eternally free (*nitya*) like Lakṣmī, those that have freed themselves from bondage (*mukta*), and those that are bound (*baddha*). Among the latter there are some souls who are eligible for release, but others who will never gain release from the experience of *saṃsāra*. Madhva's doctrine of an eternal *saṃsāra* is unique among teachers of Hinduism.

The liberation of the individual is neither through knowledge nor through works, but solely through the grace of God (*Īśvaraprasāda*). Madhva's understanding of divine grace reminded Radhakrishnan of the Augustinian view in Christianity.

> A man can never desire to be saved. It is only through grace that he can be redeemed. God is not forced by any consideration of merit. He simply elects some for salvation and others for the opposite state. The divine will sets men free or casts them into bondage. But the Hindu tradition does not allow Madhva to hold that God's choice is arbitrary, unconditioned and groundless. Though in a sense the states of the soul are brought about by *brahman*, it is also admitted that the grace of the Lord is proportioned to the intensity of our devotion.
>
> (Radhakrishnan, 1977, vol. 2: 747–8)

While Rāmānuja describes the liberated soul as similar to God in some respects, Madhva is concerned to stress the differences between God and the liberated soul. Consistent with his theology of difference, he emphasizes the distinctions in the experience of liberation, even for the emancipated soul. At the lowest level, the soul gains entry into the heavenly abode of God called *Vaikuṇṭha*. Among those who enter God's abode, some of a higher calibre attain nearness (*sāmīpya*) to God. Among those close to God, there are those who acquire the external form (*sārūpya*) of God and whose enjoyment is similar to God's. Finally, there are those souls who become united (*sāyujya*) with God and share his bliss. Their emancipation is of the highest type. This unity with God is by no means the identity of *ātman* and *brahman* advocated by Śaṃkara. Even in the state of liberation, souls are distinct from God and from each other. Rāmānuja does not distinguish gradations of bliss among souls in the state of *mokṣa*.

Conclusion

While there is clearly a plurality of perspectives on human nature and destiny within Hinduism, there is also a significant sharing of outlook. There is an optimism about human nature which is reflected in defining the basic problem as one of ignorance (*avidyā*). Liberation entails a correct understanding of ourselves in relation to that which is real in the universe. For Śaṃkara, that relationship is one of identity, while for Rāmānuja it is one of inseparability. *Mokṣa* liberates us from untruth, in the most profound sense, to truth. *Mokṣa* also implies freedom from craving and desire, and the attainment of a condition of fullness and sufficiency. It is synonymous with the attainment of bliss and peace, regarded as innate to the nature of the self. The *Bhagavadgītā* (2.70) beautifully compares the fullness of the liberated person to an ocean, the level of which is unchanged even by the waters of gushing rivers. Similarly, entering desires are absorbed in the contented mind of the liberated one.

To be human is to be part of a universal moral order in which we assume responsibility for our actions and their consequences. The doctrine of *karma*, common to all traditions of Hinduism, affirms this faith in an eternal moral order. Liberation, however, also implies freedom from *karma* and the consequent cycle of births and deaths. *Karma*, however, is only one link in a causal chain that originates with ignorance (*avidyā*) and greedy desire (*kāma*). We are liberated from *karma* and *saṃsāra* because ignorance can be overcome. All *karma*, in the words of the *Bhagavadgītā* (4.37) is destroyed by wisdom, even as a burning fire reduces fuel to ashes. The freedom from *karma/saṃsāra* means, of course, freedom from the uncertainty of change, equated in many scriptural passages with the attainment of immortality and fearlessness.

For Śaṃkara, this condition of liberation is to be attained here and now. It is a freedom from a private self into one which is shared with all existence. In the *Bhagavadgītā* (6.32) it implies a greater sensitivity towards, and awareness of, others and the ability to share their joys and sorrows:

> One, O Arjuna, who sees with equality everything, in the image of one's own self, whether in pleasure or in pain, is considered a perfect yogi.

The *Bhagavadgītā* twice (5.25; 12.4) uses the expression *sarvabhūta-hite ratāḥ* (delighting in the welfare of all) to describe the liberated person, showing clearly that its vision of *mokṣa* is one which draws us into relationships of unity and compassion with all beings.

Notes

1 The four *varṇa*s are the priests (brahmans), secular leaders (*kṣatriya*s), merchants (*vaiśya*s), and servants (*śūdra*s). The four stages or *āśrama*s are the student (*brahmacārin*), the householder (*gṛhastha*), semi-retirement (*vānaprastha*) and renunciation (*saṃnyāsin*).

2 The *Advaita* view is that the evolution of the material universe proceeds from finer and subtle forms of matter to gross forms. See chapter VII of Swami Madhavananda (trans.), *The Vedānta Paribhāṣa of Dharmarāja Adhvarīndra*. Belur Math: The Ramakrishna Mission, 1972.

3 See Swami Nikhilananda (trans.), *Ātmabodha of Śrī Śaṅkarācārya*. Madras: Sri Ramakrishna Math, 1975, v. 13.

4 See *Taittirīya Upaniṣad* II.i.1.

5 See Ganganatha Jha (trans.), *The Chāndogyopaniṣad with the Commentary of Śaṅkara*. Poona: Oriental Book Agency, 1942, VI.xvi.3.

6 For a detailed discussion of Prabhupada's views see A. C. Bhaktivedanta Swami Prabhupada, *The Bhagavadgītā As It Is*. Los Angeles: The Bhaktivedanta Book Trust, 1981.

Further reading

Chatterjee, S. (1970) *The Fundamentals of Hinduism*. Calcutta: University of Calcutta.

Chatterjee, S. and Datta, D. (1968) *An Introduction to Indian Philosophy*. Calcutta: University of Calcutta.

Gambhirananda, Swami (trans.) (1965–66) *Eight Upaniṣads: With the Commentary of Śaṅkarācārya*. Calcutta: Advaita Ashrama.

Gambhirananda, Swami (trans.) (1977) *The Brahma-Sūtra-Bhāṣya of Śaṅkarācārya*. Calcutta: Advaita Ashrama.

Madhavananda, Swami (trans.) (1978) *Vivekacūḍāmaṇi of Śaṅkarācārya*. Calcutta: Advaita Ashrama.

Olivelle, P. (1993) *The Āśrama System: The History and Hermeneutics of a Religious Institution*. New York and Oxford: Oxford University Press.

Olivelle, P. (1994) *Rule and Regulations of Brahmanical Asceticism*. Albany: SUNY Press.

Organ, T. W. (1970) *The Hindu Quest for the Perfection of Man*. Athens: Ohio University Press.

Pereira, J. (1991) *Hindu Theology: Themes, Texts and Structures*. Delhi: Motilal Banarsidass.

Prasad, R. C. (ed. and trans.) (1991) *Śrī Rāmacaritamānasa of Tulsīdāsa*. Delhi: Motilal Banarsidass.

Radhakrishnan, S. (trans.) (1976) *The Bhagavadgītā*. London: Allen and Unwin.

Radhakrishnan, S. (trans.) (1977) *Indian Philosophy*. 2 vols, London: Allen and Unwin.

Rambachan, A. (1989) 'The value of the world as the mystery of God in Advaita', *Journal of Dharma* 14 (July–Sept. 1989), pp. 287–97.

Rambachan, A. (1991) *Accomplishing the Accomplished: The Vedas As a Source of Valid Knowledge in Śaṅkara*. Honolulu: University of Hawaii Press.

Sharma, A. C. (1976) *A Critical Survey of Indian Philosophy*. Delhi: Motilal Banarsidass.

Smith, B. K. (1994) *Classifying the Universe: The Ancient Indian Varṇa System and the Origins of Caste*. New York and Oxford: Oxford University Press.

Smith, H. (1958) *The Religions of Man*. New York: Harper and Row.

Thibaut, G. (trans.) (1990) *The Vedānta Sūtras with the Commentary of Rāmānuja*. Delhi: Motilal Banarsidass.

2. Making moral decisions

Gavin Flood

Hinduism is a term covering a wide and diverse range of Indian religious traditions. Indeed some scholars, such as Wilfred Cantwell Smith, have argued that because of such diversity there is no such thing as 'Hinduism',[1] while others, such as Simon Weightman, make the point that it is legitimate to speak of 'Hinduism' as an 'umbrella concept' and to use the term because it exists in 'Hindu' self-perception.[2] This self-perception has arguably only developed with the rise of the Neo-Hindu movements in the nineteenth century and with the rise of Indian nationalism. Indeed, the idea of a 'Hindu' as a self-conscious agent with a certain set of clearly delineated beliefs and moral code may be related to the development of an educated, urban class in India (Bharati, 1982: 16–21). Bharati has contrasted this modern Hinduism with the rural Hinduism of the villages and the Sanskrit tradition of brahmanical learning and renunciation, which roughly corresponds to the distinction in anthropology between the 'little tradition' and 'great tradition' (Bharati, 1982: 6–7). Throughout its history 'Hinduism' has displayed an astonishing diversity of ideas and practices, though it could nevertheless be argued that the Sanskrit, brahmanical renouncer tradition has to a great extent determined what is normative within 'Hinduism'. Indeed, a Hindu might argue that what maintains the unity of Hinduism is *dharma*, the normative duties and ethical code which governs all aspects of life, a code which is regarded as sacred and eternal (*sanātana*).

The brahmanical view of Hindu morality is thought to be based on the revelation (*śruti*) of the Veda, articulated in various law books, the *Dharmaśāstra*s, and in various philosophical systems, most notably the Mīmāṃsā, and it becomes the practical ideology of the high-caste Hindu householder. But this practical ideology is challenged by the heterodox traditions of Tantrism, which has ethical implications for the Hindu, as we shall see.

Bharati observes that, strictly speaking, to be a 'Hindu' is to be born within an endogamous group or caste of 'Hindu' society, regardless of belief system (Bharati, 1982: 4). He notes that, at the level of belief, the only 'minimal common denominator' in Hinduism, though by no means universally agreed, is acceptance of the sacred texts called the Veda as revelation (*śruti*). This would be largely true for all three kinds of Hinduism which he identifies, namely modern or urban Hinduism, village Hinduism and the Sanskrit, brahmanical tradition, though one must be aware that the Veda as primary revelation would not be accepted in some devotional (*bhakti*) traditions nor, on the whole, in Tantrism.

If one takes the brahmanical Sanskrit tradition as in some sense normative, then apart from acceptance of the Veda as revelation, a key defining characteristic of a Hindu might be acceptance of the *varṇāśrāmadharma*, one's duty (*dharma*) in respect of class/caste (*varṇa*) and stage of life (*āśrama*), though again we must be aware that many Hindu traditions have rejected this model. Perhaps belief in the cycle of reincarnation (*saṃsāra*) and salvation or liberation (*mokṣa*) from this state might be added as common elements of Hindu ideology, though by no means universal. For example, for rural or village Hinduism, fate or the supernatural agency of malevolent spirits might be regarded as a greater cause of suffering and death than action and its effects (*karma*).

Although the ideology of caste and admittance of the Veda as revelation are not universally accepted, they can nevertheless arguably be taken as starting points in arriving at an understanding of Hinduism. Rather than belief, what is more important in delineating the boundaries of Hinduism is action: 'orthopraxy' takes precedence over 'orthodoxy'. In other words, what a Hindu does in relation to his or her social standing and context is far more important than what a Hindu thinks. Indeed, there has been a proliferation of various Hindu ideologies – monistic, theistic and atheistic – but the overarching concern of most Hindus has been the primacy of correct action in accordance with one's prescribed duties and responsibilities determined by birth.

These duties and responsibilities, incorporated within the Sanskrit term *dharma*, are concerned with the fulfilling of social obligations to one's family and wider society, and the fulfilment of one's ritual obligations to the household deities and ancestors. Indeed, traditionally the high caste or 'twice-born' (*dvija*) Hindu is born with three debts (*ṛṇa*) to be paid: the debt of vedic study to the sages (*ṛṣi*) as a celibate student (*brahmacārin*); as a householder (*gṛhastha*), the debt of sacrifice to the gods (*deva*); and finally the debt of begetting a son to make funeral offerings to the ancestors (*pitṛ*). Correct action or ethical behaviour takes primacy over belief. This ethical behaviour (*dharma*), however, varies in different social contexts for different groups: *dharma* is, as Doniger observes, 'context sensitive' (Doniger, 1991: xlvi)[3] (see below, p. 36).

Ethics and liberation

The famous Hindu law book, the *Manusmṛti*, says that once a man has fulfilled his moral (dharmic) obligations – that is, paid his three debts – he can retire to meditate and work for his liberation (*mokṣa*), though to seek liberation before he has fulfilled his moral obligations would be counterproductive and lead to hell (*Manu* 6.35–38). This points to two areas of ultimate concern, *dharma* and liberation (*mokṣa*). These two areas of concern or realms of discourse have tended to be distinct in Hinduism: *dharma* has been the concern of the law books and the majority of Hindu householders at a practical level, *mokṣa* the concern of renouncers and Hindu philosophical discourse. K. Potter has remarked that while the idea of the Good, or moral perfection, has been the dominant or even ultimate value in Western thought, in Indian thought, by contrast, liberation or freedom and control of self and environment have been the ultimate value most discussed in sophisticated philosophical discourse. He writes: 'the ultimate value recognized by classical Hinduism in its most sophisticated sources is not morality but freedom, not rational self control in the interests of the community's welfare but complete control over one's environment' (Potter, 1991: 3). Such statements, however, need to be qualified by the idea that liberation has sometimes been identified with the ultimate good (*niḥśreyasa*).[4] Indeed, liberation is minimally freedom from suffering, which is implicitly 'bad'.

While it may be true that liberation has taken priority in philosophical discourse, and is the ultimate goal of renunciation and the many spiritual disciplines of Hinduism, it is also the case that ethics or *dharma* is the basis or foundation upon which liberation is achieved.

Mokṣa, while transcending the relative opposites of 'good' and 'bad', nevertheless in orthodox Hinduism presupposes *dharma* which, at least according to the *Dharmaśāstra*s, is a necessary condition for it. Although *mokṣa* is in some sense the opposite of *dharma*, it is nevertheless not *adharma*, 'unethical' or 'bad'. Indeed, in the everyday Brahman householder's life, while liberation is perhaps a distant goal, *dharma* has taken precedence over world renunciation, as Madan (1987) has demonstrated. The Hindu householder (*gṛhastha*), while agreeing with the ideology of renunciation, has behaved at a practical level according to social and moral codes which see value not so much in their own transcendence through renunciation, but in their affirmation in daily life. Domesticity (*grāhasthya*) and its implied moral codes become more important than renunciation (*saṃnyāsa*) (Madan, 1987: 17–47). Indeed *Manu* explicitly states that of the four stages of life (*āśrama*) the householder stage is the best (*jyeṣṭha*) because the householder supports the other three stages and this vedic activity is the supreme good (*śreyaskaratara*) (*Manu* 3.77–78; 12.86).

In contrast to the renouncer, the householder Brahman's supreme duties have traditionally been to perform vedic ritual, maintain his ritual purity and fulfil his other caste obligations. Action has therefore been his central concern, especially ritual action (*karma*), which originally referred to vedic sacrifice but which in classical Hinduism came also to refer to the ritual obligations of deity worship (*pūjā*). Correct ritual action and correct patterns of behaviour determined by the tradition have become central to the high-caste Hindu's life. *Dharma* is inextricably linked with *karma* – the realm of its expression – and so is the primary concern of the Brahman householder, in contrast to the renouncer who must abandon dharmically-prescribed ritual, *karma*, in order to attain *mokṣa*. For the renouncer, *mokṣa* entails the abandonment of *karma* – both in the sense of ritual action and in the sense of accumulated merit and demerit – and so is beyond the realm of the *dharma* which governs the householder's life, beyond the ethical codes which inform all aspects of the householder's existence.

This is illustrated in the Advaita Vedāntic theologian Śaṃkara's identification of the renouncer, who has abandoned ritual action (BSB 3.4.25; for abbreviations see p. viii), with the liberated man (*jīvanmukta*) who, by definition of being liberated, no longer acts; his body merely unfolds or manifests what remains of his human destiny, his *prārabdhakarma* (see below, pp. 44–5). While the renouncer and the *jīvanmukta* have transcended the world of human transaction governed by *dharma*, the householder is obliged to maintain his household fires and pursue his worldly goals.

Traditionally, the high-caste Hindu householder has had three goals of life (*puruṣārtha*) or 'three paths' (*trivarga*): the fulfilling of social and moral obligations (*dharma*), becoming prosperous or the acquisition of profit (*artha*), and the experience of pleasure (*kāma*) (*Manu* 2.13, 224, 7.27, 12.34). These three are collectively regarded as 'the good' (*śreyas*) in *Manu* (2.224). While *mokṣa* might be the highest goal of life according to the great tradition of renunciation, and indeed is added as a fourth to the three goals at a date later than *Manu*, *dharma* is its equal in the Hindu law books and in the householder's everyday existence; the householder's practical ideology of moral obligation and action takes precedence over the renouncer's ideology of actionless freedom. There are then competing goods for the Hindu householder: the good which is *dharma* and the good which is *mokṣa*.

The primacy of ethics as *dharma*

The term *dharma*, as has been frequently pointed out, has no direct English counterpart, and we are faced with the difficulty of finding semantic equivalents which convey the various cultural resonances of the term. It has been variously rendered as 'religion', 'duty', 'justice', 'law' and 'ethics' (Coward et al., 1991: 2; Zaehner, 1966: 102–24). Although etymologies do not tell us much about the meaning of a term in the context of its use, Zaehner relates its root *dhṛ*, which means 'to hold, have or maintain', to the cognate terms in Latin *firmus*, 'firm' and *forma*, 'form'. He then defines *dharma* as 'the "form" of things as they are and the power that keeps them as they are and not otherwise' (Zaehner, 1966: 2). In other words, *dharma* can be broadly interpreted as the force or power which controls or constrains phenomena in the universe. This is a very wide definition, yet, on the other hand, the term can also refer, much more narrowly, to a person's nature or an aspect of ritual action.

Our main concern here is the sphere of ethics, of which the term *dharma* is arguably the nearest Sanskrit equivalent; though whereas in the West 'ethics' can be discussed independently of 'religion', in Hinduism *dharma* implies 'correct action', in the sense both of fulfilling moral obligations to one's kith and kin, and of fulfilling one's ritual obligations. It is therefore intimately connected with the idea of purity (*śuddha*) (see below).

Perhaps what is most striking about *dharma* is that it is both universal and particular; it refers both to a cosmic, eternal principle (*sanātana dharma*) and to specific laws and the contexts to which they are applied. *Dharma* is a cosmic principle which is responsive to different situations and contexts. This idea is illustrated in the Hindu law books, the earliest of which is the *Manusmṛti*, which reached its present form probably about the second century CE, and in the school of Hindu philosophy called the Mīmāṃsā, whose root text, Jaimini's *Mīmāṃsā-sūtra*, was composed around the second century BCE. The Mīmāṃsā, which, along with the Vedānta or Uttara Mīmāṃsā, provided in the medieval period one of the main philosophies of the Brahman householder (Sanderson, 1985: 193–7), offered an understanding of *dharma* as an eternal principle expressed at a human level as ritual obligation.

Jaimini defined *dharma* as that of which the characteristic is an obligation or injunction (*vidhi*) (MS 1.1.2). That is, *dharma* is an obligation enjoined by the Veda which specifically refers to vedic ritual action (*karma*), or 'sacrifice', and the supererogatory ritual actions for gaining wealth and happiness in this world and in the next. The performance of obligatory actions brings in itself no reward; it is expected that one should do this, for their non-performance, that is, the performance of that which is not *dharma* (*adharma*), would bring retribution or 'evil' (*pāpa*). The performance of ritual actions for a later reward in heaven, on the other hand, creates an invisible, transcendent force (*apūrva*) which produces the desired result (MS 2.1.2). *Dharma*, for the Mīmāṃsā, is identified with vedic obligation or injunction which is eternal, and also with action which is particular. Thus *dharma* has a transcendent, eternal aspect which is expressed at a human level in ritual actions which produce that which is good (*śreyaskāra*).

In order to 'produce that which is good', the Brahman's ritual action must be pure. The term 'purity' (*śuddha*), Madan (1987: 58) observes, 'refers to the most desired condition of the human body or, more comprehensively, the most desired state of being'. Such a desired state of body or being is achieved through ritual purification, for example by pouring water over the body, and through the avoidance of impurity, for example by avoiding 'polluting' castes and 'polluting' substances such as menstrual blood. 'That which is good' is also related to 'the auspicious' (*śubha*), the importance of which in Hindu culture has again been pointed out by Madan (Madan, 1987: 50–8). Thus the optimal conditions for a ritual action, a *dharma*, would be in a condition of purity (*śuddha*) at an auspicious (*śubha*) time such as a particular astrological configuration. However, as with most things in life, these conditions are rarely completely met. For example, Madan discusses the example of childbirth which, if it occurs under the right circumstances, is auspicious, yet it is also hedged about with pollution and so is impure and, in one sense, inauspicious (Madan, 1987: 60; Coward et al., 1991: 11).

The *Dharmaśāstra*s are concerned with moral obligation which, in those texts and in Hindu life generally, cannot be separated from ritual obligation and obligations entailed by one's social status and context. These texts are also concerned with *dharma* as justice, and the obligations of the just king to administer justice and punishment (*daṇḍa*) as befits the circumstance. *Dharma*, while being a cosmic principle, is at the same time particular to each situation. The *Manusmṛti* provides us with many examples of this. The religious duties are different in different ages and vary according to caste (*jāti*), family (*kula*) and country (*deśa*) (*Manu* 1.85, 119); the obligations of the servant (*śūdra*) are different from those of the higher castes – they cannot, for example, be initiated or learn the Veda (*Manu* 3.156, 4.99, 10.4, 127); and kings must judge according to the customs and particular duties (*svadharma*) of each region (*Manu* 8.41).

This idea of *svadharma*, one's own particular duty, is important in understanding the 'context-sensitive' nature of *dharma*. In the *Bhagavadgītā*, Kṛṣṇa, an incarnation of God, responds to the hero Arjuna's reluctance to fight on the battlefield by arguing first that one cannot kill the immortal soul (*ātman*) in any living thing, but secondly, and perhaps more importantly and persuasively for Arjuna, that he must fight because it is his duty, his *svadharma*, as a member of the warrior class. Duty is relative to different contexts; what is correct action for the servant might be incorrect for the warrior, what is correct for a man may be incorrect for a woman, and so on.

Let us illustrate this with reference to *Manu*'s ideas about justice. People in different castes do not have the same duties or the same rites. A good Hindu's duties are class- and caste-specific, and it is better to fulfil one's own caste obligations, however badly, than to do another's duties well. Justice, similarly, is relative to different contexts. Justice, another translation of the term *dharma*, is administered according to *Manu* by the king through 'the stick' (*daṇḍa*) or 'punishment'. Indeed, ideologically, in the period of classical and medieval Hinduism, the king is the centre of the Hindu universe, and his actions ripple down to the people. The chief function of the king was to protect the people, and to keep the four classes in order and maintain the system of the four stages of life (*Manu* 7.35). Through ensuring the boundaries of caste, the king ensured the prosperity of the communities over which he governed. Furthermore, through the practice of *daṇḍa*, which varied from community to community, he ensured the continued harmony of the state.

The particularity of *dharma* can also be illustrated with regard to marriage. One of the most important moral concerns of normative, brahmanical Hinduism has been the maintenance of caste boundaries through marriage restrictions. Marriage should be endogamous within the caste group, though exogamous within a sub-caste or 'lineage' (*gotra*), and of course marriages were, and continue to be, arranged. In India, as elsewhere throughout the world, people fall in love outside the permitted social restrictions of who is marriageable. The *Manusmṛti* recognizes this to an extent and lists eight kinds of marriage between the four social classes which vary in degree of acceptability, the highest kind being the respectable arranged marriage of a high-caste girl to a man of good character, the lowest, 'ghoulish marriage' (*paiśāca vivāhana*), being sexual intercourse with a sleeping, mad or drunken woman (*Manu* 3.21–35).

Indeed, the text is tolerant, though disapproving, of some higher-caste men marrying lower-caste women. A woman of the servant class (*śūdra*) can marry a commoner (*vaiśya*), who belongs technically to the 'twice-born' (i.e., one who has undergone vedic initiation). However, the text says that twice-born men who, because of infatuation or delusion (*moha*), marry women of the servant class, reduce their families and their descendants to the status of servants (*Manu* 3.13–16). The text, however, tends to be prohibitive of the purest caste, the Brahmans, marrying lower, more polluting, castes. Indeed a priest who sleeps with a servant girl goes to hell and loses the status of a priest if he begets a son by her. Again *Manu* recognizes the nature of fleeting sexual attraction, and allows for this in the idea of the temporary marriage (called the *gandharva* marriage) for the higher classes, when a girl and her lover make love purely out of desire (*kāmasaṃbhava*) (*Manu* 3.17). However, the text also prescribes severe punishments, ranging from the loss of two fingers to capital punishment, for the transgressing of sexual boundaries or 'sexual misconduct' (*saṃgrahaṇa*), delineated by caste (*Manu* 3.32), a category which includes adultery with high-caste women and homosexuality (*klība*). Indeed, one passage says that the king should have an adulterous woman eaten by dogs in a place frequented by many people (*Manu* 8.371).

In all these situations, punishments are more severe for a woman, and the woman is seen to be more passive than a man. In the light of contemporary Western sensibilities *Manu*, and indeed many attitudes and practices of contemporary Hinduism, might seem archaic and restrictive of women's rights. *Manu* is quite clear that a high-caste woman, whether a girl, young woman or old woman, must do nothing independently (*svatantra*), even in her own house, but must throughout her life be subject to male authority – as a child to her father, as a married woman to her husband and to her sons when her husband (or 'lord') is dead (*Manu* 5.147–148). By leading a life constantly subject to male authority, a woman will attain heaven and so reap the reward of her austerity, though she will be born in a lower form should she neglect these duties (*Manu* 5.161–164).

The ideal woman is reflected mythologically in the famous epic, the *Rāmāyaṇa*. In this text Rāma, an incarnation (*avatāra*) of the supreme God Viṣṇu, has been banished to the forest by his father in fulfilment of a promise to Rāma's stepmother. He is accompanied by his brother Lakṣmaṇa and his wife Sītā, who is often regarded as the perfect Hindu woman. Rāma and Sītā are role models for the ideal Hindu couple living in accordance with *dharma*. Rāma is robust, honest, and devoted to Sītā who is demure, modest and dedicated to Rāma, her lord. Yet she is also very strong in herself, undergoing hardship and displaying great loyalty to her husband. While in the forest Sītā is abducted by the demon Rāvaṇa who takes her to the island of Laṅka. Rāma and his brother, with the help of a monkey army, eventually rescue her, the demon is defeated and good triumphs over evil. Now although Sītā has remained faithful to Rāma, she has to undergo an ordeal by fire to prove her chastity to the world before Rāma will accept her back – a story which expresses an ambivalent attitude towards woman as a model of virtue, yet at the same time not to be trusted.

In both epic and law book we are presented with ideal images of gender roles and what is regarded as appropriate behaviour. *Manu* presents us with a normative, brahmanical view which may not have reflected social reality, but most certainly reflects the ideology of the Brahman class who composed it and who wielded influence and power in the Hindu world. We see here clearly that *dharma* is not only class-specific but gender-specific as well. The kinds of moral choice open to women are more restricted in both *Manu* and the *Rāmāyaṇa* than for men. Sītā, the exemplar of female virtue, has little choice. Although it is she who chooses to accompany her husband into the forest and who undergoes various vows of religious austerity (*vrata*), she tends nevertheless to be passive, being abducted by a male demon and rescued by her husband! Sītā is the ideal model for the Hindu woman, loyal and deferential to her husband, yet at the same time possessing immense personal strength. Sītā is, however, not the only model or image of women presented in the Hindu tradition. There are the autonomous, ferocious and erotic goddesses such as Kālī or the 'mothers' (*mātṛkā*), though these tend to be associated with Tantrism and are feared by orthodoxy. There are also historical figures such as Mahādevyakka, a Kanarese *bhakti* poet, who exhibit strength, autonomy and a breaking out of expected gender roles and male dominance, though such figures of female autonomy are rare.

Even allowing for the strength of women portrayed in Hindu mythology, ideologically women would nevertheless seem to be most constrained by the classical Hindu model of social relations. Indeed, the low-caste woman is probably the most restricted in terms of choice and opportunities open to her, while the high-caste male is the least restricted. This traditional limitation of moral choice among Hindu women is again reflected in the institution of *satī* which had developed by the fourteenth century CE, whereby a woman would die on her husband's funeral pyre if he predeceased her. This was certainly practised, though not universally, and, although illegal, is beginning to recur in contemporary India. The very word *satī* means 'good woman' and she who performed it would immediately secure heaven for both herself and her husband. Indeed, the *satī* phenomenon is complex and cannot be seen purely in terms of male oppression of women, but also must be seen in the context of female empowerment; the *satī* becomes like a *yogin*, purifying herself and her family and creating good *karma* for the next life in choosing to assert herself by dying on the pyre.[5] Such a death could feasibly be regarded from within the tradition as a noble and free choice which elevates the status of those participating in it and sanctifies the *satī*.

But to return to the central concept of *dharma* of which *satī* would be an expression. While *dharma* might be regarded as context-sensitive, responding to gender roles and caste, the author of *Manu* is not an ethical relativist. *Dharma* is an eternal principle, a natural law, but its specific laws or codes of conduct vary according to social ranking and, indeed, according to time of year and time of life.

The Hindu hierarchical social structure and the emphasis on duty with regard to class and stage of life (*varṇāśramadharma*) are absolute and sacred for *Manu*. The ideology of caste is legitimated in the first chapter with reference to the myth of the primal sacrifice of the supreme person (*puruṣa*), in the *Ṛg-veda* (10.90), from which the four classes originated: the Brahmans from his mouth, the rulers from his arms, the commoners from his thighs and the servants from his feet (*Manu* 1.31). This structure is absolute, but moral standards are flexible within it, both to allow for the different dispositions of the different classes, and to allow for human fallibility and different responses to existential situations. *Dharma* in principle is absolute, but it functions in particular, practical situations, and *Manu* recognizes the fact that people do not universally stick to it; *dharma* has to be context-sensitive in its response to human crises (*āpad*) (Doniger, 1991: liii–liv). Sex outside caste-restricted marriage is wrong, but there is nevertheless the institution of the temporary, *gandhārva*, marriage; killing is wrong, but there are circumstances in which it is permitted, for instance in defending oneself. There is then the general principle and universal moral law of *dharma*, but this must meet and adapt to the everyday reality of making moral choices for the Brahman householder. It is this level of the particularity of moral choice and prescription that is addressed by *Manu*.

We have presented a general picture of higher-caste males exercising the widest choice and lower-caste females being the most restricted. There are, however, problems here and the picture is a more complex one. The extent to which even high-caste males have been autonomous agents is open to debate. In a famous essay, Louis Dumont contrasted the Hindu social agent within the caste system, the man-in-the-world subject to *dharma*, with the world-renouncer beyond the caste system seeking *mokṣa*. The man-in-the-world, the social agent, is subordinated to the collective social order. He is not an 'individual', according to Dumont, being defined purely in terms of his place in a set of social relations. The renouncer, by contrast, is not subject to these social constraints and so is 'invested with an individuality' (Dumont, 1980: 274).

Dumont has been criticized, particularly for his idea of the 'individual' in Hindu society. The anthropologist McKim Marriott, by contrast, argues that there are no *in*dividuals in Hindu society, but rather *di*viduals, by which he means that the boundaries of 'persons' are variable and fluid within Hindu social transactions. The Hindu social agent is not individual, but subject to various transferences of his 'coded-substance', the 'form' and 'content', or 'constraint' and 'constrained' aspects of a social actor.[6] Thus the renouncer tries to minimize his transactions with the social world, while the warrior maximizes his.

The implication of this is that autonomy, the freedom to have acted otherwise, is contingent upon social standing in a scale which, as we have seen in *Manu*, is regarded as absolute and which is based on the opposition between purity and pollution. According to Dumont, the renouncer has gone beyond this dichotomy and so is outside the social world, while Marriott has argued that, on the contrary, the renouncer is still very much a part of the social matrix. The degree of autonomy of social agents in the Hindu world is important for an understanding of moral decision-making in Hinduism. There is no necessary correlation between high caste–more autonomous, and low caste–less autonomous, precisely because of the purity–pollution spectrum. Indeed, the highest, purest class and caste – the Brahmans – are arguably less autonomous than the commoner (*vaiśya*) class, who are self-supporting and to a large extent independent of the other classes. In contrast to the commoner, because of his purity, the Brahman is hedged around with prohibitions, and fear or anxiety (*śaṅkā*) of pollution and inauspicious (*aśubha*) events or times.

Manu presents a picture of the Brahman as a learned man who performs his correct ritual obligations, and who tries hard to restrain his senses 'as a charioteer his race-horses' (*Manu* 1.88). He is, then, a model of rational self-control and restrained behaviour. His ultimate, distant goal might be liberation (*mokṣa*), but his immediate concern is the fulfilling of his *dharma*, which means particularly the completion of his ritual duties, including the avoidance of pollution. These ritual injunctions (*vidhi*) are the performance of regular daily rituals (*nityakarma*), occasional rituals (*naimittikakarma*) such as birth, the investiture of the sacred thread (*upanayana*) and funeral rites in the life-cycle, or transformative rituals (*saṃskāra*) of the twice-born, and rituals performed for desired results (*kāmyakarma*) such as the obtaining of heaven upon death (Potter, 1991: 257).

Alongside these rites are the rites of expiation or restoration (*prayaścitta*) for sins (*pāpa*) committed either with awareness or inadvertently (*Manu* 12.45). By 'sins' the Brahman householder means adharmic behaviour, such as the neglect of the three kinds of ritual or the neglect of caste duties (*Manu* 12.44). Indeed *Manu* lists a variety of sins for which *prayaścitta* would need to be performed, ranging from violating the *guru*'s marriage-bed, which refers to adultery with the *guru*'s wife, to theft and murder. For example, one of the expiations for killing a Brahman would be to build a hut in a forest and live there for twelve years, begging food and using a skull for his emblem (*Manu* 12.72). Indeed this expiation is less injurious than that prescribed for violating the *guru*'s marriage-bed. Here the text offers various alternatives, including castration and walking, with the severed organs, to the south-west until death (*Manu* 12.105). It is noteworthy that expiation is for 'sin' (*pāpa*) which means 'going against *dharma*', and guilt (*enas*) is specifically related to having violated prescribed dharmic, caste-specific obligations. Indeed there is even a sense of 'conscience' about violated dharmic behaviour in that the body is freed from the wrongdoing (*adharma*), the more the mind (*manas*) despises what has been done (*Manu* 11.230).

Dharma, which embraces caste duties and moral obligations, is the governing force of the Brahman householder's life. This *dharma* is explained in the law books which, although not eternal revelation (*śruti*), are nevertheless regarded as being based on revelation: the laws which texts such as *Manu* expound, while being variable, are based on the eternal law of *dharma* and the Brahman's autonomy is totally constrained by this. The Brahman does, of course, have freedom of action, but this is constrained by *dharma*: if he performs an action which is against *dharma*, he will have to suffer the consequences in this or a future life, or pay for his action by expiation. Alternatively, the Brahman householder, should he be so inclined, could neglect his brahmanical duties and adopt the alien world-view of a tantric practitioner who, as we shall see, espouses a doctrine and practice which would be anathema from the perspective of orthodox *dharma*.

Action and moral retribution

The Brahman's ritual obligations and expiations have continued in Hinduism from the time of the Vedas to the present. The ritual act in vedic times was known as the 'sacrifice' (*yajña*), which became a synonym for many kinds of religious behaviour. Religious rituals were also known by the term *karma* or 'action'. This term initially referred to ritual and its implied invisible effects, but came to be applied, in the *Upaniṣad*s and in early Buddhism, to action generally and its consequences, which took effect not only during one life, but over several lifetimes. The theory of *karma* came to be a general explanation of human suffering and a motivation for stepping off the cycle of reincarnation (*saṃsāra*) and seeking liberation through becoming a renouncer (*saṃnyāsin*).

Manu is quite specific about the moral retribution due to action over a period of lives: action, it says, produces 'auspicious and inauspicious fruits' (*śubhāśubhaphalaṃ*) (*Manu* 12.3). An auspicious result would be due to a person having fulfilled their dharmic obligations specific to their caste and stages of life, an inauspicious fruit to their not having fulfilled their *dharma*. Actions, says *Manu*, originate in the mind (*manas*), speech (*vāc*) and body (*deha*), all of which have consequences. Mental actions, such as coveting the possessions of others, thinking about what is undesirable and believing in false ideas; verbal actions, such as lying, abuse, slander and gossip; and bodily actions, such as theft, violence which is against the law, and adultery, all result in a specific kind of retribution in a future life. An inauspicious or sinful mental act will lead to rebirth in a low caste, a sinful verbal act to rebirth as a wild animal or bird, and a sinful bodily act to rebirth as something inanimate or a plant (*sthāvaratām*) (*Manu* 12.5–10).

The text also introduces another scheme of action and its retribution based on the model of the three qualities (*guṇa*) inherent in all manifestations, namely light/goodness (*sattva*), passion (*rajas*) and darkness/inertia (*tamas*) (*Manu* 12.24). The results of actions imbued with these three qualities are reincarnations in, respectively, the realms of the gods, the humans and the animals, each of which is further subdivided into low, middle and high. Thus within the realm of goodness are included ascetics (*tāpasa*) and priests (*vipra*); within the realm of passion we have a range of beings from pugilists to rulers (*kṣatriya*); and in the realm of darkness there are animals, foreigners (*mleccha*), actors and demons (*piśāca*) (*Manu* 12.39–50). The text also deals, with graphic particularity, with the destinies for various moral misdemeanours. A violent man, for example, is reborn as a carnivorous beast; a Brahman-killer as an animal such as a dog or an untouchable; various categories of thieves are born as animals (*Manu* 12.59–68), and so on.

Perhaps what is most interesting about this list is that the punishments for misdeeds are caste-specific. That is, the retributions in lower births are due to the failure to perform one's *dharma* correctly. Thus the Brahman who has fallen from his own duty (*svadharma*) becomes a vomit-eating ghost with a flaming mouth (*ulkāmukha-preta*), the warrior who has so fallen becomes a polluted substance and corpse-eating ghost, a commoner who falls from his duty is reborn as a pus-eating ghost who sees through its anus (*maitrākṣijyotika-preta*), while a servant becomes a ghost which feeds on moths or body-lice. Conversely, the high-caste Hindu who conforms to behaviour prescribed in the Veda, that is, performs his ritual obligations (*śreyas*), becomes equal to the gods (*Manu* 12.71–90). Indeed, in other law books, Rocher notes, those who fulfil their moral obligations to their *varṇa* are reborn higher up the scale, though the texts do not tell us 'what happens upward after the Brāhmaṇa or downward after the Śūdra' (Rocher, 1980: 75–6). Presumably there would be transmigration to higher and lower non-human forms.

There are in classical Hinduism three kinds of *karma*: residues of actions performed in a previous life whose effects have not yet begun to be manifested, a 'store-house' of action (*sañcitakarma*); karmic residues whose effects become manifested in one's present life (*prārabdhakarma*); and the seeds of action sown in this life which will come to fruition in a future life (*āgamin* or *bhaviṣyatkarma*). So in each life a being is working out the results of previous actions and sowing the seeds of future action. The law of action is not therefore fatalistic since, while *prārabdhakarma* determines one's present existence, this can be changed by an act of will or by some external circumstance such as premature death. Śaṃkara likens this kind of *karma* to an arrow which will continue on its course unless obstructed by some other force (Potter, 1991: 256). Only the liberated man (*jīvanmukta*) is free from *karma*, in the sense that his liberation experience has eradicated his *sañcitakarma* and he can no longer produce *āgami-karma* through his actions in the present life. Only his *prārabdhakarma* needs to unfold, which done, there is no more return to the cycle of reincarnation. The liberated man is, therefore, beyond the realm of moral retribution. He can no longer reap the rewards of past actions, nor can he create future actions, having transcended the ethical sphere.

This figure of detachment and transcendence is not, however, the hero of the Hindu law books, which look, rather, to the householder as their exemplar. It is clear from *Manu* that the ideal Brahman householder is one who fulfils his ritual obligations, who keeps free from pollution and whose body and desires are under his rational self-control. The Brahman should make oblations every day, be non-violent (*ahiṃsā*), tell the truth, be without anger and be straightforward (*Manu* 11.222). The ideal is to become a *tridaṇḍin*, one possessing a 'triple stick', like an ascetic who carried such a trident, to control the actions of body, speech and mind. With this internalized 'triple stick' the Brahman represses emotion, controls lust (*kāma*) and anger (*krodha*), and attains perfection (*siddhi*) (*Manu* 2.10–11). Such a Brahman 'burns down' the fruits of action through knowledge of, and action in accordance with, the Veda. Indeed all other systems or doctrines outside the Veda bear no fruit for him, being based on darkness.

Dharma and the tantric traditions

In contrast to the controlled Brahman householder presented in *Manu*, other religious traditions within Hinduism, notably the tantric traditions, present very different images, at least at an ideological level. The tantric systems, which the author of *Manu* would no doubt have classified as 'based on darkness' had he known about them, claim a revelation other than the Veda, namely the Āgamas and Tantras. These texts, which generally take the form of a dialogue between the Lord (Bhagvan) as Śiva (though it can be Viṣṇu) and the Goddess as his female energy, *śākti*, can be dated from between the seventh and eleventh centuries CE, several hundred years after *Manu*, though the ideas they contain and the traditions they express may well be much older.

The locatable origins of the various tantric traditions are the ascetics living in the cremation grounds (*śmaśāna*), the most highly polluting place for the orthodox Brahman householder. These renouncers, living literally on the edges of society, were interested not in the performance of normative Hindu *dharma*, but in the acquisition of supernatural power (*siddhi*) and pleasure in higher worlds (*bhukti*) and, eventually, in liberation. These ascetics would cover themselves in ashes from the cremation ground, have long matted hair, and perhaps go naked in imitation of their terrible gods such as Bhairava, a ferocious form of Śiva (Sanderson, 1985: 201). Indeed, such people were regarded as highly polluting by the orthodox Brahman, and Sanderson cites the example of such ascetics being classified as 'unseeables': should a Brahman inadvertently see one, he would stare into the sun to purify his eyes, so polluting were they considered to be (Sanderson, 1985: 211, n. 61).

Confined to the cremation grounds, such traditions, though unpleasant and highly polluting, were not an explicit threat to brahmanical orthopraxy. However, Sanderson has shown how the ideologies and practices of these traditions became absorbed into the orthoprax and orthodox Brahman communities, particularly in Kashmir. This brahmanical tantric tradition, referred to as 'Kashmir Śaivism' or, more accurately, the Trika, drew its inspiration from the cremation ground traditions and was theologically monistic. These tantric ideologies and their concomitant practices were anathema to the orthodox, and threatened to subvert brahmanical ideology, especially once this religion had established a common base among Brahman householders.

Not all tantric traditions, however, were equally threatening, and some indeed were absorbed into quite orthodox and respectable traditions. The Pāñcarātra tradition, which is Vaiṣṇava Tantrism, based on texts called the *Pāñcarātra Āgama*s, became absorbed into the Śrī Vaiṣṇava tradition and exerted influences on the theology of the famous Vedānta theologian Rāmānuja (d. *c.* 1137 CE). The Śrī Vidyā tantric tradition became associated with the non-dualist tradition of Śaṃkara (788–820 CE) and was absorbed by the orthodox Smārta Brahman community of South India. Finally the Śaiva Siddhānta, a theistic tradition dominant in South India, initially developed in Kashmir at variance with the monistic Kashmir Śaivism, but accepted caste prescriptions and leaned towards vedic orthodoxy while accepting the dualistic Śaiva *tantra*s as its ultimate source of authority.

There have, however, been traditions and texts which have clearly remained outside the vedic fold. Such traditions and texts, which tend to be centred on Śiva and/or the Goddess in one of her forms (and which Sanderson in his publications has called 'hard' tantric traditions), advocate ritual practices involving polluting substances such as corpses, menstrual blood and semen, and polluting behaviour such as caste-free sexual intercourse. These traditions acted out the prescriptions in the tantric texts 'literally', which became known as the 'left-hand practice' (*vāmācāra*) as opposed to the 'right-hand practice' (*dakṣiṇācāra*) which took such prescriptions only 'symbolically'.[7] These 'left-hand' traditions seem so obviously incompatible with *dharma* that they raise challenging questions for the Hindu understanding of morality.

One of the claims of Tantrism is that values are relative and that transcendent reality, identified with pure, undifferentiated consciousness (*saṃvit, caitanya*) in the systems of Kashmir Śaivism, is beyond the social world and the realm of ethics. The *Kulārṇava-tantra*, a *śākta* text of the Kula tradition, says that values are inverted in the tradition; what is injurious (*bādhaka*) becomes spiritually useful (*sādhaka*) and what is unethical (*adharma*) becomes ethical (*dharma*) (KT 9.26). The 'subversive' nature of tantric traditions can be seen in the statement that one can be 'internally a Kaula (i.e., a tantric practitioner), externally a Śaiva, while remaining vedic in one's social practice' (Sanderson, 1985: 205, n. 130). That is, Abhinavagupta (*c.* 975–1025 CE), the most famous of the Kashmiri Śaiva theologians, is in one sense agreeing with the *Manusmṛti* that *dharma* is context-sensitive. Values are relative, or rather hierarchical, and here the value system of the vedic brahmanical orthodoxy is ultimately rejected or, more precisely, relegated to a low position in the tantric hierarchy of traditions. Vedic values, vedic *dharma* of the kind advocated in *Manu*, are entirely relative and of no ultimate value. What is of overarching importance for Abhinavagupta is the superiority of non-dualism over other doctrines: that Śiva is the one, non-dual reality identified with consciousness.

At first glance there appear to be parallels between the non-dualism of Abhinavagupta and the non-dualism of Śaṃkara's Advaita Vedānta. However, although, as far as I know, Śaṃkara is never mentioned by Abhinavagupta, parallels with Advaita are rejected by the Śaiva tradition on the grounds that the Vedāntic *brahman* is without *śakti* and so is powerless, a mere 'eunuch' (*ṣaṇḍha*). Furthermore, whereas Advaita Vedānta is a totally orthodox system, accepting the values of *varṇāśramadharma*, Śaiva non-dualism rejects those values and retains the hard tantric traditions at its heart. There is a disjunction here with regard to ethics between the brahmanical emphasis on *dharma*, which means the maintenance of ritual purity, and the tantric rejection of *dharma* as a norm, which means the courting of impurity and the transcending of inhibition (*śaṅkā*).

Of particular opprobrium for the orthodox is the use in tantric rituals of prohibited substances, the five *m*s (*pañcamakara*): meat (*māṃsa*), fish (*matsya*), wine (*madya*), parched grain (*mudrā*) and sexual intercourse (*maithuna*). *Manu* expressly forbids the eating of meat and fish and the consuming of alcohol, as these are substances which pollute the Brahman's purity (*Manu* 10.88). In the cremation-ground traditions of 'hard' Tantra, these substances were used as offerings to the terrible deities of the tantrika's pantheon. Liberation or power is attained through the reversal of vedic values; ritual impurity rather than purity becomes the basis for spiritual freedom. In the 'householder's Tantrism' of Kashmiri Brahmans, what became important was the religious experience of the identification of limited individual consciousness with the unlimited consciousness of Śiva. This identification could be achieved through the esoteric rite of the *kulaprakriyā*, which culminated in sexual intercourse between the male practitioner (*sādhaka*), who was ritually identified with Śiva, for only a god can worship a god (SN 50), and his female 'messenger' (*dūtī*), identified with Śakti. The emphasis in this particular rite was soteriological and, indeed, aesthetic; the bliss of sexual union transported the practitioners to the bliss of Śiva's pure consciousness. In many left-hand tantric rites the practitioners would not be married, they would not be of the same caste, and the woman would be menstruating – a very polluting condition for the orthodox Brahman. Some texts even appear to advocate incest, strictly prohibited by orthodox *dharma* (TAV 29, p. 72).

Not only were the sexual practices of Tantrism an offence to orthodoxy, but so also were the consuming of meat and the suggestion of killing. The orthodox Brahman was strictly vegetarian, which meant in a Hindu context that no meat, fish, fowl or eggs were to be consumed. *Manu*, however, does allow the consumption of meat which has been offered in vedic sacrifice, though there is some ambivalence about this, given the general emphasis on non-violence (*ahiṃsā*). A Brahman is on the one hand urged to perform vedic sacrifice, yet on the other to befriend all creatures (*Manu* 2.87, 6.75). But, given the ambivalence towards killing in his own tradition, it is little wonder that the tantric rites were quite unacceptable to him. The Brahman's ritual purity would be threatened by the consumption of non-vegetarian food, which had possibly been offered to non-vedic deities, and of alcohol, which would threaten his self-controlled equilibrium.

Tantric ideology is generally an affront to vedic orthodoxy. The

Trika Śaivism of Kashmir undermines the social balance and implicitly questions the hierarchical models of the orthodox tradition, offering in their stead initiatory hierarchical models of its own, with its own system at the apex (PH v. 8). Caste, as having any ontological and soteriological significance, is rejected – both implicitly in tantric ritual's eschewing of sexual controls, and explicitly in saying that tantric initiation eradicates caste (Sanderson, 1985: 205). Indeed, there are wider questions here concerning different conceptualizations of the self or person in the two traditions. For orthodox ideology, represented by *Manu*, the person is *prima facie* an actor defined completely by his or her social matrix, in which the highest ideal is the detached, controlled Brahman; for the Kashmir Śaiva the person's true identity is unconstrained consciousness, and the highest ideal is the liberated *yogin*.

Such differences are also reflected in gender. Sanderson points out that there are great differences in models of women presented in the orthodox and tantric traditions (Sanderson, 1985: 202). In the former, as we have seen above, they are models of docile dependence, without autonomy, whereas in tantric traditions, women have been regarded as channels of esoteric power and knowledge. The *dūtī* was the 'door' through which the power of the divine was transmitted (TA 29.122–123), and should, according to Jayaratha, Abhinavagupta's commentator, be intelligent, beautiful and displaying signs of possession (TAV 29, p. 68f.). Although the respect and ideological function of women in tantric traditions are higher than those of the orthodox, the extent to which this has been reflected as a social reality is questionable.[8]

Tantric traditions consciously break orthodox taboos in order to offer worship to unorthodox deities and to attain the religious experience of union with Śiva. Indeed, for the tantric ritual to work, Abhinavagupta says that the practitioner must be without desire (TA 29.99–100), which would keep him attached to the world from which he wishes to escape. The end is identification with pure consciousness, and the means is the stripping away or deconstruction of limiting social identities through their transcendence. This is significant because here we see how a monistic ideology takes precedence over brahmanical social reality: ethics becomes subordinated to ontology or even aesthetic experience (and the true identity of the person becomes, not the limited subject of first person predicates, but the unlimited subject of universal consciousness).

Ethics and ontology

R. C. Zaehner argued that the monistic philosophies which uphold the idea of the union of opposites, the absolute or ultimate reality conceived as a union of masculine and feminine principles, tend towards unethical behaviour. If the absolute is beyond good and evil, then these are relative concepts which have no bearing on that ultimate state or on the means of achieving it. Thus, conventionally 'wrong' or 'evil' behaviour could lead to or express a transcendent state. Zaehner cited a passage from the *Kulārṇava Tantra* which describes an ecstatic orgy in which usual social codes of behaviour have been abandoned.[9] He then went on to draw parallels between this and the behaviour of the 'Family', a twentieth-century quasi-religious group led by Charles Manson which undertook a number of murders in California in the late 1960s, arguing that such behaviour is a consequence of belief in a transcendent state of being beyond good and evil. In *Our Savage God*, Zaehner wrote:

> There is much nobility and probably much truth in the theory of the 'union of opposites' proclaimed by Heraclitus and the Upanishads alike . . . But it needs to be rigorously checked by the rational mind which it would destroy. If not then 'all things are lawful'. And is it a coincidence that this particular sect called itself the 'Family' as Charlie Manson called his own devoted band? Or is there a mysterious but real solidarity in what Manson called the 'total experience', which for this Tantric family was 'Bliss' and 'participation in the Divine'?
>
> (pp. 102–3)

The issue of the relation between behaviour and ideology, between action and belief, needs to be addressed here. This is a complex subject and our remarks will be confined to Zaehner's claim in respect of Hinduism. Put simply, Zaehner would seem to be arguing that ethical behaviour is dependent upon belief systems or, more precisely, upon ontology. On this account, dualist ontologies as in Śaiva Siddhānta, in which there is a distinction between the absolute and the particular soul, are more conducive to ethical behaviour, whereas non-dualist ontologies as in Kashmir Śaivism are not. Indeed, according to Zaehner, non-dualist ontologies when pushed to their logical extreme produce murderers.

It should perhaps be remarked that Zaehner was perceptive to an extent, for it is the Śaiva and Śākta monistic *tantras* which tend to advocate 'left-hand' practices such as caste-free sexual intercourse, whereas the softer Śaiva dualist *tantra*s and the *Pāñcarātra Āgama*s do not. Indeed, monistic texts of Kashmir Śaivism state explicitly the logical development of a pure monism: if everything is identical with the pure consciousness of Śiva then, from that absolute perspective, the ideas not only of subject and object, but of purity and impurity are invalid. As has been shown above, ethics in the sense of brahmanical *dharma* are subordinated to a monistic ontology. The *Spanda-kārikā* says that 'whether in thought (*cit*), word (*śabda*) or object (*artha*), there is no condition which is not Śiva. The enjoyer always and everywhere abides in the condition of the enjoyed' (SK 2.4). If all is identical with Śiva, then the mind cannot escape from this condition in any state. The *Vijñāna-bhairava* (116) says: 'Wherever the mind goes, whether without or within, there is the condition of Śiva. Because of his all-pervasiveness where [can the mind] go?' This sentiment is again echoed in a verse quoted by Ksemaraja, the student of Abhinavagupta: 'O dear one, if there are no knowers (*vedaka*) how is there any object of knowledge (*vedya*)? Knower and object of knowledge are one. Thus there is no reality (*tattva*) which is impure (*aśuci*)' (SSV 8).

This terminology is uncompromisingly non-dualistic. The term *tattva*, which I have rendered as 'reality', can be taken both as 'appearance to consciousness' in a phenomenological sense, and as referring to the hierarchical cosmos comprising the emanation of thirty-six *tattva*s. In saying that there is no *tattva* which is impure, because of the ontological identity of subject and object, the text is saying that there is no appearance to consciousness which is impure and, by implication, no action which is impure or against the 'truth'. Such passages are, therefore, denying the orthodox distinction between *dharma* and *adharma* as a consequence of their non-dualist ontology. The absolute consciousness of Śiva is beyond the distinction of *dharma* and *adharma*.

It has been argued that, far from undermining brahmanical Hinduism, tantric practices serve to reinforce it. Caste restrictions on sex and impurity are suspended during the left-hand rites, but these only serve to underline the differences during everyday worldly transactions. The high-caste Brahman in a left-hand rite would not mix with the low-caste woman outside the ritual context. Yet on the other hand it could be argued that left-hand tantrism is surely subversive of brahmanical norms, in so far as it reacts against an ethical and social code perceived to be highly restrictive, particularly of low-caste groups and of women. Indeed, caste distinctions are said to be eradicated by the Kashmir Śaiva tantric initiation, which is given rational back-up by the uncompromising non-dualism of some tantric scriptural authorities. As Sanderson has observed, the distinction between orthodoxy and heterodoxy is not relative in a tantric context (Sanderson, 1985: 211, n. 61).

From the perspective of 'orthodox' and 'orthoprax' vedic Hinduism, tantric non-dualistic ideas might lead to 'immorality' in the sense of adharmic behaviour, and Zaehner might be correct here. However, it is not clear that adharmic behaviour would necessarily be the direct consequence of a non-dualist ontology. The most orthodox of Hindu philosophies, Advaita Vedānta, would never advocate adharmic behaviour. Indeed Advaita Vedānta is deeply concerned with the fulfilling of moral and social obligations.

Among the 'great sayings' (*mahāvākya*) from the revealed scripture (*śruti*), namely the *Upaniṣad*s, of the Advaita Vedānta tradition are such statements as: 'I am the absolute' (*aham brahmāsmi*), 'you are that' (*tat tvam asi*) and 'truly this all is the absolute' (*sarvam khalvidaṃ brahma*). Such passages express similar sentiments to those of Kashmir Śaivism cited above, in that both traditions present a non-dualist ontology. However, Advaita Vedānta places itself squarely in the orthodox vedic tradition. While such statements can be existentially realized in the experience (*anubhava*) of liberation, the ultimate identity of subject and object is also known from the vedic scriptures, one of the valid means of knowledge (*pramāna*). For Śaṃkara, the most famous exponent of Advaita Vedānta, knowledge (*jñāna*) is undoubtedly superior to action (*karma*), and sections in the Veda concerning knowledge of the absolute (*jñānakāṇḍa*) are more important than those concerning action (*karmakāṇḍa*). It therefore follows that knowledge of the absolute, which is liberation, is of a higher order than action and, by implication, ethics as *dharma*. Potter's remarks mentioned at the beginning of the chapter are apposite here: *mokṣa* is for Śaṃkara the highest value, higher than ethical duty, though this does not mean that ethical duty is unimportant. For Śaṃkara there are two levels of truth. From the highest perspective (*paramārtha satya*), the liberated person (*jīvanmukta*) has realized the identity of his self (*ātman*) with the absolute (*brahman*), while from the relative level (*saṃvṛtti satya*) of everyday transaction (*vyāvahāra*), he is a renouncer (*saṃnyāsin*) who behaves in an appropriate, i.e. dharmic, way. Indeed,

Śaṃkara says that precisely *because* of the identity of subject and object in *brahman*, the realizer of this cannot perform faults (*doṣa*) such as not doing good (*akaraṇa*) (BSB 2.2.21).

Unethical behaviour as defined within the context of *dharma* does not necessarily follow from a monistic ontology. Advaita Vedānta, which maintains a non-dualistic ontology, has been one of the central ideologies of the Brahman householder. Perhaps one way of looking at this would be to say that Advaita Vedānta, or indeed the Mīmāṃsā, provided the Brahman householder with a belief system while the *Dharmaśāstra*s provided him with a code of ethics and appropriate styles of behaviour. There would be no 'cognitive dissonance' here, for the philosophical systems would not contradict the dharmic system of action. For the Mīmāṃsāka *dharma* is an eternal natural law which is not dependent upon any theistic reality. Indeed, here we have an atheistic tradition which advocates strict ethical codes of behaviour in accordance with the eternal *dharma*, a fact which militates against Zaehner's claim that theistic systems are more conducive to ethical behaviour.

Zaehner, in his criticism of tantric systems, seems to have been appealing to some universal sense of morality. But the universality of moral statements is in itself a highly contentious issue and its assumption methodologically unjustifiable if understanding rather than judgement is one's aim.[10] To explain and understand tantric traditions and their codes of behaviour it is necessary to locate them in their Indian contexts, rather than discuss them in the light of a presupposed moral discourse.

We can say then that Tantrism might well produce or even advocate adharmic behaviour, but this is not necessarily as a consequence of a non-dualist ontology. Non-dualism, in itself, is neither a necessary nor a sufficient condition for an action to be regarded as unethical in Hinduism. As we have seen with the example of Advaita Vedānta, non-dualism does not entail adharmic behaviour, nor even does atheism. It is not simply non-dualism which creates adharmic behaviour in left-hand *tantra*, but rather a different soteriology in which value is located in the ultimate experience of liberation, and in which liberation and pleasure or joy, particularly sexual pleasure, are not seen to be incompatible.

By way of conclusion, I have tried here to locate the semantic equivalent of 'ethics' in the term *dharma* and pointed to some of the term's applications for the brahmanical householder, with particular reference to the *Manusmṛti*. *Dharma* provides the resources for the making of moral decisions in Hinduism. It both refers to a cosmic, eternal principle, and, more importantly, operates within particular situations which require moral choice. *Dharma* is the context in which moral choice operates, determining the kinds of moral choice available. These moral choices are constrained in brahmanical ideology by a person's location in a hierarchical and gender-specific social structure. This brahmanical understanding of *dharma* can be contrasted with some tantric traditions, such as the monistic Śaivism of Kashmir, in which vedic values are undermined and even reversed. Here, while orthodox norms might be superficially adhered to, we have an ideology and practice which directly threaten brahmanical orthodoxy by undermining caste and elevating women to an ideologically higher status. The brahmanical ideology of ritual duty and eventual liberation through control and purity is contrasted with the tantric ideology of transcending accepted moral codes in its aspiration for total freedom.

Notes

1 W. Cantwell Smith (1962) *The Meaning and End of Religion*. New York: Macmillan, pp. 64ff.

2 S. Weightman (1978) *Hinduism in the Village Setting*. Manchester: Open University, pp. 5f.

3 For the application of the idea of context-sensitive rules to ritual acts prescribed by vedic *dharma*, see F. Staal (1989) *Rules Without Meaning*. New York: Peter Lang.

4 B. K. Matilal (1991) *Perception*. Oxford: Clarendon Press, p. 17.

5 See H. G. Coward, J. J. Lipner and K. K. Young (1991), p. 19; J. Leslie, 'Suttee or *satī*: victim or victor?' in J. Leslie (ed.) (1991) *Roles and Rituals for Hindu Women*. London: Pinter.

6 M. Marriott, 'Hindu transactions, diversity without dualism' in B. Kapferer (ed.) (1977) *Transaction and Meaning: Directions in the Anthropology of Exchange and Symbolic Behavior*. Philadelphia: Institute for the Study of Human Issues.

7 There is a problem with the terms 'literal' and 'symbolic', in so far as the 'literal' use of the five *m*s is also 'symbolic'.

8 S. Gupta, 'Women in the Śaiva/Śākta ethos' in Leslie, op. cit.

9 R. C. Zaehner (1974) *Our Savage God*. London: Collins, pp. 102–3.

10 See P. Donovan, 'Do different religions share common moral ground?' in (1986) *Identity Issues and World Religions*. Australia: Australian Association for the Study of Religion.

Further reading

(I have not given bibliographical information about Sanskrit texts. For details see the bibliographies of Doniger, Potter and Sanderson.)

Bharati, A. (1982) *Hindu Views and Ways and the Hindu–Muslim Interface*. Santa Barbara: Ross-Erikson.

Biardeau, M. (1989) *Hinduism, the Anthropology of a Civilization*. Oxford: Oxford University Press.

Coward, H. G., Lipner, J. J. and Young, K. K. (1991) *Hindu Ethics*. Albany: SUNY Press.

Doniger, W. D. (1991) *The Laws of Manu*. London: Penguin.

Dumont, L. (1980) *Homo Hierarchicus*. Chicago: University of Chicago Press.

Guha, R. and Spivak, G. (1988) *Selected Subaltern Studies*. New York and Oxford: Oxford University Press.

Halbfass, W. (1991) *Tradition and Reflection: Explorations in Indian Thought*. Albany: SUNY Press.

Madan, T. N. (1987) *Non-Renunciation*. Oxford: Oxford University Press.

Potter, K. (1991) *Presuppositions in India's Philosophies*. Delhi: Motilal Banarsidass.

Rocher, L. (1980) 'Karma and rebirth in the Dharmaśāstras' in W. O'Flaherty (ed.) *Karma and Rebirth in Classical Indian Traditions*. Berkeley: University of California Press.

Sanderson, A. (1985) 'Purity and power among the Brahmans of Kashmir' in M. Carrithers et al. (eds) *The Category of the Person*. Cambridge: Cambridge University Press.

Zaehner, R. C. (1966) *Hinduism*. Oxford: Oxford University Press.

3. Women in Hinduism

Sharada Sugirtharajah

Hindu women come from diverse cultural, linguistic, geographical and social backgrounds, and their roles have been varied in history, literary tradition and society. This chapter looks at the varied scriptural, mythological, sociological and philosophical perspectives on women.

Women in *śruti* literature (1500–500 BCE) (the Vedas, *Brāhmaṇa*s, *Āraṇyaka*s and *Upaniṣad*s)

The Aryan pastoralists who came to India from the north-west around 1500 BCE were part of the Indo-European patriarchal tradition. The religion they brought with them involved elaborate rituals, including the sacrificial use of fire. It was patriarchal, family-based and life-affirming. The vedic pantheon is dominated by male deities whereas the pre-Aryan and post-vedic traditions are replete with feminine images of the Divine.

THE VEDAS

The earliest scripture of the Aryans, the *Ṛg-veda*, throws some light on the position of upper-class women in ancient India. Despite the family being patriarchal and patrilineal, women were accorded a significant place within the family and society. Although the roles of wife and mother were of supreme importance, women's intellectual and spiritual quests were recognized. The rite of initiation (*upanayana*) which marked the beginning of vedic studies was open to both men and women. In contrast to later periods, education was not an obstacle to marriage. On the contrary, it was essential, as some knowledge of rituals was required in order to be able to participate in religious activities, which were jointly performed by the husband and wife.

Despite male dominance, women seers, poets and philosophers were held in high esteem in the vedic period. A few of the hymns in the *Ṛg-veda* are attributed to women seers such as Ghoṣā, Apālā, Viśvavārā and Lopāmudrā.

Even though the *Ṛg-veda* shows a marked preference for sons, daughters were not devalued as in the *Atharva-veda* and later scriptural texts. The vedic deity Usha, goddess of Dawn, is described as a beautiful maiden who never grows old. There is reference to young maidens and women participating in a recreational festival called *Samana* and mixing freely with men and women. It appears that both the sexes had some freedom in the choice of marriage partners, although parental guidance and protection played an important part. References suggest that marriage was not compulsory for women and that very early marriages were not prevalent during the vedic period. Ghoṣā figures as an unmarried woman living in her father's house (RV 1.117.7).[1] The few references to the life of a widow suggest that widowhood did not pose any serious problems as it did in subsequent periods. The vedic texts indicate that the widow could marry her brother-in-law (RV 10.40.2).[2] The rite of *satī* (self-immolation of widows) was merely symbolic during the vedic period (see pp. 74–5).

Despite patriarchal orientation, the Ṛg-vedic marriage hymn (8.31.5–9)[3] emphasizes the equality of wife and husband. This is also indicated by the use of the term *dampati*, meaning the married pair (although in some contexts it may signify the 'Lord of the house'). Even to this day the term is used when blessing a newly married couple. The new bride is called *sumaṅgalī* (fortunate). Her presence is considered auspicious and she is associated with prosperity, well-being and happiness. She is warmly welcomed and accorded an honourable position in the family. The Ṛg-vedic marriage hymn welcomes her arrival to take charge of the entire household and to take care of the physical and spiritual welfare of all its members. Her varied roles are indicated by terms such as *Jāyā*, *Janī* and *Patnī*: 'Jāyā has the special sense of a sharer of the husband's affections; Janī, the mother of children; and Patnī, the partner in the performance of sacrifices.'[4]

Marriage being the ideal upheld in the vedic religion, and home being the centre of religious practice, the woman was indispensable from both the domestic and religious point of view. She was important for bearing children, especially male children, and her presence and participation in religious activities were essential. In the Ṛg-vedic marriage hymn, the couple are described as jointly performing ritual acts. They both wash and press the *soma* juice and pluck the sacred grass for sacrifice (RV 8.31.5 and 6).[5]

THE *BRĀHMAṆAS*

Women's ritual and educational roles came gradually to be marginalized in the *Brāhmaṇa* texts, which were primarily concerned with the ritualistic side of sacrifice. With ritual specialists becoming teachers, the gap between men and women widened. Sons came to be valued more highly and rituals were performed to prevent the birth of a daughter. The birth of a son came to be seen as a blessing as it was thought that he alone could ensure the future well-being of the family. Although vedic education was open to women, few were able to undertake it as it became extensive and complicated and the period of study was extended to twelve to sixteen years. Without a proper vedic education participation in sacrifices was not possible.

Women came to be trained in domestic activities and a minimal ritual knowledge was imparted to qualify them for their participation in the sacrifices. They also came to be seen as being impure during menstruation and pregnancy. This no doubt affected the ritual status of women as in other traditions.

THE *ĀRAṆYAKA*S AND *UPANIṢAD*S

In the *Āraṇyaka*s and the *Upaniṣad*s there is a shift from ritual to 'knowledge', or wisdom, which came to be seen as the means to salvation. While the Ṛg-vedic texts exalt marriage and family, the *Upaniṣad*s extol the ascetic life. The emphasis on meditation, knowledge and asceticism affected the later position of women in Hindu society. With the emergence of Buddhism in the sixth century BCE, challenging Brahman ritualism and priesthood, an uneasy tension arose between vedic orthodoxy and the ascetic ideal (upheld by both the *Upaniṣad*s and the Buddha). Unlike Buddhism, in which nuns have a place, Hinduism was not favourably disposed towards women embracing the monastic ideal. Although learned women figure in the

Upaniṣads, women ascetics were less common. In the later vedic period there were two classes of educated women: *brahmavādinīs* and *sadyodvāhās*. For the former, education remained a lifelong pursuit and they were initiated into vedic learning. The latter studied only until they got married. Although the rite of initiation (*upanayana*) was open to both, it was nominally performed for those who desired to get married.

In the *Brāhmaṇa* texts women were already marginalized. Their eligibility to take up the monastic ideal was almost a closed issue except in the case of the few women who remained single and pursued religious studies. The two well-known women in the *Upaniṣads*, Gārgī and Maitreyī, display their critical skills in philosophical discourses, but there is little evidence to suggest that they desired to become ascetics.

In the *Bṛhadāraṇyaka Upaniṣad* (2.4.1–5),[6] Maitreyī and her husband Yājñavalkya discuss how to attain immortality. Yājñavalkya, who is about to take up the life of an ascetic, desires to settle his property between his two wives, Maitreyī and Kātyāyanī. Maitreyī asks her husband whether she would become immortal if she owned the whole earth and all its riches. Yājñavalkya tells her that there is no hope of immortality in wealth. She then asks her husband to enlighten her with his knowledge. Then Yājñavalkya goes on to expound the nature of the true Self which alone could lead to immortality.

In the same *Upaniṣad* (3.6)[7] Gārgī Vācaknavī emerges as the leading figure in the philosophical debate that takes place in the court of King Janaka of Videha. She challenges the learned sage Yājñavalkya on abstruse and esoteric topics.

Although there were a few female ascetics, the monastic ideal was primarily associated with men. The life of a man came to be divided into four stages: student (*brahmacārin*), householder (*gṛhastha*), forest dweller (*vānaprastha*) and renunciant (*saṃnyāsin*). Marriage was important in the stage of a householder, when a man shared his domestic and religious duties with his wife. The desire for the ascetic way of life and *mokṣa* (salvation) diverted his attention from family to other-worldly concerns. In the legal texts women could accompany their husbands into the forest only if the husbands so wished. Even in the forest women's ascetic way of life was devoted to serving their husbands selflessly and observing chastity. While men were entitled to seek *mokṣa* or salvation, women's goals were seen in terms of marriage and rebirth.

Women in myths

The two Hindu epics, the *Mahābhārata* and the *Rāmāyaṇa* (probably compiled around 400 BCE to 200 CE), offer a variety of images of ideal womanhood. The epics focus on the fidelity of women and the ordeals they are prepared to undergo for the sake of their husbands. Even though the *Mahābhārata* has contrasting feminine images, the image of Sītā in the *Rāmāyaṇa* has had a greater impact on Hindu society. The epic figures such as Sītā, Savītrī and Draupadī are known for their wifely devotion and marital fidelity.

SĪTĀ

Sītā figures in the *Rāmāyaṇa* as a devoted wife to Rāma. She chooses to follow her husband into the forest and live in exile with him for fourteen years. When Rāma dissuades her she tells him that a woman's place is with her husband. While in the forest she is abducted by the demon King Rāvaṇa and held captive in his palace. He desires to marry her but she does not succumb. Her devotion to Rāma remains steadfast and finally he rescues her from Rāvaṇa with the help of Hanumān (the monkey-god) and his tribe.

The story reaches an unexpected climax when Rāma renounces her. Although he knows that Sītā is chaste and devoted to him, there is no means of proving it to his subjects. Against his personal wishes he is forced to renounce her. Society will not consider her acceptable, because she has lived in another man's house. In the classical version of the *Rāmāyaṇa* Rāma's rejection of Sītā is linked with the notion of the ideal king whose duty (*rājadharma*) it is to respect the sentiments and wishes of his subjects at the cost of personal suffering. Sītā is shocked at Rāma's behaviour towards her but that does not make her less devoted, though wifely devotion does not prevent her from questioning Rāma's attitude to her abduction by Rāvaṇa:

> If some are faithless, wilt thou find
> No love and truth in woman-kind?
> Doubt others if thou wilt, but own
> The truth which all my life has shown.
>
> (*Rāmāyaṇa* 118.8)[8]

Her honour is at stake. She decides to prove that she is pure and blameless by asking Rāma's brother Lakṣmaṇa to prepare a funeral pyre for her. When she emerges unharmed from the fire her chastity is affirmed and Rāma and Sītā are reunited.

The story does not end there. Rāma is again forced to renounce her, though he knows she is pregnant, as society, despite the fire ordeal, seems reluctant to accept Sītā fully. While in the forest, in the cottage of the sage Vālmīki, Sītā is blessed with twins, Lava and Kuśa. When Rāma comes to know that they are his children, he calls for Sītā. Sītā makes her appearance but decides to follow her own course of action. She prays to the Mother Earth to swallow her up and disappears into it – an appropriate ending as she was found in a 'furrow' by her father and named Sītā, meaning furrow.

In the oral tradition Sītā shows her anger and disapproval of Rāma's treatment of her, and her sons are given a matrilineal heritage. While Sītā's earlier decision to follow Rāma into the forest fulfils traditional expectations of an ideal woman, her role towards the end of the story can be seen as a departure from traditional norms. She emerges as a woman who is capable of shaping her destiny and affirming her deeper self.

Sītā is not worshipped in her own right, as Lakṣmī, Sarasvatī and Pārvatī are. She is always seen with Rāma and his brother Lakṣmaṇa. Although she has popular appeal, she plays an intermediary role – devotees approach her to seek Rāma's grace.

SĀVITRĪ

In another legend in the *Mahābhārata*, Princess Sāvitrī, like Sītā and Draupadī, emerges as a devoted wife and a woman of great spiritual strength. She shows remarkable fortitude and firmness in accomplishing her ideal. She chooses her own husband, Satyavan, although she knows that he has only a year to live. When Yama, the Lord of Death, takes him away, she pleads with him to restore Satyavan to life. Yama commends her wifely devotion and is prepared to offer her any boon other than bringing Satyavan back to life. Sāvitrī requests Yama to grant her the boon of offspring and cleverly argues that her duties as a wife do not end with the death of her husband. Finally, Yama is persuaded to grant her boon and she is reunited with Satyavan and gives birth to many sons. By her wifely devotion she conquers death and brings Satyavan back to life.

Although the main emphasis is on Sāvitrī's fidelity and devotion to her husband, the legend also illustrates the powerlessness of the male without his female counterpart. In other words, *śakti*, the feminine consciousness and energy, is seen as necessary for man to achieve immortality. Sri Aurobindo (a twentieth-century mystic and philosopher) has transformed the legend of Sāvitrī into a spiritual symbol in his monumental epic *Sāvitrī*. The birth of Sāvitrī indicates 'the arrival of the New Dawn, the descent of a new consciousness' into humanity.

DRAUPADĪ

Draupadī is strikingly different from other epic figures in some respects. In the *Mahābhārata* she is married to the five Pāṇḍava brothers. Although monogamy was seen as the ideal norm, polygamous and polyandrous marriages were not unknown in certain parts of India.

Draupadī's polyandrous marriage, which is explained and justified in a variety of ways (both figuratively and literally), is not the central theme of the story. Arjuna, one of the five Pāṇḍava brothers, wins the hand of Draupadī, the Princess of Pañcāla, at a contest held by her father King Draupada. The Pāṇḍava brothers return to their home in the forest (where they were living in disguise as begging Brahmans and sharing alms) and tell their mother of the 'alms' they had obtained. Kuntī, without looking up to see what Arjuna had won, asks them to share it. The five sons fulfil their mother's wish.

Draupadī is visible in both the domestic and public spheres. She is both ideal wife and queen. She emerges as a dynamic and devoted wife. She follows her husbands into the forest after all their wealth is lost in gambling with their cousins. She not only offers them comfort and solace, but also rouses them to action when their spirits are low. But she does not hesitate to show her rightful anger when one of them, Yudhiṣṭhira, pawns her after having forfeited his brothers and himself. Her refusal to yield to the command of Duryodhana (the cousin of the Pāṇḍavas) that she should work as a servant in his household, shows her as a woman of courage and determination. She sends off the charioteer who has come to fetch her, saying:

> O charioteer, return. Ask of him who played the game whether in it he first lost himself, or his wife. Ask this question in the open assembly; bring me his answer and then you can take me.
>
> (*Mahābhārata* XXV)[9]

Draupadī is forcibly dragged by her hair to an assembly of elders. On regaining her composure she points out to the assembly that Yudhiṣṭhira was tricked into this game and that, after having lost all his wealth and freedom, he had no right to pawn his wife and moreover she belonged to all five Pāṇḍava brothers. She questions the integrity and justice of the Kauravas who resorted to unfair means to achieve their goals.

Draupadī suffers the worst form of humiliation in the court of Duryodhana. His brother insults her by stripping off her sari but she is miraculously saved by Lord Kṛṣṇa, who restores it. Seeking to avenge herself, Draupadī does so on the battlefield where she smears Duryodhana's blood on her hair. She emerges as a powerful person who will not allow others to dictate to her.

Conformity to tradition

In a predominantly patriarchal culture women's roles are defined and interpreted by men. Although the idealized images of women in the epics belong to the aristocratic class, their experiences have some relevance to all women in Hindu society.

While these images of women have been a source of great comfort to some Hindu women, others find them less liberating. Like the epic heroines, some women see themselves in terms of giving rather than receiving. Their happiness and well-being are seen in terms of encouraging their husbands to achieve success.

It is a common belief among devout Hindu women that their fasts and vows will protect their husbands and children. Even young unmarried women fast so that they may be married to suitable partners. While in worship devotion is directed to God, in marriage it is directed to one's husband.

Feminists in the Hindu tradition look to Draupadī, who challenges her husband's right to pawn her, or to the goddess Kālī who inspires terror and awe.

Women in the *bhakti* tradition

With the emergence of *bhakti*, devotional movements centred on Śiva and Viṣṇu in South India (sixth and seventh centuries CE) and later in

North India, the religious status of women improved considerably. The impact of these movements was not significant at the social level but women were allowed greater participation in the religious realm. Being non-Brahman in origin, the *bhakti* cults challenged the hierarchical caste structures, Brahman orthodoxy and ritualism. They were open to all regardless of caste or sex. *Bhakti* required only an intense personal relationship with one's chosen deity. Most of the devotional literature has non-Brahman authors, including women. The songs of the Vaiṣṇava saint Andal are sung in Vaiṣṇava shrines and homes even today.

Bhakti allows different kinds of relationships with one's deity. The exact form it takes is less important. One could conceive of God as lord, master, father, mother, friend, child, and even as one's beloved, but here God is the male and the worshipper is the female. In the *madhura bhava* relationship (God as beloved and the devotee as lover), God is the only male and both male and female devotees are spiritually female.

Strangely enough, in the *bhakti* tradition a reversal of gender-related roles is called for. A male who seeks union with Kṛṣṇa will have to transform himself psychologically into a woman and identify with her love and longing for Kṛṣṇa. In devotional literature one finds poets identifying themselves with *gopīs*, cowherd girls who yearn for Kṛṣṇa. Anyone who desired an intimate relationship with Kṛṣṇa had to become one of his *gopīs*. History provides examples of male devotees such as Jayadeva (twelfth century CE) and Caitanya (fifteenth century CE) who suspended their masculinity in order to relate to Kṛṣṇa as their beloved. Even Sri Ramakrishna, the nineteenth-century saint, dressed like a woman and identified with Rādhā. Another significant aspect that emerges in the relationship with Kṛṣṇa is the illicit love-affair of the *gopīs*, who are already married but flock to him when they hear the sound of his flute. To identify with Kṛṣṇa's *gopīs* verges on adultery. This also means transcending social norms and becoming natural and spontaneous as the *gopīs* did in their relation to Kṛṣṇa.

Among women devotees of Kṛṣṇa two saints stand out. Andal, a saint well known in South India (sixth century CE), is the only female saint among the twelve devotees of Viṣṇu called Āḻvārs. Even from her early years she began to look upon herself as the bride of Kṛṣṇa. She imagined herself to be Kṛṣṇa's *gopī*, pining for his love and suffering from pangs of separation. Her *Song Divine* (*Tiruppāvai*) speaks of her devotional love for Kṛṣṇa. Her spiritual yearning finds expression in her *Sacred Utterance* (*Tirumozhi*). In the South Indian classical dance, *Bharatanatyam*, Andal's love and yearning for Kṛṣṇa are given a unique place.

Mirabai (sixteenth century CE), a Rajput saint, was devoted to Kṛṣṇa even as a young child. Although married at a young age to a Rajput prince, she continued to look upon Kṛṣṇa as her husband and spent most of her time in the company of saints singing the praises of Kṛṣṇa. Her fervent devotion to Kṛṣṇa enraged her in-laws, who tried unsuccessfully to poison her. While her early poems express her agony over separation from Kṛṣṇa, her later poems speak of her spiritual identity with him. Her devotional songs have captured the hearts of musicians, dancers and ordinary householders.

The traditional ideal of womanhood did not mean much to Mirabai. On becoming a widow she did not, like most Rajput princesses of her time, opt for self-immolation on the funeral pyre of her husband, but proclaimed that she was wedded to Kṛṣṇa.

Women saints in the Śaivite tradition

In the long list of canonized saints in the Śaivite tradition in South India, women are held in high esteem. Of the three women saints, Karaikkal Ammaiyar is the best known.

Even as a young child she was devoted to Lord Śiva. She was a devoted and dutiful wife to her husband but at the same time her devotion to Lord Śiva never diminished. According to legend, Karaikkal Ammaiyar prayed to Lord Śiva to transform her beautiful body into a ghostly one (symbolic of her severance from the world), afterwards continuing to sing his praises in her new form. She composed verses in praise of Śiva, known in Tamil as *Arpuda Tiruvantādi* and *Tiru Iraṭṭai Maṇimālai*, which are included in the scriptures of Śaivism.

Modern women saints

Modern Hinduism also has examples of such saintly figures. One of them is Sarada Devi, who was married at an early age to Sri Ramakrishna, a well-known saint of nineteenth-century Bengal. He recognized the spiritual eminence of his wife and looked upon her as an equal partner in his spiritual mission or journey. She became his disciple, helpmate and spiritual partner, and combined the roles of wife, ascetic, mother and *guru*. Sri Ramakrishna taught her not only the sacred *mantras* for the worship of the Divine Mother, but also how to initiate people into them. After the death of Ramakrishna she became the spiritual guide to all disciples – monks as well as laypeople – of the Ramakrishna Order.

There are a few well-known contemporary female *gurus* such as Mother Jnanananda and Sati Godavari Mataji. The final stage of *saṃnyāsa* (renunciation), normally not open to women, was taken up by Mother Jnanananda. She is perhaps the only woman to be initiated into *saṃnyāsa* by the present Śamkarācāraya (follower of the advaitic or non-dualistic philosophy of Śaṃkara) of Kanchipuram in South India. Now Mother Jnanananda herself initiates both men and women into *saṃnyāsa*. Sati Godavari Mataji trained young girls, women and widows to read the Vedas in Sanskrit, perform religious rites and follow the path of selfless service.

Women in the law books

The *Dharmaśāstras*, the legal texts, were composed some time during the first two centuries CE by Brahman men. The contradictory views on women in the law books are attributed to the sage Manu, the legendary author of the *Mānava Dharmaśāstra*, or Law Code, under whose name there exist heterogeneous legal views from different ages.

In the law books women are classified with the lowest class, irrespective of their social class or origin, and are stripped of their ritual and social status. They are considered ritually impure and therefore not entitled to study or recite the sacred *mantras* (*Manu* 9.18).[10] Increasingly, marriage came to be equated with initiation into religious studies, and devotion and service to one's husband came to be equated with the period of study under a *guru* or spiritual teacher. Women's domestic duties were equated with rituals performed by men in the stage of householder (see p. 59).

AMBIVALENT ATTITUDE TOWARDS WOMEN

The authors of the legal texts reflect a profound sense of ambivalence in their attitude to woman. On the one hand, she is elevated to the status of a goddess, but on the other, she is seen as a temptress and seducer. A woman's love and devotion to her husband are extolled but at the same time she is seen as incapable of these virtues (*Manu* 2.213–214).[11] Women are both deified and dehumanized. As mother she is most revered, but as sexual partner she is seen as an obstacle to man's spiritual quest. Sexual love has mystical connotations in Indian art, but in the legal texts it is a hindrance to man's religious pursuits. While in the stage of a householder, a man is considered incomplete without a wife. In the third and fourth stages of life he is free to withdraw from the world of senses and take up the life of an ascetic. There are references to women ascetics such as Sulabhā in the *Mahābhārata* and Sramaṇī and Śabarī in the *Rāmāyaṇa*, but the legal texts restrict women to domestic roles.

FREEDOM AND SUBSERVIENCE

In the law books women are accorded dependent status. A woman is seen in relation to her husband and family. She should be guarded by her father in childhood, her husband in youth and her sons in old age (*Manu* 9.3).[12] But, on the other hand, Manu seems to allow considerable freedom to women in matters of marriage. A woman has the freedom to choose her own partner if her parents fail to arrange her marriage within three years of her attaining puberty (*Manu* 9.90–91).[13] An ideal wife is one who serves her husband with love and devotion, even if he is lacking in these virtues (*Manu* 5.154).[14] The ideal of *pativratā*, devotion to husband, came to be seen as the only *strīdharma* or duty of the wife. Her individuality was merged in his and she had no separate existence apart from him. This ideal perhaps later gave rise to and commended the practice of *satī* (see pp. 74–5). Even though the authors of the legal texts disapprove of polygamy and men deserting their wives, men are allowed to remarry on the death of their wives but women are forbidden to remarry except in certain circumstances (*Manu* 9.65 and 69).[15]

As mother, a woman is more venerable than the teacher or the father (*Manu* 2.145).[16] She is seen as the best spiritual teacher of her children, but as wife she is expected to do the will of her husband. Furthermore, motherhood is seen as enhancing the value of a woman even more if she gives birth to a male child. This preference is rooted in the Hindu belief that a male child ensures the salvation of the father and the family. Hindu folk tales and myths are replete with the imagery of motherhood and maternal love.

Since women have been led to believe that to be mothers is their prime duty, any departure from it produces guilt and anxiety. Pregnancy delivers a woman from the fear of infertility and establishes her adult identity. It is interesting to note that it is men who idealize their mothers. There are numerous folk legends and myths about the mother–son relationship. Rāma willingly goes into exile to fulfil his father's promise to his stepmother. The marriage of the five Pāṇḍava brothers to Princess Draupadī is partly the outcome of Kunti's unwitting declaration that her sons should share what they had won.

Although the law books reflect the social conditions of the times to some extent, they are more a description of what society ought to be like. The commentators of later periods formulated rigorous laws to ensure the protection of women from foreign tribes who entered the country in the early centuries CE. With the advent of Islam in the tenth century, the status of women underwent further changes in North India where Islamic culture was dominant. The Islamic custom of purdah, or the seclusion of women, was adopted by upper-class Hindus in North India. This further intensified the seclusion of Hindu women, who were already segregated from men. Although it restricted the freedom of women, it came to be seen as a mark of high status and prestige.

In a traditional North Indian family, especially in a village, women still observe purdah to some extent. The daughter-in-law veils her face in the presence of male members of the family and in public, though in her parental home she is not required to cover her face. Purdah restricts a woman's involvement in social activities, but on the other hand it offers a new bride some privacy and protects her from the close scrutiny of her in-laws and neighbours. In the domestic sphere she may gain power and authority as she gets older. In South India, where Islamic influence was not strong, the relationship between the two sexes is more relaxed, especially among the lower sections of the community. It is also more informal between men and women in matrilineal families in certain parts of South India. Today, in urban India, purdah is rarely observed by Hindu women.

Feminine images of the Divine

The Divine is conceived of in both masculine and feminine categories. In the *Upaniṣads*, one finds the idea of male and female as equal halves of one divine substance, each completing and fulfilling the other (*Bṛhadāraṇyaka Upaniṣad* 1.4.3).[17] From the ultimate philosophical point of view, the Divine is neither male nor female as it transcends both without negating them. Furthermore, the concept of *ātman* (the deeper or inner self in man and woman) being the 'sexless self', the question of gender does not arise. On the contrary, it affirms the spiritual equality of both male and female.

The feminine dimension of the Divine is exalted in the tantric tradition (500–1800 CE) and in popular worship. The Divine is primarily seen in feminine categories such as *śakti*, or the divine energy, from which all forms of life emerge and by which they are sustained. Since *śakti* is latent in both the masculine and feminine, she is not dependent on anything outside herself. Without the activating power of *śakti* (feminine principle), Śiva (masculine) is powerless. In Tantrism, the male principle is subordinated to the feminine, which has an independent status and in which all contradictions are resolved in interaction with the male (see Kālī and Durgā below).

Goddesses in myths appear in both traditional and unconventional roles. Goddesses relate to gods in a variety of ways – as consort, lover, mother – and they also appear in dominant roles or as equals who are fiercely independent. Although the goddesses Sarasvatī, Lakṣmī and Pārvatī figure as consorts to male deities, they are worshipped in their own right. They are associated with knowledge, wealth and power, which are traditionally male preserves.

Pārvatī (consort of Śiva) has many forms. In the form of Pārvatī she represents the domestic ideal. She figures as a benign and devoted wife. Her role is to lure Śiva from his ascetic ideal into the worldly life of a householder. In the forms of Durgā and Kālī, however, she departs from the traditional model of an ideal wife. Durgā was created by the male gods to subdue the demon Mahiṣāsura, who was immune to all opponents except woman; however, she does not depend upon their support to defeat the demon. Durgā's role, despite being married to Śiva, is not in the home but on the battlefield. Standing on the fringes of civilized society, she challenges the traditional norms of womanly behaviour and yet is regarded as a benevolent mother. Although inseparable from Śiva, in the myths she has an autonomous function and freedom.

In Tantrism Kālī is seen as the dominant force or *śakti*, from whom all else evolves. Kālī's role is to draw Śiva into the world of dynamic activity – of destroying evil in all its forms. Although Kālī is terrible and bloodthirsty, she is also maternal and compassionate. She creates and destroys, nourishes and starves, comforts and challenges the traditional norms of Hindu society. She reverses the traditional norms of purity and pollution. She reminds us that death, being part of life, cannot be dissociated from birth or creation.

Although Durgā and Kālī are not typical examples of ideal womanhood, they nevertheless help to put things into perspective. All notions of gender-based ideology and assumptions are called into question. They indicate that feminine roles need not necessarily be confined to being a daughter, wife, sister or mother. Contemporary Hindu women have found in Kālī a hope for liberation from various forms of oppression. The publishing house Kali was set up in Delhi by two women for women. Ritu Menon and Urvashi Butalia say: 'Kali stands for the destruction of ignorance in order to recreate. ... This positive aspect of Kali is what we are all about.'[18] Hindu women can look to these dynamic models to resolve the conflict between conformity and individuality.

In contrast to the orthodox tradition, where menstruation is seen in terms of pollution, it is not a taboo in Tantrism. In fact, a menstruating woman is accorded a special place in the ritualism of Tantrism. Furthermore, Tantrism does not subscribe to patriarchal conceptions and standards of feminine beauty and conduct. Any woman, irrespective of age, status and looks, is regarded as the representation of *śakti*. Evidence of this can be seen in the high-priest and poet called Chandidas of Bengal (fifteenth century CE); he loved a maid called Rumi despite society's disapproval.

While at the philosophical level the spiritual equality of male and female principle is acknowledged, there is tension between the two at the mythological level, which is finally reconciled in a higher principle. Śiva, in the representation of *Ardhanārīśvara* (half man and half woman), symbolizes harmony and the union of all opposites. At the social level the relation between the two is highly ambivalent. In myths, goddesses are associated with knowledge, wealth and power; in society, a woman's power or *śakti* is largely confined to the domestic sphere. While women's *śakti* is recognized, it is also believed that it should be controlled. Female children are less desired, for religious and economic reasons. The oppressive social custom of dowry continues to affect all classes of women, including educated women with professional careers. The status of a girl in her husband's family in some cases depends on the amount of dowry she brings with her. It is a status symbol among some urban middle-class families. Although forbidden by law, the practice continues, and it badly affects parents who have daughters. But there are also a few enlightened families who are against this dehumanizing practice.

Of all the feminine images of the Divine, the mother image is the most significant. The worship of the Divine as Mother dates back to the prehistoric period of the Harappan civilization. India is known as *Bhārat Mātā* or Mother India, and the river Ganges, sacred to Hindus, is known as Gaṅgā Ma (Mother Ganges) – all that is nourishing and sustaining is seen in feminine categories. The image of mother goddess became a focus during the Indian freedom struggle. India's political liberation was tied up with the concept of *śakti*. Both men and women were involved in recovering the feminine principle which was violently abused by both foreign powers and Indian social structures (see pp. 72–3).

While the Hindu literary tradition is predominantly male-dominated, worship at the popular level is centred on the feminine dimension of the Divine, especially in the form of Mother. Another feminine principle closely linked with *śakti* is *prakṛti* (nature), which has both philosophical and popular connotations. Nature, in all her forms, both animate and inanimate, evolves from the feminine principle (*prakṛti*) in interaction with the masculine principle (*puruṣa*). Women in rural India affirm their links with *prakṛti* through their veneration of nature in all her varied forms.

On the ecological front, rural women in India have played a significant part in protesting against the cutting of trees which are venerated as *Vana devatā*s (forest deities). Forests are venerated as the Earth Mother – one who creates, nourishes and sustains life. Some 300 years ago the followers of a Hindu sect called Bishnoi in Rajasthan, led by a woman, Amrita Devi, protected the trees by embracing them and thus allowing the wood-cutters to harm them instead of the trees. Women sacrificed their lives to prevent the abuse of nature in the name of development. This event was the origin of the Chipko (hug-the-tree) movement which later became an ecological and feminist movement.[19]

Women's ecological movements in rural India challenge the conventional categories of patriarchy which do not make any ontological link between humanity and nature. From the standpoint of Hindu ontology, violence to nature implies violence to women, as all forms of life are seen as evolving from the feminine principle.

Women in modern Hinduism

Women's issues in the last two centuries have been tied up with Indian political resistance to British imperialism and social reform movements which aimed at rectifying oppressive social practices. Women became the focus of attention in the nineteenth century, initiated by British colonial attitudes to issues such as child marriage, infanticide, polygamy, widow remarriage, women's property rights, and especially the socially oppressive custom of *satī* (self-immolation of widows). Hinduism came under severe attack from Christian missionaries and others when it was at a low ebb. Some Hindus, although supportive of reforming measures, felt that they should come from within. While seeing merit in reform, they also saw reflected in the attack attitudes about the cultural and moral superiority of British ways.

Both colonialism and nationalism brought into sharper focus the status of women in Hindu society, thus giving it a significant place in the national struggle for freedom. Indian social reformers and nationalist historians tried to show that women had a high status in ancient India. They challenged the advocates of *satī* and condemned corrupt practices by going back to ancient texts to justify the need for reforms. The historical reconstruction of the image of women, however, was largely based on the ancient religious texts that had to do with the upper strata of society.

Indian reformers were actively involved in women's issues, ranging from *satī* to property rights. For example, Raja Rām Mohan Roy (1772–1833), the founder of the reform movement Brāhmo Samāj, along with other progressive thinkers, created a favourable climate for the abolition of *satī* and other corrupt practices which affected women. Ishwar Chandra Vidyasagar (1820–91) and others campaigned for the right of widows to remarry, which resulted in legalizing the marriage of Hindu widows in 1856. Dayananda Saraswati, the founder of the Ārya Samāj, opposed caste and child marriage and spoke in favour of women's education. Bengali writers, playwrights and reformers denounced polygamy. The Property Act of 1874 allowed women a share of their husband's property.

Indian reformers had to contend with British imperialism, the colonial portrayal of Indian women, and Hindu traditionalists who resisted change. Although in favour of women's education, they saw it in terms of producing good mothers and efficient wives. In their view, social evils affecting women could be effectively tackled by revitalizing family structures and according women a respectable place within the family. Education should, therefore, reinforce women's role in the home. English-style education did, however, prepare the ground for women's participation in the national movement. By the late nineteenth century there were a good number of educated middle-class women who, alongside political leaders, fought against imperial rule. Women like Sarojini Naidu (a well-known poet and orator), Tagore's sister Swarnakumari Devi (co-editor of a Bengali journal) and Kamaladevi Chattopadhyaya were active members of the Indian National Congress. Women from various backgrounds (urban and village) responded enthusiastically to Gandhi's call to participate in the national struggle for freedom. They organized marches and political demonstrations, boycotted foreign goods and gave generously of their time and energy.

Gandhi himself saw a link between women's capacity for self-sacrifice and endurance and the non-violent resistance (*satyāgraha* or 'soul force') against the British. He was well aware of the traditional orientation of women in Hindu society. The *strīdharma* (duty of a wife) involved steadfast devotion to her husband, and a woman committed to this goal undertook fasts and vows for the welfare of her husband and family. In the domestic sphere she was well-versed in the art of self-denial, self-sacrifice and suffering. This kind of single-minded devotion and commitment was essential for engaging in the non-violent struggle against imperial rule. Gandhi was able to divert women's *śakti* from the domestic to the national sphere. This is described in Kathleen Young's essay 'Hinduism' in *Women in World Religions* (1987).

Although Gandhi was using traditional categories to encourage women to take part in the national movement, it had important implications. It called for the redefinition of roles within the family. Both men and women became equal partners in a common cause. Women were able to come out into the open and thus break the barriers of caste and sex. Since then women have played a significant role in Gandhi's ashrams and in the secular sphere. Women availed themselves of educational opportunities and qualified for professions such as law, medicine, teaching, social work and the like. There are colleges exclusively for women in Indian towns and cities, and the teaching staff are mostly women. Men hardly figure in women's institutions except in non-professional roles such as laboratory technicians, porters or caretakers.

Satī

The word *satī* means a 'virtuous woman'. One does not 'commit *satī*' but can only become a *satī*, i.e., a virtuous one – sometimes through immolation on the funeral pyre of one's husband. It is possible that this act, which was symbolically performed by a widow during the vedic period, may have paved the way for the actual practice of *satī* in later centuries.

Despite minimal warrant or justification for the rite in the *smṛti* literature, *satī* seems to have gained ground in certain parts of India, particularly Rajasthan and Bengal. It was largely confined to the women of high castes, particularly *kṣatriyas* (warrior class) and Brahmans (priestly class). *Satī* is different from the *Jauhar* custom prevalent among Rajput (martial class) widows, who opted for collective widow-burning on a mass scale to save their honour rather than submit themselves to the Mughal conquerors.

While Lord William Bentinck deserves the credit for abolishing *satī* (1829), the efforts of various opponents of the custom created a favourable ground for the effectiveness of reforms. Among Hindus there were both upholders and critics of the rite. It was denounced by Bana, a well-known Sanskrit scholar (600 CE), *tāntrikas* (who hold women in high esteem), *bhakti* poets such as Ramananda, Kabir and Sikh *gurus*. In the early nineteenth century, reformers like Rām Mohan Roy challenged the traditionalists' view that the woman who became a *satī* was assured of a place in heaven. Arvind Sharma[20] shows that he refuted such statements by quoting the *Gītā*, which sets a high value on the concept of *niṣkāma karma*, actions performed without any desire for their fruits or reward. According to the *Gītā*, women are entitled to salvation, and to subject them to an inferior mode of action ('reward-oriented act') therefore smacks of male superiority.

The religious dimension of *satī*

The wife who chose to become a *satī* on the death of her husband was considered auspicious, and the widow by contrast was inauspicious, though they both sought the same goal – reunion with their husbands. While the *satī* was glorified, the widow was looked down upon despite her self-disciplined life. Whether women chose to become *satīs* or widows, their sexuality was controlled by their dead husbands. Total fidelity to their husbands was expected of women and this could be established by becoming a *satī* or a widow. Women's salvation came to be seen in terms of being reunited with their husbands and hence was rebirth-oriented. Men's salvation came to be seen in terms of release from the cycle of births and deaths.

Widows

In orthodox families a widow was required to shave her hair, wear a white sari and give up her ornaments (toe and ear rings, bangles and the red dot in the middle of her forehead), which symbolize auspiciousness (*śubha*). Her economic well-being and status were those of dependence on her sons. Despite a widow's austere life and religious orientation (fasts, vows and prayers), she was not favourably looked upon. Her presence at festivals, social and religious ceremonies was considered inauspicious. It is therefore not surprising that women placed in these circumstances might prefer *satī*. Although the practice is now banned, there are a few advocates of *satī* even today. It is ironic that a tradition that reveres the feminine aspect of the Divine should consider the widow inauspicious.

Although some degree of inauspiciousness may be associated with widows today, attitudes have changed to some extent. India had a Prime Minister (Indira Gandhi) who was a widow, and then had an Environment Minister (Maneka Gandhi) who was also a widow. Indira Gandhi participated in social functions and sought the advice of *gurus*, and she was given a grand funeral ceremony.

Two earlier women who did not conform to the traditional orientation of a widow were Pandita Ramabai (1858–1922) and Kamaladevi Chattopadhyaya (born in 1903). Widowhood did not stop Pandita Ramabai (who later converted to Christianity) from being involved in women's education and rights. Kamaladevi became a widow soon after marriage and later married the Bengali playwright Haridranath Chattopadhyaya, and she was actively involved in the national movement for Indian independence.

Widow remarriage

The remarriage of widows was not uncommon in earlier times. The custom of *niyoga* which allowed a widow to be married to her husband's brother is mentioned in the vedic and post-vedic literature but went out of vogue in the early centuries CE. Although a Hindu widow can remarry today (The Hindu Widow Remarriage Act was passed in 1856), very few opt for it, for reasons such as family honour and social acceptability. Moreover, since marriage is seen in broader categories, involving not merely two individuals but two families, remarriage poses problems. There have been few cases of widow remarriage among the upper castes, whereas it is more socially acceptable among the lower castes.

*Devadāsī*s

In the *Kāmasūtra* (*The Book on the Art of Love*), composed in the early centuries CE, women are neither idealized nor held in contempt. Courtesans in ancient India were women of great artistic accomplishments and cultural refinement. They were to a great extent independent and not bound by the norms that applied to upper-class women.

To the class of courtesans belong *devadāsī*s (female servants of god), who were dedicated to the temple at a very early age. *Devadāsī*s in South India were associated with both royal and village temples. They enhanced worship by their repertoire. They also functioned as ritual specialists in the village temples. The female village deities were both malevolent and benign. Since a *devadāsī* was associated with the female aspect of the goddess, she was seen as specially qualified to deal with the ambivalent Divine.

In later years the *devadāsī* tradition came to be associated with prostitution. The practice of dedicating a female of any age as a *devadāsī* was declared illegal in 1947. But the artistic dimension of the tradition was revived by Balasaraswati, who belonged to a *devadāsī* family. She was one of the best exponents of the South Indian classical dance, *Bharatanatyam*. Her performances in Varanasi, the centre of Hindu orthodoxy, gradually gained favour for the dance among upper- and middle-class Hindus. The ritual and folk songs of the *devadāsī*s are still sung in South Indian temples.

Women in religious practice

The question of women priests has not been an important issue in Hinduism. Few women aspire to officiate at public religious ceremonies and they do so out of personal interest. Women do not see priesthood in terms of a full-time profession as men do. However, priesthood not being a remunerative profession, Brahman men tend to choose it only if there is a strong family tradition. Even male priests have only a marginal status outside the ritualistic context.

As with other traditions, women's menstruation is seen as making them impure and therefore unfit for the role of a ritual specialist. At the popular level women have relatively greater freedom and authority and can function as religious specialists. Women exorcists and shamanesses are prominent in the oral traditions.

Despite strong opposition, a group of Brahman women in Pune have set up a school for women priests. The Thatte school charges no fees and is open to non-Brahman students. It was the result of the efforts of an elderly couple, Pushpa and her husband Shankarrao, who were disenchanted with the quality of service offered by male priests who often have to officiate at several places on the same day.

Women are important in religious practice in a more fundamental sense. The home is the centre of religious practices such as daily worship, life-cycle rituals, festivals and fasts. The temple, almost wholly the domain of male priests, is not central to Hindu religious practice. The daily worship (*pūjā*) is usually performed by the mother on behalf of the family. It is mostly the women in the family who take care of the religious education of children. As well as daily *pūjā* and numerous festivals in which women take leading roles, there are rituals for women's welfare. Pre-natal rituals such as *sīmanta*, performed during the early months of a woman's pregnancy, are meant to ensure the emotional and physical well-being of the child. Gujarati women perform a special rite called 'inviting the Mata' or goddess during a woman's first pregnancy. It is also performed on other occasions. The rite involves honouring a *goyani* (an unmarried woman or a married woman whose husband is alive) who is treated as if she were a goddess. In identifying a woman with a goddess, this rite affirms the creative energy or *śakti* which is inherent in woman.

Hindu women can look to the concept of *śakti* (latent in both the masculine and the feminine) to challenge the patriarchal images of women and thus recover the feminine principle in both woman and man.

Notes

1 R. T. H. Griffith (trans.) (1920) *Hymns of the Rig Veda*, vol. I. 3rd edn; Benares: E. J. Lazarus, p. 158.
2 Griffith (1926), op. cit., vol. II, p. 438.
3 R. Panikkar (1989) *The Vedic Experience: Mantramañjarī*. 2nd edn; Pondicherry: All India Books, p. 265.
4 S. R. Shastri (1954) *Women in the Vedic Age*. Bombay: Bharatiya Vidya Bhavan, pp. 17–18.
5 Panikkar, op. cit., p. 265.
6 R. C. Zaehner (trans.) (1966) *Hindu Scriptures*. London: J. M. Dent & Sons, pp. 45–6.
7 Ibid., p. 52.
8 R. T. H. Griffith (trans.) (1963) *The Rāmāyaṇa of Valmiki*. 3rd edn; Varanasi: Chowkhamba Sanskrit Series Office, p. 496.
9 C. Rajagopalachari (1978) *Mahābhārata*. 21st edn; Bombay: Bharatiya Vidya Bhavan, p. 92.
10 G. Bühler (trans.) (1886) *The Sacred Books of the East*, vol. XXV, ed. F. Max Müller. Oxford: Clarendon Press, p. 330.
11 Ibid., p. 69.
12 Ibid., p. 328.
13 Ibid., p. 343.
14 Ibid., p. 196.
15 Ibid., p. 339.
16 Ibid., pp. 67–72.
17 Zaehner, op. cit., p. 35.
18 R. Sarin (1985) 'Kali's crusade against ignorance', *Sunday* 13(7) (22–28 December), Calcutta, p. 20.
19 V. Shiva (1988) *Staying Alive: Women, Ecology and Development*. London: Zed Books, p. 67.
20 A. Sharma, A. Ray, A. Hejib and K. K. Young (1988) *Satī: Historical and Phenomenological Essays*. Delhi: Motilal Banarsidass, pp. 67–72.

Further reading

Altekar, A. S. (1959) *The Position of Women in Hindu Civilization*. 2nd edn; Delhi: Motilal Banarsidass.

Gupta, B. (1987) 'The masculine–feminine symbolism in Kashmir Saivism' in B. Gupta (ed.) *Sexual Archetypes: East and West*. New York: Paragon House, New Era Books.

Hawley, J. S. (ed.) (1994) *Satī, the Blessing and the Curse: The Burning of Wives in India*. New York and Oxford: Oxford University Press.

Hawley, J. S. and Wulff, D. M. (eds) (1982) *The Divine Consort: Rādhā and the Goddesses of India*. Berkeley: University of California Press.

Hawley, J. S. and Wulff, D. M. (eds) (1996) *Devi: Goddesses of India*. Berkeley: University of California Press.

Kakar, S. (1989) *Intimate Relations: Exploring Indian Sexuality*. Delhi: Viking.

Kersenboom-Story, S. C. (1987) *Nityasumaṅgalī: Devadasi Tradition in South Indian*. Delhi: Motilal Banarsidass.

King, U. (1989) *Women and Spirituality: Voices of Protest and Promise*. Basingstoke: Macmillan.

Kingsley, D. (1987) *Hindu Goddesses: Visions of the Divine Feminine in the Hindu Religious Tradition*. Delhi: Motilal Banarsidass.

Knott, K. (1987) 'Men and women, or devotees? Krishna consciousness and the role of women' in U. King (ed.) *Women in the World's Religions: Past and Present*. New York: Paragon House, New Era Books.

Leslie, J. (1980) 'The religious role of women in ancient India'. Unpublished MPhil thesis, University of Oxford.

Leslie, J. (1989) *The Perfect Wife: The Orthodox Hindu Woman According to the Strīdharmapaddhati of Tryambakayajvan*. Oxford University South Asian Series. Delhi: Oxford University Press.

Leslie, J. (ed.) (1991) *Roles and Rituals for Hindu Women*. London: Pinter.

Mookerjee, A. (1988) *Kali: The Feminine Force*. London: Thames and Hudson.

Mukerjee, Prabhati (1978) *Hindu Women: Normative Models*. New Delhi: Orient Longman.

Parikh, I. J. and Grag, P. K. (1989) *Indian Women: An Inner Dialogue*. New Delhi: Sage.

Pintchman, T. (1994), *The Rise of the Goddess in the Hindu Tradition*. Albany: SUNY Press.

Swami Ghananda and Stewart-Wallace, J. (1979) *Women Saints: East and West*. Hollywood: Vedanta Press.

Young, K. K. (1987) 'Hinduism' in A. Sharma (ed.) *Women in World Religions*. Albany: SUNY Press.

4. Attitudes to nature

Anuradha Roma Choudhury

In discussing Hindu understandings of nature, we come across a wide range of ideas: on the one hand, we find ideas which reflect very early human encounters with natural phenomena, such as we find elsewhere in the world (i.e., the initial sense of awe and humility towards the natural forces), and on the other hand, we find lofty philosophical ideas which are undoubtedly the product of a mature analytical mind.

In the early period, numerous invaders or settlers entered India from outside. Among them, the Aryans (*Ārya*) contributed most to the Hindu way of life. They brought with them their well-developed language, Sanskrit (*Saṃskṛta*), their ritual worship, their sacrificial fire. The world's oldest literature, the Vedas (*veda* meaning knowledge), followed by the *Brāhmaṇa*s, *Āraṇyaka*s and *Upaniṣad*s, are the product of the Aryan intellect.

From the scriptural literature it is evident that the initial urge for appeasing the forces of nature with rituals and hymns of prayer gradually turned into a quest for unravelling the mysteries of nature. Out of adoration for nature grew a faithful search for a creator, the cause or root of this magnificent creation. From this search evolved Hindu theories of cosmology: the universe, its creation and dissolution. Several schools of philosophy developed as the mature analytical mind probed deeper into the secrets of nature and also attempted to establish a relationship between the created phenomena and their creator.

To get the complete picture of how Hindus view nature, one has to consider two perspectives. One is the wider perspective of the creation as a whole – the universe, its stars and planets, and its relationship with its creator; and the other is the intimate perspective of the Mother

Earth – her plants and animals, and her relationship with the humans.

Concept of creation (*sṛṣṭi*)

As with other early civilizations, very basic questions were addressed: How is the world created? Who is the creator? Is there a creator? In answering these questions each civilization created its own theories of cosmology in general and cosmogony in particular. Many of them assume that the phenomenal world, despite its apparent permanence, did not exist throughout eternity. It had an origin at a certain time in the past and it would go into oblivion at some future date. Like mortal beings, the world too has been born and is destined to die.

The Hindu thinkers went a step further, and stated that the universe has no single birth nor an ultimate death. The creation and dissolution of the universe is a cyclical ongoing process. A variety of sources is available in the sacred writings to show the kinds of attempts made through the ages, both in vedic and non-vedic fields, to explain how an individual creation takes place and how it goes into oblivion.

The early speculations to resolve the mystery of creation refer back to records which were pure myths. To start with a non-vedic cosmological myth, the narrative of *Śrī Chaṇḍī* (a part of the *Mārkaṇḍeya Purāṇa*) (I.66–104) states that the universe, prior to the creation, was filled with *kāraṇa-salila* (*kāraṇa*/cause, *salila*/water/fluid) or causal/primordial fluid. In the infinite expanse of primordial fluid, Nārāyaṇa, the Supreme Being, was lying in deep slumber (*yoga-nidrā*) on the coils of *Ananta-Nāga* (*ananta*/infinite, *nāga*/snake; stands symbolically for an infinite dimension of time length). A lotus (*padma* – often associated with mystic symbolism) sprang up from the navel of Nārāyaṇa (also known as Viṣṇu). Over the lotus was seated Brahmā, the deity who, according to puranic legend,[1] is considered to be the creator. Next, two demons (*asuras*) emerged from Nārāyaṇa's *karṇa-mala* (*karṇa*/ear, *mala*/dirt/wax). They were Madhu and Kaiṭabha. The demons started attacking Brahmā. Brahmā sought Nārāyaṇa's help. Rousing Nārāyaṇa from his yogic slumber was a hard task, and Śrī Chaṇḍī's help was needed. Eventually Nārāyaṇa woke up and, after a long fight, killed the demons. The fatty substance (*meda*) that oozed out of the huge corpses solidified in the vast expanse of the primordial fluid to form the earth. That is why one of the names of the earth is *medinī* (from *meda*).

In the Vedas there appears a much more sophisticated form of myth. Underneath the superficial external account there is a symbolism which adds a new dimension to the myth. Frequent references are made to a war between Indra (leader of the gods/*suras*/*devas*) and Vṛtra (leader of the demons/*asuras*/*dānavas*). On the surface the story is of a war between the gods and the demons. *Ṛg-veda* (X.147.1 and II.12.3) praises Indra, who killed Vṛtra and slit open his belly and consequently let loose the seven torrential streams. Laying the great mountain open, Indra set free the floods that were obstructed before. This 'war episode' turns out to be a creation myth. It has been interpreted as the struggle between the forces of chaos, disorder and inertia on one side, and those of harmony, order and progress on the other. *Sura* means concord and *asura* means discord. *Vṛtra* means darkness. The killing of Vṛtra symbolizes the uncovering of darkness and inertia. As a result, streams of light and progress are freed and bring order in place of the chaos that prevailed prior to the creation. The torrential streams represent the primordial fluid out of which the creation materialized. Clearly, Indra is the creator according to this myth.

There are other myths where the credit of creation goes to other deities. One such deity is Prajāpati, meaning the Lord (*pati*) of the people/creatures (*prajā*). From within the belly of Prajāpati emerged the primordial fluid out of which the creation materialized. Then there is Viśvakarman (*viśva*/all/world, *karman*/maker), whose very name proclaims him as the maker of all or the architect of the world.

Next came the early metaphysical period, reflected in portions of the Vedas and some other writings. The idea of the uniqueness of a Supreme Creator evolved during this period. The singularity behind the superficial pluralism has been expressed in several hymns (e.g., *Ṛg-veda* VIII.58.2 and *Yajur-veda* 32.1), as in the following:

> They speak of Indra, Mitra, Varuṇa, Agni,
> and there is the Divine, winged Suparṇa.
> The One Being the wise call by many names
> as Agni, Yama, Mātariśvan.
>
> (*Ṛg-veda* I.164.46 and *Atharva-veda* IX.10.28)

A different class of thinkers emerged in the field of cosmogony, who might be called 'theologian naturalists', as Bhattacharjee (1978: 63) puts it. They were mystified by the unfathomable nature of this universe. The puzzled state of their analytical mind is apparent from the hymn which is hailed as the Hymn of Creation (*Nāsadīya Sūkta*). According to Macdonell (1972: 207), in this 'cosmogonic poem the origin of the world is explained as the evolution of the existent (sat) from the non-existent (asat). Water thus came into being first; from it was evolved intelligence by heat. It is the starting point of the natural philosophy which developed into the Sāṃkhya system.' (This is explained on pp. 85–6.) The frequent use of questions in the composition of the hymn itself emphasizes the unresolved nature of the thinker's quest.

> There was neither the non-existent nor the existent then. There was no air nor the heavens beyond it. What lay covered and where? In whose protection? Was there then the unfathomable cosmic water? There was neither death nor immortality then. There was no sign of night nor of day. The One breathed, windless, by self-impulse. Other than that there was nothing beyond.
>
> At first there was darkness and all this was undistinguishable water. That One arose at last, born of the power of heat (*tapas*). In the beginning desire (*kāma*) came upon it. It was the primal seed, born of the mind. The sages, in their wisdom, discovered the bond of the existent in the non-existent.
>
> Who knows truly? Who can declare? When and how did this creation happen? He, the surveyor of the highest heaven, surely knows; or may be even He does not!
>
> (*Ṛg-veda* X.129.1–7)

Two important ideas appear in this hymn: the role of desire (*kāma*) as the first initiating factor, and the part played by heat (*tapas*) in materializing the creative process. In addition, 'the symbol of water is the most pertinent one: the primordial water covers all, . . . it is the first condition of life, the place of the original seed, the fertilizing milieu' (Panikkar, 1979: 56).

But the climax of the *Ṛg-veda* in the field of cosmogony is considered to be the concept of *hiraṇya-garbha*, which was widely accepted and elaborated by later thinkers in subsequent works: the *Brāhmaṇa*s, the *Upaniṣad*s and the *Purāṇa*s. The term (*hiraṇya*/gold, *garbha*/womb) stands for an object whose interior is extremely bright. According to the hymn *Hiraṇya-Garbha* (*Ṛg-veda* X.121) and other sources, the first creation appeared out of primordial fluid as an object with an extremely bright interior, and from it the present form of the universe evolved in stages.

The *Brāhmaṇas* also have passages on the creation process. The creation of *mahābhūtas* (the fundamental physical elements, namely, earth, water, heat, air and space) has been described in some. The *Aitareya Brāhmaṇa* (V.32) suggests a picture of successive creation of the gross elements.

In the upanisadic stage, again several points of development emerged. The *Muṇḍaka Upaniṣad* (I.1.7–8) says:

> As the web comes out of the spider and is withdrawn, as plants grow from the soil and hairs from the body of man, so springs the universe from [within] the Eternal.
>
> With the will to multiply Brahman [the Supreme Being] expanded and then came the primeval matter out of him. From this came the primal energy. From that came mind, from mind the subtle elements, from elements the many worlds.

Six systems of philosophy (*darśana*)

Following the theologian naturalists, there appeared a class of rationalist thinkers or philosophers in the proper sense. They attacked the whole riddle of cosmology with a new type of precision in methodology, introducing intellectual analyses of the subject. The diversity of opinion resulted in the development of six main schools. But there is one very basic underlying factor which is common to all these systems, and that is an emphatic declaration that their aim is not to pursue knowledge for knowledge's sake, but to find a way of eliminating suffering,[2] or to find the cause of suffering in human life and to eliminate the causative factor.

The six main schools of philosophy can be put into three groups according to the individual cosmological theories they follow.

- Nyāya
- Vaiśeṣika
- Sāṃkhya
- Yoga
- Mīmāṃsā
- Vedānta

Three of these schools, Vaiśeṣika, Sāṃkhya and Vedānta, have distinctive theories of creation.

VAIŚEṢIKA

Vaiśeṣika claims that all material objects are made of atoms (*paramāṇus*). Different combinations of atoms with special qualities make up different materials. There are four such special qualities:

- odour (*gandha*)
- taste/flavour (*rasa*)
- form/appearance (*rūpa*)
- touch/feel (*sparśa*).

A combination of all four qualities makes up earth, i.e., all earthy objects have some kind of odour, taste and appearance and are tangible. Water has three special qualities: taste, appearance and touch/feel. Fire has two qualities: appearance and touch/feel. Air has only one: touch/feel.

The Vaiśeṣika school accepts a personal God (*Īśvara*) who created the world, but not out of nothing. The elements existed before the world was formed. He fashioned them into an ordered universe. *Īśvara* is thus the creator of the world, but not of its constituents.

SĀṂKHYA

This school of philosophy deals prominently with the creation of the material universe. It holds that to know an object fully one has to know all its components. The system is dualistic, recognizing two basic principles of creation: *puruṣa* (the male principle) and *prakṛti* (the female principle).

Prakṛti is the primal substance or matter out of which the entire creation evolves. Its constituents are the three *guṇa*s (properties/attributes): *sattva* (purity/harmony), *rajas* (passion/energy) and *tamas* (inertia/darkness). These three *guṇa*s are responsible for all change, and form the basis of evolution. But *prakṛti* lies dormant when its three *guṇa*s are in equilibrium. While *prakṛti* has the potential of creating and destroying the universe by itself, without *puruṣa*'s initiation the process of creation cannot start. As opposed to *prakṛti*, *puruṣa* is *nirguṇa* (without any *guṇa*/attribute) and does not change. As soon as *prakṛti* is united with *puruṣa*, the equilibrium of the *guṇa*s is broken. The agitation of the three *guṇa*s starts the creative process.

Through several stages of creation the five *mahābhūta*s (the fundamental elements) finally appear:

- *kṣiti* (earth)
- *ap* (water)
- *tejas* (fire/heat)
- *marut/vāyu* (air)
- *vyoman* (space).

From the *mahābhūta*s the phenomenal world eventually evolves.

VEDĀNTA (OR UTTARA MĪMĀṂSĀ)

Vedānta means the 'End of the Vedas' (*anta*/end), i.e., the definitive knowledge of the Vedas. It is also known as Uttara Mīmāṃsā (*uttara*/later; *mīmāṃsā*/investigation), which means that it is the investigation into the later chapters of the Vedas, that is, the *Upaniṣad*s.

From a cosmic standpoint, Vedānta explains the relationship of *brahman*, the unmanifested Absolute Reality, with the manifested creation by introducing the principle of *māyā*. *Māyā* means illusion – that which is not real but which appears to be real. According to Vedānta, only *brahman* is real; the phenomenal world is unreal (*māyā*), and beings are no different from *brahman*. As Bhattacharjee (1978: 69) points out, it is a bold antithesis of all creation hypotheses. If the phenomenal world is illusory, there need not be any creative process. This world is only an apparent transmutation of *brahman*. Under the influence of *māyā* this material world appears to be real, but with true knowledge and diligent investigations, one can see through the unreal world and find *brahman* in everything.

All the *Upaniṣad*s agree that *brahman*, the ultimate unchanging reality, lies behind this constantly changing (therefore unreal/*māyā*) material world. Regarding the nature of this Absolute Reality (also known as *ātman*/self), the *Upaniṣad*s are quite specific. The *Kaṭha Upaniṣad* (I.2.20) says 'It is smaller than the smallest and greater than the greatest'. The *Śvetāśvatara Upaniṣad* (V.9) says 'If the tip of a hair is split a hundred times and that fine part again split a hundred times, then that equals the Self and that is at the same time infinitely extended'.

Brahmāṇḍa

This is a term frequently used in Hindu cosmology. It means the universe in general. Etymologically it means the Egg of Brahman (*aṇḍa*/egg). Both vedic (the *Brāhmaṇas*, the *Upaniṣads*) and non-vedic (the *Purāṇas*) sources give vivid descriptions of this egg. The *Chhāndogya Upaniṣad* (III.19.1–2) says:

> The non-existent became existent in the form of an egg. Then it lay motionless for a year. Then it got divided. One part of the egg was silvery and the other golden. The silvery one became the earth and the golden one the heaven.

The *Viṣṇu Purāṇa* (I.2.51) and the *Kūrma Purāṇa* (I.4.36) say:

> Gradually that material-egg expanded like a water bubble. The unmanifested Viṣṇu made himself manifested and rested in the egg as Brahman.

Two striking points emerge from these two quotations. The first hints at the fragmentation of the original body, and the second supports the theory of the expanding nature of the material-egg (or the universe) as suggested by the *Upaniṣads* (e.g., the *Muṇḍaka Upaniṣad*) at an earlier period.

There are passages in the *Purāṇas* which indicate that a very large number of *brahmāṇḍas* are in existence. The *Kūrma Purāṇa* (II.6) says:

> The innumerable brahmāṇḍas of the past, the present brahmāṇḍas made up of the combination of all material elements, and the future brahmāṇḍas whose elements are resting in spirit [soul] level are all dependent on Īśvara's [God's] will/command.

In the same *Purāṇa*, mention has been made of fourteen types of *brahmāṇḍas* (I.44.1).

The term *brahmāṇḍa*, in these cases, may be compared with galaxies. It is not just one *brahmāṇḍa* that was created, once, a very long time ago, and that we know here and now, but it is a continuous process of creation and dissolution of *brahmāṇḍas* throughout eternity.

The Hindu scholars had clear concepts about the position of the earth in the universe and its relation with the other stellar bodies. Ārya Bhaṭṭa (fifth century CE) wrote: 'The stars in the firmament and the sun are static, it is the earth that by its own rotation is causing either the rising or the setting of the planets and stars' (quoted by Bhattacharjee, 1978: 6).

Theory of evolution

The Hindu treatises that deal with creation, evolution and dissolution are called the *Purāṇas*. The term *Purāṇa* (*purā*/ancient) signifies 'dealing with ancient topics'. It is the *Purāṇas* that claim for the first time that the process of creation and evolution is a purely physical one. The *Viṣṇu Purāṇa* (I.4.52) says:

> The matter [the universal stuff] evolves into the material form by virtue of its own potentialities and that requires no other agency to effect the transformation.

Regarding evolution, both the *Viṣṇu Purāṇa* (I.5.18–23) and the *Agni Purāṇa* (XX.1–6) say that there are several stages (*sargas*), and that the highest form of evolution is yet to come.

1 *Mahat sarga* – the creation of infra-physical entities.
2 *Bhūta sarga* – the creation of the fundamental physical elements, namely, earth, water, fire, air and space.
3 *Vaikārika sarga* – the formation of the stellar bodies from the fundamental elements.
4 *Mukhya sarga* – during this stage the inanimate creation (mountains, etc.) was complete.
5 *Tiryak-srotā sarga* – the creation of the first living things that are mobile and grow as a result of taking food, but have no thinking ability or motivation.
6 *Ūrdhva-srotā* (or *Deva*) *sarga* – the creation of deities who are givers of happiness and love.
7 *Arvāk-srotā sarga* – the creation of human beings.
8 *Anugraha sarga* – subdivision of humans into two groups: motivated and positive (because of *sattva guṇa*); and ignorant and negative (because of *tamas guṇa*).

9 *Kaumāra sarga* – the period of evolution of 'supermen' (like Sanatkumāra, one of the sons of Brahmā).

Apart from this complete theory of evolution, comprising both inanimate and animate creation, there is a myth prevalent in Hindu literature which needs to be mentioned here since it describes, through its narrative, the successive appearance of higher forms of life on this planet. It is the story of the ten *avatāras* (*daśāvatāra* – *daśa*/ten; *avatāra*/incarnation) or incarnations of Viṣṇu. According to Hindu ideas, God is not different from the created objects. The phenomenal world forms part of the Supreme Being. In times of need, to restore balance or to regain harmony of the world, God manifests himself in the form of a created being. The story is found in several scriptures, and all ten *avatāras* were recognized by about the eleventh century CE. According to Jayadeva's *Gīta-Govinda* (I. 5–14), Lord Viṣṇu saved the earth repeatedly from its predicament.

The narrative, as rendered by Bhattacharjee (1978: 29), starts with the early condition when the surface of the earth was covered with water. In the watery environment, there appeared the first *avatāra*, in the form of a fish (*mīna*/*matsya*). Next, as the water level receded, the second *avatāra* appeared, in the form of a tortoise (*kūrma*). This marks the amphibian stage. This was followed by the appearance of a boar (*varāha*), a pure mammal. The next *avatāra* appeared in the form of a lion-man (*narsiṃha*), a form intermediate between animal and human. Then came a dwarf (*vāmana*), a short-statured man. The next *avatāra* was Paraśurāma or Rāma with the axe (*paraśu*), a fierce warrior-like character, fully human in form but not humane in nature yet. His warring missions and the murdering of his own mother hint at the brutality of his nature. Then came Rāma, the hero of the epic *Rāmāyaṇa*. He belonged to the *kṣatriya* (warrior) caste, showing that fighting was a way of life for him. Next was Balarāma, the bearer of the ploughshare (*haladhara*), signifying the settled agricultural phase of society. In a variant form, Kṛṣṇa (the deliverer of the *Bhagavadgītā* in the epic *Mahābhārata*), the younger brother of Balarāma, is the eighth *avatāra*, not Balarāma. The ninth *avatāra* was the Buddha who preached non-violence. The whole evolution from the first aquatic life to the extremely human, compassionate Buddha is symbolically expressed here. The tenth *avatāra*, called Kalkin, is yet to come. It is predicted in the narrative that his weapon for destroying evil will be something as fierce as a comet (*dhūmaketu*).

Pralaya

Nature, like living creatures, is subject to decay and destruction. But in Hindu thought there is no ultimate destruction or dissolution. It is a continuous cycle of creation, dissolution and re-creation from the dissolved state. *Pralaya* (or *laya*) is the term used for dissolution in general, but various degrees of dissolution are recognized by Hindu thinkers and described in great detail in various sources.

We start with the story of the deluge of Manu. Descriptions of it are found in both vedic and non-vedic literature. The basic narrative, found in the *Śatapatha Brāhmaṇa* (I.8.1.1–10) and the *Mahābhārata* (*Vana-parva* 187), runs as follows.

There was an ancient sage named Manu who passed his days in religious pursuits. One day when he was washing himself in the river, a little fish came into his hand. The fish asked the sage to save him from the immediate danger of being devoured by a bigger fish. He explained that in the fish community the law of 'might is right' prevails. So a small fish lives in perpetual danger from a bigger fish. The fish also instructed Manu how to tend him carefully. Manu kept him in a jar of water as instructed. When the fish outgrew the jar he was transferred to a pond and later to the sea. Once saved, the fish warned the sage about an imminent great flood that would wash away the whole creation, and asked him to build a large boat and take seeds of all plants and animals with him in the boat. In time the prediction was fulfilled. The water level rose and rose. The fish towed the boat, and anchored it to a peak of the Himalayas. After the destruction, all was created again from Manu. The term for 'human' is *mānava*, which literally means 'of Manu' – descended from Manu.

The destruction described here is not a full-scale one. Compared with other kinds of *pralaya*s vividly described in various *Purāṇa*s, this is only a mini-*pralaya*. According to the *Kūrma Purāṇa* (II.43), a *pralaya* takes place after a specific length of time called a *kalpa*.[3] When the time arrives, the process starts with a prolonged drought. The fragile beings of the earth decay fast and the seven rays of the sun become intense. The water in reservoirs evaporates and the sun looks like seven suns. Gradually the sun's seven rays become a thousand rays, pouring in all directions. In that intense heat everything melts and becomes a single blazing mass. The whole of it then bursts into a larger flame called *saṃvartaka* which starts consuming the worlds (*loka*s). The magnitude of the catastrophe suggests that it would be an astronomical event.

The description goes on to say that, gradually, large columns of highly electrically-charged clouds appear in the empty space. These clouds look white, black, yellow, red, grey and deep blue. The fury of the catastrophe goes on for a long time, then slowly things start to change. From within the smoky clouds appears rain, and the space becomes flooded. From that fluid gradually emerges a new creation.

The whole of this process takes another *kalpa* to complete. Two *kalpa*s make a day and a night of Brahmā. The *kalpa* during which creation takes place is the 'day of Brahmā', and the *kalpa* of dissolution is the night. This cyclic process of dissolution and creation goes on against the backdrop of the eternally flowing *kāla* (time).

In these narratives of *pralaya* there is no mention of the element of degeneration of, or sins perpetrated by, humans. But, during the period of the epic *Mahābhārata*, the idea gained ground that in ancient times there lived on earth an ideal race of humans. It was the age of the great sages. Then gradually there is a progressive deterioration of morality and degeneration of human society that need to be dealt with. The era is brought to a climax of dissolution by a great deluge, as there was a need for a complete clean-up, so to speak. This deterioration from the ideal to the vile state takes a very long time and happens very gradually, through four stages or eras (*yuga*s): *satya*, *tretā*, *dvāpara* and *kali*. The general concept behind these divisions is that in *Satya yuga*, the whole humanity is truthful and its moral values are intact; in *Tretā yuga*, three-quarters of human society are truthful and one quarter degenerate; in *Dvāpara yuga*, only a half are moral; and in *Kali yuga*, only one quarter are truthful. There are specific references to the present era being the *Kali yuga* of the current creation (e.g., in the *Viṣṇu Purāṇa*).

The theory of *daśāvatāra* is based on the same criteria of morality (*dharma*) and right conduct. Lord Kṛṣṇa's utterance in the *Bhagavad-gītā* (IV. 6–8) makes it clear:

> Though I am unborn and of imperishable nature, though Lord of all beings, yet remaining in my own nature I take birth through my own power of creation. Whenever *dharma* is in decay and *adharma* flourishes, O Bhārata, then I create myself. To protect the righteous and destroy the wicked, to establish *dharma* firmly, I take birth age after age.

The natural environment

To trace the development of the Hindu attitude towards the natural environment, one has to go back to the vedic literature, where the earliest hymns dedicated to the natural elements are found. The powerful forces of nature inspired human awe and bewilderment, and consequently a whole culture grew up glorifying and appeasing them. Natural phenomena were revered and personified as various deities, for example, the sun, fire, storm, lightning. On the one hand, people were offering oblations and chanting hymns to glorify the deities, and, on the other, they were asking favours from them in return, in the form of a good harvest, cattle, children and well-being in general. Vedic worship seems to have been the performance of sacrifices in the open air around a fire. Worship in relation to nature was clearly a preoccupation in this period.

The most intimate, beneficent, household deity was Agni (fire). He was considered to be a friend, a father, and a messenger from humans to the other deities in the heavens. The ascending flames and smoke of the sacrificial fire seem to have given him the status of heavenly messenger or mediator. Some two hundred hymns were addressed to Agni. The very first hymn of the *Ṛg-veda*, the central part of the entire vedic revelation, is an invocation to Agni (I.1). Here he is described as the domestic priest (*purohita*), the divine minister (*ṛtvij*) of the sacrifice. He is the mediator who transforms all material and human gifts into spiritual and divine realities, and delivers them to the heavenly deities, bringing back the divine blessings to the human worshippers. Agni has a priestly role and a three-fold composition, his nature being divine, human and earthly at one and the same time.

Reverence is due to Parjanya (rain cloud), Vāyu (wind), Maruts (storm gods), Savitṛ (solar god) and Sūrya (the sun), among many other vedic deities who are in some way or another linked with natural occurrences. Of these, Sūrya is the most concrete of the solar deities – since the name specified the orb of the sun as well as the deity, his connection with the luminary was always present in the minds of the sages.

> The golden gem of the sky, far-seeing rises, whose goal is distant, speeding onward, shining. Now may men, aroused by the Sun, attain their goals and perform their labours.
>
> (*Ṛg-veda* (VII. 63.4), trans. Macdonell, 1972: 127)

Vedic people not only composed hymns to glorify the natural phenomena, to appease them or to thank them for their earthly gifts, but also composed pure poetry inspired by the sheer beauty of nature. The hymns to Uṣas (dawn) are among the most beautiful of all hymns of the *Ṛg-veda*. Some twenty hymns are addressed to Uṣas, the Daughter of Heaven, who is born of Dyu (sky). She is the Lady of Light, consort of the Sun, who follows her as a young man follows a maiden (*Ṛg-veda* I.115.2). The Goddess of Hope, the elder sister of Niśā (night), Uṣas is mentioned more than 300 times in the *Ṛg-veda*.

Besides the natural elements and the heavenly bodies, humans see themselves surrounded by nature near at hand, complete with its plants and animals and other, apparently inanimate, objects. They feel akin to this environment, so much so that they develop an animistic view of nature, believing that there is life or soul in every little thing in nature. Even apparently inanimate rivers and mountains are believed to have some kind of hidden consciousness, according to the *Kālikā Purāṇa* (22.10–13), just as a shell seems lifeless but contains a living being inside. Humans see themselves not as isolated beings but as a constituted relationship, incorporated with the rest of the living community. The following hymn from the *Ṛg-veda* (I.90.6–8), known as the *Madhumatī Sūkta*, shows how vedic people recognized and appreciated nature's beneficence.

> For one who lives by Eternal Law [*ṛta*]
> the winds are full of sweetness;
> the rivers pour sweets;
> so may plants be full of sweetness for us.
> Sweet be the night and sweet the dawns;
> and sweet the dust of the earth.
> Sweet be our Father Heaven to us.
> For us may the forest tree be full of sweetness,
> full of sweetness the sun,
> and full of sweetness the cows for us.

This may be called vedic 'paganism' – the joy in the earth, but a joy sanctified under the control of Eternal Law (*ṛta*), as Bose (1970: 253) points out. The expression 'Eternal Law' here is significant. *Ṛta* means, on the one hand, the regular order of the universe/nature, such as the unvarying course of the sun and moon, and the seasons; on the other, the moral order. The hymn then emphasizes that only the person who abides by the natural law (i.e., who does not exploit nature) and keeps harmony with nature may be blessed by all things in nature and make a heaven of the earth. Hence the human relationship with nature is not one of exploitation but of harmonious participation. Nature is never left out in human social ceremonies. The final chant or the *śānti-vachana* (words of peace) at the end of all Hindu rituals or celebrations captures the spirit of the entire natural world:

> Peace of sky, peace of mid-region,
> peace of earth, peace of waters, peace of plants.
> Peace of trees, peace of all gods, peace of Brahman,
> peace of the universe, peace of peace,
> May that peace come to me.
>
> (*Yajur-veda*, VS 36.17 and *Atharva-veda*, XIX.9.94)

From these vedic hymns it is evident that the natural world, with its animate and inanimate components, is not to be ignored by humans; on the contrary, it is welcomed ceremonially at most rituals. The attitude is one of recognition of the fact that humans are only a part of the whole natural world. Hence all should co-exist and complement one another. The destruction of one may put the balance of this whole world into jeopardy.

The reverence for the earth takes literal form in India. The earth is the foundation, the basis from which emerges all that exists and on which everything rests. Not surprisingly, the earth is Mother. She is the basis of life and, when considered as a divine being, she always occupies a special place among deities. Though only one hymn in the *Ṛg-veda* is addressed to Pṛthivī (earth) specifically, she is praised in several hymns conjointly with Dyu (sky). Dyu and Pṛthivī are called father and mother not only of terrestrial creatures, but of the gods too. Worshipping earth is not idolatry. It is the veneration shown, so to speak, to an ancestor, continuing even today; the simple tradition of *Bharatanāṭyam* (a classical dance form of South India) – with the dancer's first gesture of touching the earth and thereby begging forgiveness for treading upon her – reveals this veneration.

One of the most beautiful hymns of the Vedas, the famous prayer to the earth called *Bhūmi Sūkta*, consisting of 63 verses, is found in the *Atharva-veda* (XII.1). The earth is here called *bhūmi* (ground/land) and not *pṛthivī* (literally, the broad one). This hymn depicts the universal mother, giver of every sort of good. It presents a striking cosmogonic sequence, as can be seen from Panikkar (1979: 121–2):

The description starts with the origin of the earth. She was hidden in the fluid state in the bosom of the primordial waters and the sages were seeking her through meditation. Then comes a geographical description, a highly poetical vision of nature. The earth is composed of hills and plains, of snow-clad peaks, of deserts, oceans and rivers, of lakes and streams, trees and plants, rocks and stones. The seasons appear with unfailing regularity and bring to her their own gradations of climate. Her fragrance emanates from plants, from water, from animals, from humans, even from the gods. She is rich with underground treasures of jewels and gold. Earth is the dwelling place of people. The first humans were scattered upon her, and upon her they sing and dance and find their happiness. It is she who diversifies human speech into different languages. She is the dwelling place of all living creatures. She is the home of lions and tigers, the beasts of the forest, of deer and birds, reptiles and two-legged creatures. Mention is made even of snakes and scorpions that viciously bite and, chilled by winter, lie lazily hidden, and of tiny wriggling worms that stir in the rain. She is, finally, the Mother, a cosmic power, the receiver of prayers and the bestower of blessings, and the protector.

As the human role evolves from being a passive receiver of earth's produce to being an active toiler on the land, the relationship with nature matures into a partnership. Human involvement in the process of producing food is an act of collaboration with the earth/nature – we learn to work with nature. On the other hand, the earth is happy to be worked by those who are helping her to produce more and to reach her own plenitude. It is not a relationship of dominion or of exploitation. A hymn addressed to Kṣetra-pati (lord/*pati*; of the field/*kṣetra*) as a friend, expresses this reliance on the earth as a partner. The reciter of the hymn begs the spirit of the field to watch over the ploughman's toil and to cause the earth to produce bountifully.

> Having the Lord of the Field as our friend and helper, may our cattle and horses have food in plenty. May men and oxen both plough in contentment, in contentment the plough cleave the furrow. Auspicious Furrow, we venerate you. We pray you, bless us and bring us abundant harvests.
>
> (*Ṛg-veda* IV.57)

When the tilling of the soil is over, then come the prayer for a bountiful harvest (*Atharva-veda* VI.142) and the harvest song (*Atharva-veda* III.24). The last verse of the harvest song, called *Samṛddhi-prāpti*, mentions even reaper and garnerer as the two distributors or attendants of Prajāpati (lord/*pati* of the creatures/*prajā*).

Any civilization which is mainly dependent on agriculture has a special relationship with its Mother Earth, who is the eternal provider of food. Timely rain, rivers and tributaries, seasonal changes in nature, are all of primary importance. To an agricultural community, nature is a living reality; at times harsh and cruel, at other times loving and generous. That is why earth is an object of worship and not of exploitation. This is how the Hindus of the past saw nature.

India today is still a country very much dependent on nature. Even in the present age of vast industrialization and high technology, 70 per cent of its population depend on agriculture. Yet the necessity for economic development has led India to look for desperate measures, at the expense of natural resources that took hundreds of years to establish; the felling of trees is one of them. Unexpected floods, the increase of barren desert areas and environmental changes are all linked with deforestation, and are signs of disharmony with, and exploitation of, nature. The ideals preached by the ancient Hindus are not always followed in actual practice in modern India. But at grass-roots level, a predominantly rural population still looks up to the Mother Earth as the life-sustaining living reality. The 'Chipko' (hug-the-tree) movement, which started in 1974 and spread all over India, proves the point. It is a movement that grew from the simple act of hugging the trees by the village women of Reni in Garhwal, thus stopping the hired workers who were about to cut down the trees for a sports-goods company.

The plant world

Forests have always played a central part in Hindu civilization. Forest life (*vānaprastha*) is the third of the four *āśrama*s. The term *vānaprastha* is derived from the word *vana*, meaning woodland. In this third stage, the individual takes leave of society and retires to a forest life for reflection and self-searching. As Jyoti Sahi (1986: 43) points out, 'forest' has a particular symbolic meaning in Hindu thought, rather like the 'wilderness' of Jewish and Christian thought. The forest is seen in contrast with the cultivated land. In a way, the individual must return to the way of life of the pre-agricultural, food-gathering societies. It is not that a Hindu has no experience of a developed urban life (names of very many cities could be cited), but he consciously chooses to model human life in close proximity to nature, where the process of rejuvenation goes on perpetually. According to Rabindranath Tagore, the uniqueness of Hindu ideology consists in recognizing life in the forest as the highest form of cultural evolution. He writes (in *Tapovana*, as quoted by Shiva, 1989: 55):

> Indian civilization has been distinctive in locating its source of regeneration, material and intellectual, in the forest, not in the city. India's best ideas have come where man was in communion with trees and rivers and lakes, away from the crowds. The peace of the forest has helped the intellectual evolution of man. The culture of the forest has fuelled the culture of Indian society. The culture that has arisen from the forest has been influenced by the diverse processes of renewal of life which are always at play in the forest, varying from species to species, from season to season, in sight and sound and smell. The unifying principle of life in diversity, of democratic pluralism, thus became the principle of Indian civilization.

The vedic poet even worships Araṇyānī (Sprite of the Forest/*araṇya*) as a deity. The hymn to Araṇyānī (*Ṛg-veda* X.146.2, 6) shows that the woodland is not merely appreciated for its generous gifts of shelter, food and pure air, but is venerated for its inspiring quality of sight, sound and smell. The hymn is a piece of pure poetry without any motivation attached to it.

> When the cicada emits his shrill notes
> and the grasshopper is his accompanist,
> it's the Sprite of the Forest they hail with their praises,
> as with cymbals clashing in procession.
>
> Adorned with fragrant perfumes and balms,
> she needs not to toil for her food.
> Mother of untamed forest beasts,
> Sprite of the wood, I salute you!
>
> (Quoted from Panikkar, 1979: 276)

Apart from the *Saṃhitā* (hymn) period, there is a whole set of vedic literature called *Āraṇyaka*s (forest texts) that contain the knowledge which comes from direct participation in the life of the forest. The forest 'nurtured an ecological civilization in the most fundamental sense of harmony with nature' (Shiva, 1989: 56).

In non-vedic literature also, plant life is venerated and associated with divinity, e.g., in *Śrī Chaṇḍī* (a part of the *Mārkaṇḍeya Purāṇa*) (XI.48), the primordial Mother Chaṇḍī proclaims that she nourishes the whole world with the life-sustaining vegetation that grows out of her own body.

The Hindu ideal of elevating plant life to the level of divinity is evident from the common practice of tree or plant worship in India. There are certain trees or plants that are considered sacred for various reasons. For example, the banyan tree is considered to have a benign effect on people searching for spiritual enlightenment. The Buddha, believed by Hindus to be the ninth incarnation of Viṣṇu, achieved his enlightenment meditating under a type of banyan tree called *aśvattha* (*Ficus religiosa*), subsequently known as the *bodhi* tree (tree of knowledge), in the city of Bodh Gaya. The nineteenth-century saint Ramakrishna achieved his vision under another type of banyan tree, called *vaṭa* (*Ficus benghalensis*), in Dakshineswar in Bengal.

The daily worship of the sacred plant *tulasī* (*Ocymum sanctum*) is prevalent all over India. It is a little plant which has medicinal value and is used in herbal (Āyurvedic) treatments. But besides its beneficial properties, it has a religious significance for its devotees. It is a symbol of Lord Viṣṇu. Women, when they water the *tulasī* every morning and light a lamp at its altar in the evening, do not think of it as a mere plant, but are filled with veneration and humility, as in the presence of a deity. In the form of a small plant, nature is elevated to divinity.

Similarly, other trees, plants and flowers are associated with particular deities. *Bilva* (*Crataeva religiosa*), *javā* (hibiscus) and *kamala* (*Nymphaea lotus*) are associated with Śiva, Kālī/Durgā and Lakṣmī respectively. There are even special dates in the Hindu calendar for the worship of particular plants.

ĀYURVEDA (LIFE-SCIENCE)

People in the vedic period recognized their indebtedness to the plant world for an additional reason. The medical science based on the knowledge of herbs and plants is called Āyurveda (*āyur*/life, *veda*/knowledge). It is often known as the fifth Veda or an *upaveda* (a part or sub-group) of *Atharva-veda*, showing the high regard it attracted as a life-science. Herbal medicine flourished in India for centuries. Even in today's India there are a large number of followers of Āyurveda, which in the West is considered to be one of the alternative medicines.

The main basis of Āyurveda lies in the concept of the balance of elements in the human body. Like any material body, the human body is made up of five elements: earth (*kṣiti*), water (*ap*), heat (*tejas*), air (*marut/vāyu*) and space (*vyoman*). When all these elements in their particular proportions are working in proper balance, the body is fit. When somehow these respective proportions go wrong and the balance is not perfect, the body becomes ill. The Āyurveda prescribes various plants and roots for rectifying different kinds of imbalance.

There are hymns in the *Atharva-veda* (e.g., IV.17) addressed to plants for their power of curing particular diseases, thus acknowledging humanity's indebtedness to the plant world for its contribution towards human welfare.

From a study of Āyurveda one can see how detailed was the vedic knowledge of medicinal properties of herbs, and how delicately medicine was administered in each individual case. The *Atharva-veda* mentions about 110 plants used in the cure of various ailments, and most of these remedies came to occupy a significant place in the ayurvedic literature of later periods. In the *Ṛg-veda* also, there is a hymn addressed to *Oṣadhi* (herbal plant) (X.97) which mentions several herbs, and distinguishes between herbs bearing flowers and fruits and herbs without them. Vegetation itself is divided into various categories, e.g., *vanaspati* is the forest tree that bears fruit without any blossom, and *oṣadhi* is the annual plant that dies after the ripening of fruits.

That the Hindus had a detailed knowledge of various species of trees and plants is also evident from terms like *vanaspati-vidyā* (*vidyā*/knowledge/science), meaning tree-science; and *vṛkṣāyurveda* (*vṛkṣa*/tree, *āyurveda*/life-science), meaning the science of treatment of trees, which shows that treatments for trees were practised.

The animal world

While the Aryan deities were mostly personifications of natural phenomena or heavenly bodies, the indigenous non-Aryan peoples had rituals of image worship of male and female deities. Several mystic animals also had their place in the rituals. Various animals or birds are associated with particular deities as their vehicles (*vāhana*) and companions. One deity (Kārtikeya – male) is mounted on a peacock, another (Sarasvatī – female) on a swan, a third (Śiva – male) is carried by a bull, a fourth (Durgā – female) by a lion, and so on. Because of their association with the deities, these animals and birds are considered sacred. Apart from the peacock, swan, bull and lion, others belonging to this sacred list include goat, buffalo, elephant, tiger, serpent, rat and owl. Together with the deities, the respective animals are worshipped and praised.

The clash of cults (in the present context, Aryan and non-Aryan) or the contacts of cultures do not necessarily result in a complete domination of one by the other. There may be an interchange of concepts, with old concepts being given new significance. There are stories in the epic literature (the *Rāmāyaṇa*) indicating the reconciliation of the vedic and the non-vedic faiths. As Radhakrishnan (1971: 30) pointed out, 'The enlistment of Hanumān, the monkey-general, in the service of Rāma, signifies the meeting-point of early nature worship and later theism'.

In Hindu mythology, the frequent occurrences of transformations of humans into animals and vice versa show the recognition that animal life is as valid as, and thus interchangeable with, human life. The Hindu theory of transmigration of the soul accepts the logic that a soul being born into several forms may take animal forms as well as human. Though it may seem strange, this hints at the acceptance of the idea that, in the strata of living creatures, humans are not necessarily put on an unchallenged pedestal. The positions of humans and animals are interchangeable when circumstances demand or *karma* (the consequence of deeds from previous lives) dictates.

In the story of *Daśāvatāra* (ten incarnations), Lord Viṣṇu himself takes several births into animal forms before taking human ones. It is significant that Hindus do not find it hard or unnatural to think of their God in animal forms. On the contrary, they find it most natural and plausible if they are to believe that creation is an evolutionary process, and that life began in its minutest forms. If their God himself can take up the humble forms of a fish (aquatic), a tortoise (amphibian), a boar (terrestrial) and a lion-man (half-human) before human forms, it shows the kind of regard or reverence Hindus feel towards the animal world. This story puts humans in their proper perspective. They are just one of the creatures created during the process of evolution; they owe their existence to their predecessors, the creatures of the animal kingdom.

There are also other areas of human indebtedness to the animal world recognized by the Hindu scriptures. References have been made to animals' knowledge of the medicinal properties of herbs. It is not only humans who have familiarity with the plant world for health and cure; the animals perhaps have a priority over humans in this context. In *Atharva-veda* (VIII.7.23–24), where various plants are invoked to cure human ailments, mention is made of individual plants being known to boars, hawks, eagles, swans, birds and wild beasts.

In the puranic literature (e.g., in the *Mārkaṇḍeya Purāṇa – Śrī Chaṇḍī* I.49–51), it is recognized that the birds and animals have intelligence of some kind. The difference between the intelligence of animals and the intellect of humans lies in the fact that humans can, if they wish, develop spiritual wisdom beyond the inborn, instinctive, material sense. To begin with, humans are no wiser than animals. Without the Ultimate Knowledge, humans are equal to animals in intelligence because both are ignorant, knowing merely the sensual world.

The 'sacred cow' of the Hindus is a familiar phrase in the West. The sanctity of the cow has probably been acquired by its association with Lord Kṛṣṇa, a deity and an incarnation of Viṣṇu. The mythology has it that Kṛṣṇa was brought up as a dairyman's son who used to graze the cattle. The cow is even worshipped in some parts of India on an auspicious day called *Goṣṭhāṣṭamī* in the month of Kārttika (in November), a special day set aside for the cow. 'Whatever origin or value we may ascribe to the sanctity and worship of the cow in India, the fact remains that for a predominantly agricultural civilization the worth of the cow cannot easily be over estimated' (Panikkar, 1979: 286). The herd of cattle is an asset to the farmer. The oxen are used for ploughing, the cows produce milk from which come all kinds of dairy products. Cows are not only the source of almost inexhaustible riches, they also symbolize maternity, endurance and service. It is common knowledge that a Hindu does not eat beef. The ban on the slaughtering of cows involves not only religious but also economic factors in an agricultural Hindu society.

VEGETARIANISM

The Aryans enjoyed the meat of sacrificial animals. There are references which show that, in vedic culture, great honour was shown to a guest by offering a young calf's meat for his meal (e.g., the sage Vaśiṣtha was served with veal in the hermitage of the sage Vālmīki –

Uttara-Rāmacharita), though they seem to have admired the cow as a very useful animal. The ideals of vegetarianism and non-violence (*ahiṃsā*) developed under the influence of Buddhism and Jainism, and flourished in the sixth century BCE, though the first seeds of non-violence were sown in the *Upaniṣads*. The upanisadic concept of all living creatures being part and parcel of *brahman* emphasizes the sacredness of all forms of life, and thus the killing of animals is unjustifiable. During the developing period of Buddhism and Jainism – two contemporaneous ideologies – this moral issue gained ground. Gradually they evolved into two similar but distinct faiths. As Sen (1973: 64) pointed out, the vedic interest in gods had by then been replaced by interest in humanity and in human greatness. The vedic ideal of a pleasant life on earth had been challenged by believers in renunciation, ego-lessness and selfless work. Jainism contributed to Hindu thought and practices to a great extent, and the vegetarianism of some sects of Hindus may be due to Jain influence. A strong sense of love and compassion for animals and other sub-human species led to vegetarianism. One must remember though, in this context, that not all Hindus are vegetarians, e.g., Bengalis are non-vegetarians. That vegetarianism was widespread in India from a very early period is known from the accounts of the ancient Greek traveller Megasthenes (fourth century BCE), and those of Fa-hsien (fifth century CE), a Chinese Buddhist monk who travelled to India to obtain authentic copies of the Buddhist scriptures.

The fact that animals were treated compassionately in Hindu society is documented by the sixteenth-century English traveller Ralph Fitch, who came across a veterinary hospital in Cooch Bihar. As quoted by Sen (1973: 25):

> I went from Bengala into the country of Couche. Here they be all gentiles and they will kill nothing. They have hospitals for sheepe, goates, dogs, cats, birds, and for all other living creatures. When they be old and lame, they keep them until they die. If a man catch or buy any quicke thing in other places and bring it thither, they will give him money for it or other victuals, and keepe it in their hospitals or let it go.
>
> (*Early Travels in India*, ed. William Foster (1921). Oxford University Press, pp. 24–5)

This shows that social or public service was not restricted to humans, but was extended to other living creatures. The continuation of the same trend can be noticed in the preachings of Swami Vivekananda, the Hindu visionary and social reformer, at the turn of the nineteenth century (1863–1902):

> Where do you seek your God,
> overlooking Him in various forms, in front of you?
> He serves God best,
> who is kind to all His creatures.

Notes

1 The *Purāṇa*s are the bulk of literature dealing with ancient (*purā*) accounts. They are not directly based on the Vedas, but accept their authority. There are eighteen *Purāṇa*s in all.

2 There are three types of suffering:
   (a) *Ādhyātmika* – mental or spiritual suffering rooted in the soul (*ātman*);
   (b) *Ādhibhautika* – physical suffering caused by imbalance of material elements (*bhūta*) in the body;
   (c) *Ādhidaivika* – accidental suffering caused by fate (*daiva*).

3 More information concerning *kalpa*s, *yuga*s and the Hindu concept of time can be found in Chapter 5.

Further reading

Bhattacharjee, S. (1978) *The Hindu Theory of Cosmology*. Calcutta: Bani Prakashani.

Bose, A. C. (1970) *The Call of the Vedas*. 3rd edn; Bombay: Bharatiya Vidya Bhavan.

Gupta, L. (1993) 'Ganga: purity, pollution, and Hinduism' in C. J. Adams (ed.) *Ecofeminism and the Sacred*. New York: Continuum.

Halbfass, W. (1992) *On Being and What There Is: Classical Vaiśeṣika and the History of Indian Ontology*. Albany: SUNY Press.

Macdonell, A. A. (1972) *A Vedic Reader for Students*. 3rd edn; London: Oxford University Press.

Panikkar, R. (1979) *The Vedic Experience – Mantramañjarī: An Anthology of the Vedas for Modern Man and Contemporary Celebration*. 2nd edn; London: Darton, Longman & Todd.

Radhakrishnan, S. (1971) *The Hindu View of Life*. 16th edn; London: Unwin Books.

Sahi, J. (1986) *Stepping Stones*. Bangalore: Asian Trading Corporation.
Sen, K. M. (1973) *Hinduism*. 8th edn; London: Penguin Books.
Shiva, V. (1989) *Staying Alive: Women, Ecology and Development*. 2nd edn; London: Zed Books.

5. Myth and history

Jacqueline Suthren Hirst

It is often said that Hinduism is not interested in history, that it is ahistorical. Historians, both European and Indian, have followed Rawlinson in suggesting that, before the coming of the British, the pre-Muslim history of India did not exist.[1] On the other hand, Hinduism has rarely been accused of lacking myths. Retellings, anthologies and analyses of Hindu myths abound. It might be expected, then, that this chapter would be largely concerned with myth, giving perhaps passing consideration to histories of India. However, the matter is not that simple.

'Myth' and 'history' are, of course, Western terms, both of which are used in many ways with different nuances of meaning. Put very crudely, the distinction is sometimes assumed to be this: where myths deal with God or the gods and 'events' which may not literally have happened, history deals with past facts and so reports what actually did happen. The impression may be given that myths are, at least in some senses, 'false', whereas historical accounts are 'true'. This is implied by Walker when he says of the brahmanical court chronicles 'Mythology is the framework of their fanciful outpourings, replete as they are with eulogies of patrons and heroes, and theological and moral didacticism'.[2] Not exactly a sympathetic view!

Yet the kind of crude opposition implied here will not do. The interests of myth and history converge in so far as both are concerned with human existential questions about meaning, values, a sense of identity, causation, continuity and change. Without denying their differences, this chapter will explore some of these common concerns as they are expressed in Hindu traditions, whose variety at any one period and across the centuries is well known. It will also try to show how different senses of history have affected Hindus' self-understanding. First, though, we shall look at two key terms and types of textual source for myth and history in Hinduism.

Itihāsa-purāṇa

Itihāsa is used in some modern Indian languages as the word for 'history'. *Purāṇa* is frequently rendered as 'myth'. So it looks as though here are neat Hindu equivalents for 'history' and 'myth'. However, because the words often occur in a compound (*itihāsapurāṇa*) meaning 'history and myth', it has been suggested that Hinduism makes no great distinction between the two, backing up the view that it is fundamentally ahistorical.

To the question of ahistoricality, we shall return. For the moment we shall look more carefully at the usages of *itihāsa* and *purāṇa* in some key textual traditions.[3] Both words appear together in the *Śatapaṭha Brāhmaṇa* and the *Bṛhadāraṇyaka* and *Chāndogya Upaniṣads*, for types of oral wisdom. They seem to refer to entertaining stories which were recited during the Horse Sacrifice to keep the sacrificer alert!

Śaṃkara, the most famous exponent of classical Advaita Vedānta (seventh or eighth century CE), gives examples for each within the Veda. For *itihāsa* he refers to the story of Urvaśī and Purūravas, found, among other places, in the *Śatapaṭha Brāhmaṇa* (11.4.4.1). This is the famous story of a nymph and a king who marry, which later inspired a play by the great poet Kalidasa. Because the king, Purūruvas, fails to keep one of the conditions of their marriage, Urvaśī disappears. The heartbroken Purūruvas is finally granted a boon by the *gandharva*s (celestial musicians) through which he becomes the initiator of a crucial fire ritual. In calling this story *itihāsa*, Śaṃkara is probably referring to its aetiological function, explaining how the particular sacrifice came to be. *Itihāsa* literally means 'thus it was'.

For *purāṇa*, Śaṃkara quotes *Taittirīya Upaniṣad* (2.7): 'This universe was in the beginning Non-being.' The passage goes on to describe how Being emerged from Non-being to form itself into *ātman* (the self), with bliss as the quintessence of its being. It is, then, an origination story or 'creation myth'. *Purāṇa* literally means 'ancient'.

Others suggest different interpretations. Yaska (a grammarian of the fifth century BCE) discusses many vedic etymologies in his *Nirukta*. In one example, he is trying to ascertain the identity of the

Aśvins, twin celestial gods (12.1). He points out that some people identify them with sun and moon or with day and night, but that the *aitihāsikas* (specialists in *itihāsa*) say they are two famous kings. The *aitihāsikas* look for a historical basis for the Aśvins, whereas others look for a mythological basis in parts of the cosmos. What is important is that there is awareness of story of various kinds, whose interpretation is open to discussion.

In devotional Hinduism, the terms refer to particular texts which may well be based on the earlier *itihāsas* and *purāṇas*, at least in part. *Itihāsa* comes to denote the epic *Mahābhārata* and, often, the *Rāmāyaṇa* as well, though strictly the latter is a *kāvya* (poem). The *Mahābhārata* has as its centre the legendary history of the war between two sets of cousins, one side, the Pāṇḍavas, aided and abetted by (Lord) Kṛṣṇa. In many ways, it acts as a key source of historical consciousness for (Hindu) Indians, as we shall discuss further below.

The *Rāmāyaṇa* tells the story of Rāma, his birth, marriage and banishment into the forest, accompanied by his wife, Sītā, and his loyal half-brother, Lakṣmaṇa. Sītā's kidnapping by Rāvaṇa, the ten-headed demon king of Laṅka, gives rise to a great search and battle in which Rāvaṇa is defeated. At this, Rāma reclaims Sītā, puts her through a fire ordeal which proves her purity, and returns with her victorious to be enthroned in Ayodhyā. Sītā subsequently goes into exile once more, suspected of unfaithfulness. She dies, swallowed up by the earth which finally attests her innocence. The *Rāmāyaṇa*, especially in its various vernacular versions, may well be the best-known story in India, particularly since its serialization on Indian television in 1987–88. In both past and present, its narration has been bound up with issues of social and political identity, some of whose implications will be discussed towards the end of this chapter.

The *Purāṇas* are the sources from which many of the well-known stories of the gods and goddesses are drawn. Traditionally, there are said to be eighteen major *Purāṇas* and eighteen minor, though in fact there are many more. According to Vaiṣṇava tradition, six of the major *Purāṇas* belong to each of the Vaiṣṇava, Śaiva and Śākta devotional schools. This is certainly an oversimplification, but it does indicate the (sometimes competitive) devotional milieux of these texts.

The following story is from the *Kūrma Purāṇa* (quotations from Dimmitt and van Buitenen, 1983: 205–6). It will give a flavour of the kind of stories to be found in the puranic literature. For collections of other puranic stories, Dimmitt and van Buitenen (1983) and O'Flaherty (1975) make excellent introductions (in the following, square brackets indicate my own summary).

> [Long ago, when the cosmos was in a period of dissolution, Śiva appeared to awaken Lord Viṣṇu and Lord Brahmā. Both claiming to be the creator of the worlds, they argued about who was greater.] While the argument was going on like this there appeared by the illusion of the supreme god a matchless *liṅga* whose self was Śiva. ... It was bright as the fire of Doomsday, wreathed with garlands of flame, free from growth and decay, without beginning, middle or end.
>
> [Brahmā and Viṣṇu agreed to explore the limits of this fiery pillar but could find no end though they searched for a hundred years. Chanting *Oṃ*, they praised Śiva, who manifested himself as the great Yogin, with trident, tiger-skin and snake for sacred thread. Then the great god spoke:] 'I am pleased with you both, O best of the gods. Now see that I am the greatest god and fear no more! Ages ago the two of you eternal ones were produced from my limbs. Brahmā, Grandfather of the worlds, lies in my right side. Viṣṇu, the protector, dwells in my left. And Hara [a form of Śiva] is born in my heart. ... I will give to you both whatever you desire.'

Prostrating themselves, Brahmā and Viṣṇu claim their boon. It is constant devotion to Śiva. The myth thus makes a clear statement about the identity of the Supreme Lord and also provides an explanation of the significance of the *liṅga*, the aniconic form in which Śiva is generally worshipped. While many other myths (and indeed sculptures) stress the *liṅga*'s phallic form, the symbolism of the ungraspable nature of Ultimate Reality is often preferred by Hindus in the West who feel the balance of male and female in *liṅga* and *yoni* can be misunderstood by outsiders.

Traditionally, a *Purāṇa* is said to cover five topics: the origination of the world cycle, its dissolution, genealogies, world ages and the successive deeds of the descendants of the dynasties mentioned. Klostermaier notes that scholars are increasingly prepared to accept the historical value of some of these dynasty lists (1989: 91). Besides these topics, not all of which feature in every *Purāṇa*, is a wealth of other material covering religious observances, image worship, pilgrimage, astrology, the aims of life, the nature of *brahman* and so on. Iconography, ritual and a sense of time and tradition are thus underpinned by the puranic stories. To see how these stories of *itihāsa* and *purāṇa* are viewed, we shall turn to the ways they are told.

Telling the stories

In the villages of India, besides perpetual informal family retellings, it is the *paurāṇika*, the storyteller, who keeps these stories alive. R. K. Narayan describes such a figure, living in conformity with the *śāstra*s and knowing by heart the 24,000 verses of the *Rāmāyaṇa*, the 100,000 of the *Mahābhārata* and the 18,000 of the *Bhāgavata Purāṇa*. For him, he says:

> The characters in the epics are prototypes and moulds in which humanity is cast, and remain valid for all time. Every story has implicit in it a philosophical or moral significance. ... To the storyteller and his audience the tales are so many chronicles of personalities who inhabited this world at some remote time, and whose lives are worth understanding, and hence form part of human history rather than fiction.
>
> (Narayan, 1987: 5)

In her delightful book *Storytellers, Saints and Scoundrels* (1989), Kirin Narayan shows the reverse process employed by the holy man whose stories she recorded. Swamiji's audience is drawn into his stories as his listeners hear themselves featured among the characters in his tales, individual human histories becoming part of fiction in order to be perceived more truly as they are. Story is about self-perception and identity. Its sources need not be limited to the epics and *Purāṇa*s, but may include traditional *kathā* (narrative) collections, like the *Hitopadeśa* fables, regional stories in local languages and tales told to accompany and explain particular practices like a fast for a certain goddess.

Storytelling is not simply a rural phenomenon. Jackson and Killingley describe a South Indian storyteller, many of whose recitations are for town dwellers, helping them to keep in touch with their religious traditions (1988: 114–16). Hearing a *Purāṇa* acts as an efficacious substitute for the highest and most complicated rituals. It is said to yield many benefits, including purity and the removal of the contamination of the *Kali* Age. Puranic recitations provide the easy path of *bhakti* (devotion) for busy urban people, and bring refreshment and inspiration into their lives.

Increasingly, such narrations are gaining popularity in the West. Storytellers from India undertake tours which draw thousands of Hindus, some choosing to spend their annual holiday in this way. The tellers may narrate in Sanskrit or Hindi with commentary in Gujarati and English, say, and draw in the younger generation with competitions and jokes as well as more serious teaching. The *Rāmāyaṇa* and *Bhāgavata Purāṇa* are particularly popular texts. Based on his oral retellings, Morari Bapu's *Mangal Ramayan* is the English translation of his Gujarati commentary on the sixteenth-century Hindi version of the *Rāmāyaṇa*, the *Rāmcaritmānas* of Tulsidās.[4] He emphasizes that this is not just a story or a recitation, but the wish-fulfilling tree, the bodily incarnation of God Almighty. To hear it helps to build up inner purity and moral conduct which lead to nearness to Lord Rām. To bring out its significance, Morari Bapu has a fund of stories, some emphasized as true anecdotes – life really is like this. With others, it is the 'hidden message' which is 'very appealing'. However, this should not be taken to imply that the events of the epic may or may not have occurred. The link with actual geography (and hence with a current pilgrimage location) is stressed in the following:

> It is not only a belief but a substantiated fact that the Lord himself had his permanent abode in Chitrakoot [Rāma's first home in exile] . . . Chitrakoot was and is, thus, a permanent abode of Lord Ram.
>
> (p. 7)

It was in Chitrakoot, explains Morari Bapu, that Rāma established *Rāmrājya* (reign of all for the benefit of all), where he denied himself all luxury in food, transport and shelter till he could provide amply for all his subjects. In such a place, chanting of his name is particularly efficacious. Yet Morari Bapu also speaks of the 'Chitrakoot of our hearts' where God can dwell. For this reason, the return of Rāma and Sītā to Ayodhyā is for him the climax of the whole story. There the ideal of selfless service flourishes as, joyfully, the couple are enthroned together, just as they can be in our hearts today. Morari Bapu believes that Tulsidās wisely ignores the end of Vālmīki's saga where Sītā goes off into exile, accused again of unfaithfulness, because 'it is not useful to humanity at large'. Events in themselves are not enough for him; nor is their narration in esteemed versions from the past. It is their continuing uplifting significance which makes them retellable.

'So indeed it was'

In 1989, Peter Brook launched his massive nine-hour English stage version of the *Mahābhārata*, based on Jean-Claude Carrière's French retelling. It subsequently became a televised film. With an international cast, Brook made it clear that his intention was to show the epic's story as the story of the world, of all humans, of universal concern. This is 'how things are'.

Many Hindus preferred the Hindi version, shown in 91 episodes on British television, with interpolations from other texts like the *Bhāgavata Purāṇa*. As one friend of mine put it, 'Krishna really looked like he does in the Hindi version. He just didn't look like God in the other one.' He also did not look Indian, played as he was by Bruce Myers, an Englishman. My friend is not naive. She would be quick to agree that God is beyond all human ideas. Yet her vision of Kṛṣṇa is shaped by the *Bhagavadgītā*'s description of his four-armed form, holding conch and discus and represented iconographically with the equivalent of a halo around his head. The Hindi version which reproduced this rang more true for her, though she agreed with Brook that the epic story deals with the fabric of all human experience.

The *Mahābhārata*, 'the Great [Epic] of India', sees itself as *itihāsa*. It portrays itself fundamentally as Vyāsa's account of the victory of the Pāṇḍavas over their cousins, the Kauravas. This is retold on two subsequent ritual occasions, augmented by a mass of material on *dharma* and other topics. It even says 'Whatever is written here, may also be found elsewhere; but what is not found here, cannot be found anywhere else either' (quoted in Klostermaier, 1989: 78).

The *Mahābhārata*, then, infuses awareness of past events in its hearers but goes well beyond this in a claim to comprehensiveness which works at several different levels. Madhva, the great thirteenth-century Dvaita Vedānta teacher, believed that the *Mahābhārata* conveys three different layers of meaning: *āstikādi*, 'in so far as it is a relation of the facts and events with which Śrī Kṛṣṇa and the Pāṇḍavas are connected'; *manvādi*, 'by which we find lessons on virtue, divine love . . . sacred duty and righteous practices, on character and training, on Brahmā and the other gods'; and *auparicara*, 'by which every sentence, word or syllable' names or glorifies 'the Almighty Ruler of the universe' (see Klostermaier, 1989: 78).

Modern commentators have found allegorical as well as political significance in the war, as the struggle between *dharma* and *adharma*, or between the higher and lower natures of the self. Gandhi's interpretation of the *Bhagavadgītā*, part of Book 6 of the *Mahābhārata*, works with the latter view. It would, then, be incorrect to say that the *Mahābhārata* has been understood simply as history. On the other hand, to deny that it is in some sense 'historical' ignores one of its most vital dimensions. In his foreword to a book entitled *Mahābhārata: Myth and Reality: Differing Views*, Niharranjan Ray writes:

> And the people of traditional India have been believing that the *Mahābhārata*, despite its being a store house of legends and stories, is an *itihāsa* or history according to their conception, since it records at its core the story of the Kuru-Pāṇḍavas, the Pañcālas and a host of other contemporary *janas* [tribes], as faithfully as the live story of a fraternal feud leading to a devastating war could be, but all put in a literary form by an imaginatively effective poet. They have been singing and reciting it through the ages and allowing the characters, events and situations presented in it, affect their lives very deeply and widely ... the *Bhāratayuddha-kathā* [Vyāsa's poem] has been, through the centuries, woven into the very texture of India's life and culture, and is thus an important and inalienable part of the lives of countless millions of people of this land, and hence an essential fact of Indian history, and this, even from the point of view of the modern concept of history.
>
> (Gupta and Ramachandran, 1976: vii)

Ray suggests that the original historical events have been mythicized and that this myth has then become part of history. This latter point cannot be stressed too strongly. However, because of this, attempts to confirm the *Mahābhārata*'s historicity by straightforward archaeological means seem, to Ray, futile. Nonetheless, this does not render all historical exploration useless. Even more importantly, he stresses that there is no need to choose between myth and reality.

> In actuality [myth] is a 'true story' of the life of any society, the essence extracted out of the very process of human life of a given time and space. ... [Myths] incorporate deep-rooted traditions and provide 'living' entities in the sense that they supply models of human behaviour, and by doing so, give meaning and value to the flowing current of life in a given social situation. ... A myth is a socio-psychological phenomenon, and hence a reality which historians can hardly afford to ignore.
>
> (Gupta and Ramachandran, 1976: xiv)

Ray, then, makes two points. First, there is a historical core to the *Mahābhārata*, though this is not recoverable in any easy way. Secondly, the *Mahābhārata* has become inextricably bound up with Indian (Hindu) self-consciousness and therefore has become part of

Indian history. The collection of articles following Ray's balanced introduction stems from a controversy which raged in the front pages of the Indian press during 1975 over the date of the Bhārata war. Romila Thapar, a prominent Indian historian, relates the storm to cultural nationalism at a time of social and political change. She suggests that the contenders are caught in their own battle, one side trying to dismiss the epic as valueless because not historically authentic, the other seeking to verify its authenticity with what are thought to be the most up-to-date scientific methods. The limits of these she sharply delineates. However, elsewhere she rejects a view of history which limits it to a modern Western form and seeks to explore what she calls 'embedded history' and 'externalized history' in an Indian context. The *Mahābhārata* she finds to carry the seeds of a more conscious (hence externalized) and less embedded approach than earlier myths and eulogies. In her view, 'it is a later age reflecting on an earlier one' as a state system replaced the pastoral-agricultural world of the epic's heroes.[5]

Is Hinduism ahistorical?

Thapar's work brings us back to the question of the supposed ahistoricality of Hinduism. As indicated above, many Orientalist writers clearly thought it was ahistorical, condemning such a stance as sorely inadequate. They based their views on observations of the following sorts. Hindu texts show a decided lack of interest in recording dates of any sort. Accordingly, it is difficult to date even such major events as the entry of the Aryans into India (supposing that there was such an entry). Texts, too, are notoriously difficult to date, partly because of the lack of records and partly because they are often oral composites (see above on the three 'tellings' of the *Mahābhārata*). Dates that are given are often based on the accounts of foreigners, Chinese pilgrims, for example, or on Indian Buddhist material. The *Rājataraṃgiṇī*, a Kashmiri work dated to 1160 CE, 'represents the only Sanskrit chronicle which can lay claim to being regarded as history'.[6] Texts of a 'properly' historical kind are to be found only after the Muslim conquests in the thirteenth century CE.

This lack of historical writing is linked with the often-mentioned Hindu cyclical view of time which is contrasted with Western linear views of history as moving from a beginning to an end. If events repeat themselves from cycle to cycle, the argument goes, they are not really significant in themselves nor open to historical explanation in terms of socio-economic conditions, for example. Another argument points to the denial of change in the transmission of texts and their interpretations. Thus a sub-commentator claims merely to reproduce the views of the earlier major commentator who in turn was simply elaborating on the meaning of the text itself, say *Upaniṣad* or *Bhagavadgītā*. Yet the various works show clear evidence of differences which might be linked with changing social conditions, so this again shows a lack of historical awareness.

It is possible to challenge the deductions drawn from the above points in a number of ways. For example, the assertion that a writer is simply being faithful to the original texts whose authority is beyond question, is commonplace across religious traditions before the modern period. The contrast between linear and cyclical views of time may be overdrawn, as we shall consider in more detail below. Hindu texts may well contain embedded historical records, for example, in the puranic genealogies. Historical consciousness in terms of a present shaped by a past tradition is wholly characteristic of, for example, the *Mahābhārata*, past and present! Moreover, it can be shown that a sense of cumulative progress, of freedom and contingency of human action, is present in the myths and concepts of Hindu classical traditions (Lipner, 1994: ch. 11).

Histories of (Hindu) India which have been written by or under the influence of modern Western writers also have their own advantages and drawbacks. K. M. Panikkar, in his *Survey of Indian History*, published in 1947, urges: 'Today when we talk of the Mauryas, the Guptas, the Chālukyas and the Pallavas, let it be remembered that these great ages of Indian history were recovered to us by the devoted labours of European scholars.' Thapar acknowledges such work in providing a chronological framework 'around which fresh interpretations can be constructed which will place the ideas and institutions of Indian civilization in their correct perspective' (Thapar, 1966: 22). Yet she indicates how the concerns of nineteenth-century Western scholars (mis)shaped Indian history, concentrating as they did on dynastic histories, brahmanical (idealized) texts and comparisons with Greek achievements. If such history claims to report 'events as they really happened' in contrast with the testimony of despised eulogy and myth, it deceives itself.

One response, then, to the contention that Hinduism is ahistorical is to challenge the basis on which that claim is made and the notions of history that are associated with it. Another response, typified by Pratima Bowes, is to accept the basic data, especially the lack of interest in chronology and the cyclic view of time, but to reject the deductions that may be drawn from these points. She strongly denies that the Hindu intellectual tradition 'took history to be meaningless or even life itself to be so' (Bowes, 1977: 15). She rather takes the *yuga* theory of the four ages to be a sign of profound interest in progress and decline in human affairs and one which does not adopt the simplistic view of progress found in much Western history. Granting that the Hindu view of the four ages takes a mythological approach and may involve a 'relative devaluation of history' (Bowes, 1977: 17), she feels that in compensation it gives a greater breadth and resilience to a civilization which can accept decline as part of a larger pattern.

A third response is given by Madeleine Biardeau, who also points out the many difficulties faced by historians using modern historical methods to construct early histories of India. She shows how the theory of the Aryan invasion and suppression of Dravidian peoples has great appeal because of its supposed explanatory properties. Thus the *varṇa* system of four 'social groups' (see below) is understood as the product of the dominance of pure Aryans (twice-born) over impure vanquished Dravidians, now *śūdra*s (later, untouchables as well). The many features of devotional Hinduism which seem strikingly different from those of the sacrificial vedic religious system are explained as Dravidian resurgences. Perhaps, Biardeau allows, such an incursion did take place.

> But what if this seemingly historical structuring only existed in our minds; and perhaps even implicitly took its model from our most recent history? Between the assertion that ethnically and culturally different peoples must have learnt over the centuries to coexist, and the assertion that their cohabitation explains the present-day socio-religious structure of Hindu India, there is a gulf which cannot be crossed without examination.
>
> (Biardeau, 1989: 6)

In writing her book on *Hinduism: The Anthropology of a Civilization*, Biardeau therefore eschews 'the historical overview' and 'linear continuity that is visibly lacking' (Biardeau, 1989: 14). Rather, she seeks to find the 'complex, stable system of values, beliefs and practices that still underlines [*sic*] the surface variations [of different forms of

Hinduism, including those affected by the impact of the West] and which alone makes them comprehensible' (Biardeau, 1989: 15).

For some, Biardeau's proposal will liberate Hinduism from a Western historical straitjacket. For others, it will seem like another Western denigration of India, denying it the 'proper history' of the West. For still others, it will undercut their very claims about self-identity. Dalit consciousness, for example, is based on a view which sees themselves as the 'oppressed', the original people subordinated as untouchables by the Aryan invaders, from whom they wish to distinguish themselves sharply. In South India, such views are reinforced by readings of the *Rāmāyaṇa* such as that of the Tamil writer E. V. Ramasami. He heard its story as 'a thinly disguised historical account of how North Indians, led by Rāma, subjugated South Indians, ruled by Rāvaṇa'.[7] Writing in a political context before and after Indian Independence in 1947, in which anti-Northern, anti-brahmanical feeling ran high, he received enthusiastic support from his Tamil audience. His book *Characters in the Rāmāyaṇa* is now translated into English and Hindi, and hence has wider impact. Against such interpretations, Biardeau points out that Rāvaṇa is himself an *ārya*, a Brahman, though one who has overreached himself. Followers of Ramasami would simply point out how ensnared she has become in a brahmanical view of history.

What is certain is that the question of (a)historicality and the relation between myth and history in Hinduism is not simple, nor of merely academic interest. It is highly complex, affects people's sense of identity and has political and social ramifications too. We shall explore some of these below. First, though, we shall return to a few key concerns shared by history and myth – origins, time, causation, continuity and change – and see how these are approached in various Hindu traditions.

Stories of beginnings

In her book *The Origins of Evil in Hindu Mythology*, Wendy O'Flaherty notes that many of these myths use a pseudo-historical framework to tell how evil arises. So, for example, in this story from the *Vāyu Purāṇa* (1.8.77–88), corruption comes simply through the power of time (*kāla*).

In the beginning, people lived in perfect happiness, without class distinc-

> tions or property; all their needs were supplied by magic wish-fulfilling trees. Then because of the great power of time and the changes it wrought upon them, they were overcome by passions and greed . . . the wishing-trees disappeared; the people suffered from heat and cold, built houses, and wore clothes.
>
> (Quoted in O'Flaherty, 1980: 24)

However, as O'Flaherty rightly emphasizes, though the myths are often set 'in the beginning', 'implicit in them is a concern for the way things *are*' (O'Flaherty, 1980: 9). They help explore and explain the kind of cosmos in which we live and hence may contain recommendations for human behaviour now.

One famous origin myth is found in the *Puruṣasūkta* in the *Ṛg-veda* (10.90.1–16). It tells of the Cosmic Person, who is dismembered in a sacrifice by the gods. From parts of his body spring the four social groups of human society and elements and regions of the cosmos. 'His mouth was the brahmin (*brāhmaṇas*), his arms were made into the nobles (*kṣatriyas*), his two thighs were the populace (*vaiśyas*), and from his feet the servants (*śūdras*) were born' (O'Flaherty, 1975: 28). Thus the *varṇa* system is legitimated as being part of the very structure of the universe. By implication, human beings should uphold that system to maintain cosmic order. But because there is a legitimating myth, that is not to say there has been no further discussion about what constitutes a person's *varṇa*. From the *Upaniṣads* on, it was stressed, in a number of important texts, that a Brahman was not a Brahman simply by birth, but by behaviour befitting a Brahman. When, in the 1990s, European members of the Hare Krishna movement claim Brahman status, they are tapping into the latter emphasis in this ancient tradition as developed within the Caitanya movement and made explicit by the two teachers who preceded their leader Prabhupāda (A. C. Bhaktivedanta Swami). In their rejection of the (multiple *jāti*) caste system, they follow the trend of many nineteenth- and twentieth-century reform movements. Retaining the four *varṇas* as suitable for people of different intellectual abilities, they stress the vedic grounding of the *varṇāśrama* system of four social groups and stages of life. The underlying myth continues to provide an ideal for society, variously interpreted (or rejected) in modern Hindu contexts.

Such myths are not limited to the Sanskrit tradition. David Shulman gives an interesting analysis of some Tamil stories about the legendary figure Agastya, author of the first Tamil grammar. The Agastya legend, he says, 'is in essence an origin myth explaining the beginnings of Tamil culture' (Shulman, 1980: 6). Since Agastya is a vedic seer who is said quite explicitly to have come from the North, the legend shows that the Tamil tradition looks to the North as the source of its inspiration and prestige.

There was once a dispute, runs one story, between Agastya and Vyāsa over who was the greater. Agastya worshipped Śiva, who told him to worship in two places for a year, one famous as a Sanskrit place of study, and then return to Śivagiri to be instructed in Tamil by Śiva's son Murukan. When Agastya returned to the sages, they, with Vyāsa, greeted him, saying 'You have enabled all to taste the divine drink of Tamil'.

Shulman comments 'Agastya is thus a symbol of Tamil learning, not as independent from or opposed to Sanskrit, but rather in harmony and conjunction with it' (Shulman, 1980: 8). Here is a somewhat different picture of the relation of Tamil and Sanskrit from that which Ramasami, for example, espoused.

Many stories of beginnings are on a much smaller scale. They relate not to society or a whole culture, but to local places of worship or pilgrimage. Thus many temples have their own *sthalapurāṇa* or story of founding, sometimes in Sanskrit, sometimes in the vernacular. Shulman gives Tamil examples. Such stories of founding are not confined to the past. Maureen Michaelson records the story of a Lohāna man from Uganda, who settled with his family in Leicester.[8] One night, in Uganda, he dreamed that Jalarām, a nineteenth-century Gujarāti saint revered for his devoted service to others, would appear to him. The following night, after a lightning storm, an image of Jalarām appeared on the white kitchen tiles. Many people came to take *darśan* (seeing the manifestation and realizing the presence of the divine). When the family were driven out of Uganda, they brought the tiles to England. Their house remains a centre for a Jalarām *satsaṅg* (group singing devotional songs). Parents also take their children there for their first outing, so it has become a small place of pilgrimage. In explaining its origin, a historian would have to acknowledge that for this family and the other devotees, the explanation lies in a perception of Jalarām's self-manifestation.

The three previous stories have been about the origins of society, culture and devotional practice. Many other myths deal with the origin of all things: from the Cosmic Egg, from the desire of a lonely creator or, more metaphysically, from Non-being or Being or the disruption of the cosmic equilibrium. Śaṃkara, the great Advaitin teacher, was not inclined to mistake origin myths as accounts of the way things came to be. For him, the various upanisadic origin myths are usually classified as *ākhyāyikā*, stories, a form of secondary passage or *arthavāda*. For Śaṃkara, the stories of *arthavāda*, though they may be truthful, are there to direct people's thoughts to the true Self, identical with *brahman*, Ultimate Reality, goal of realization and hence liberation. So a story which speaks of fire, water and food arising from Being (*sat*) (*Chāndogya Upaniṣad* 6.2) directs the mind to the source of everything, *brahman*, and hence to the desire to realize one's identity with that Ultimate Reality. As Śaṃkara comments on the origin myth in the *Aitareya Upaniṣad*:

> There is no worthwhile result from knowing the story of origination (*sṛṣṭyākhyāyikā*). But the result from knowing the proper nature of the one Self is immortality, well-known from all the *Upaniṣads*.
>
> (*Aitareya Upaniṣad Bhāṣya* 2.1)

Within Hindu traditions, then, stories of beginnings are interpreted in a range of different ways: as literal accounts of the way certain things came to be; as stories conveying crucial values shaping actions now; as pointers to the deepest truth about the way things are. In many ways, historians have played similar tunes, albeit in different keys.

Concepts of time

At this point, we shall turn back to examine the view that the Hindu understanding of time is cyclical. Roger Hooker suggests that the observation of the recurring seasons is one key factor in Hindu concepts of time, which is balanced by the sense of linearity found in each individual's movement from birth to death. Certainly the pattern of the mythological and ritual year is strongly affected, for example, by the monsoon. Thus Viṣṇu is said to sleep for four months from the eleventh of the bright half of Āshāḍha to the eleventh of the bright half of Kārttika, roughly mid-July to mid-November, spanning the rains. This is the time of rife disease, when Viṣṇu is absent, yet also the marriage season in some parts of India, for other activities are suspended. The great autumn festival of *Navrātrī* takes place once the rainy season has ended. C. J. Fuller has shown how royal celebrations of *Navrātrī* at once identified the ruler with, and subordinated him to, the Goddess who slew the buffalo demon and so allowed order to be restored under proper kingship.[9] He suggests that the king was also identified with Rāma, as still clearly happens in Vāranāsi (Benares). Thus the festival legitimates rightful rule, through myth and ritual, and marks the commencement of the battle season once the rains are over. Myth, time and history are interwoven in a complex repeated pattern.

In mythology, it is said that one human year is just a day to the gods. Their year comprises 360 human years. In this way, suggest Dimmitt and van Buitenen, observations of days, lunar months and solar years are 'given divine and universal significance' (1983: 20). Besides this pattern of time based on observation is another scheme, that of the four *yuga*s (explained below). A third scheme involves the *manvantara*s – fourteen ages of the earth, each having an original ruler called a *Manu*. Dimmitt and van Buitenen suggest that there may have been a connection with actual human rulers, the *Manu* acting as the legitimating source of kingship. Here seems to be another example of human history being underpinned by a mythological view of time.

Whereas the *manvantara* scheme fits uneasily with the other two schemes, the relation between observed years and the *yuga*s is quite straightforward. Jackson and Killingley (1988: 137) give a chart (adapted in Table 5.1) to show how 12,000 years of the gods make up a cycle of four ages or *yuga*s.

Table 5.1

Name of *yuga*	Years of the gods	Human years
Kṛta or *Satya*	4800	1,728,000
Tretā	3600	1,296,000
Dvāpara	2400	864,000
Kali	1200	432,000
Total:	12,000	4,320,000

The ages are named after the four throws of the dice in ancient Indian games. The *Kṛta* Age is perfect. It is represented by a cow standing on four legs. Each subsequent age gets shorter and worse. Humans live shorter lives, there is less food and morality declines. By the *Kali* Age, in which we now live, the cow is left wobbling precariously on only one leg. The *Kaliyuga* opened with the war of the *Mahābhārata*, traditionally dated to 3102 BCE. In this sense, our current period of world history is shaped by the aftermath of these events. It will end when Kalkin, Viṣṇu's tenth *avatāra*, comes to begin a new *Kṛtayuga* or perfect age. Then the cycle of the four *yugas* will start all over again. After 1000 cycles, a *kalpa*, or cosmic day, the world will end through fire and/or flood and undergo a cosmic night of similar time. Then it will be manifested again, a cosmic day. And so on, *ad infinitum*.

With this immense time perspective, it is not surprising that a modern Advaitin can write:

> Advaita Vedānta and the Hindu tradition in general, unlike almost all other traditions, had long been familiar with vast time periods and scales; for this reason, the modern cosmological estimate of the age of the universe – the time since the Big-bang to the present – as approximately eighteen billion years is neither shocking nor blasphemous to Advaita Vedānta.[10]

The impression is sometimes given that a biblical view of history with a beginning and an end just needed a little stretching to make it into a modern scientific view of time. Authors like the above claim, rather, that the view of time found in Hindu mythology accords more readily with a modern scientific world-view.

We saw earlier that Bowes argues that the Hindu view of *yugas* also gives a more realistic attitude to the rise and fall of civilizations within the historical process. Some, though, have been inclined to draw on the *yuga* pattern to idealize as a perfect age the time before Muslim and British domination. Other commentators have felt that the idea of the *Kaliyuga* has led to a rather fatalistic acceptance of events, since decline is programmed into the times, so to speak. Only when Kalkin appears will things improve. Yet others have found the idea more flexible, galvanizing people into political action. Orators in the Panjab in the 1920s spoke in a traditional manner of the evils of the *Kaliyuga*, time of food shortages and falsehood. But then they urged that the perfect age would be restored once the British were overthrown. That their hope was not borne out has not discouraged others from urging political action to improve the state of the age.

The concept of cyclical world ages or *yugas* is developed in texts like the epics and *Purāṇas*. It is not found in the *Upaniṣads* or other vedic texts. In consequence, ideas like the *mahāpralaya* or destruction of the world at the end of a cycle are not found in the Pūrvamīmāṃsā school. Moreover, sophisticated metaphysical discussions about the nature of time take place in other classical schools without overt reference to this mythological background. These discussions are concerned with such matters as the origin of time, its relation to *brahman*, the nature of continuity between past, present and future, the role of memory in perception and error, and the way in which the results of actions are experienced by an individual in future embodiments.

For most of these writers, the *yuga* framework is an implicit part of their 'mental furniture'. However, this does not usually mean that their thought is dominated by a cyclic view of time where the events of this age become insignificant because they are in some sense repeated. Rather, such writers emphasize the importance of one's present human birth, for their concern is ultimately soteriological. Liberation of the self from *saṃsāra*, the entrammelling world of rebirth, is most easily or only achievable from a human birth, however that liberation is conceived. In future cycles, there is no duplication of events happening in this *yuga*, and hence no evasion of the present moment.

In the *Bhagavadgītā* (8.19), it is said that all beings come into existence again and again, and are then dissolved into the Unmanifested at the coming of the (cosmic) night. Śaṃkara explains that this verse has at least two purposes. One is to remind people that they will not escape from the consequences of their actions, for they will be reborn again and again in different births. Another is to create detachment from this interminable process of *saṃsāra*. So, again, such teachings serve primarily to foster the desire for liberation. It is often alleged that this in itself devalues the significance of the world and hence of history. If it does, it is not for the reason that the cyclic view of time is seen as repetitive, but that it is unrelieved. Moreover, since the very structures of this world provide the clues for realizing the Ultimate Reality within, their importance should not be too lightly dismissed, even for the Advaitin.

From a rather different angle, the idea that cycles of time necessarily diminish the importance of the historical present can be challenged by looking at the modern Brahmā Kumārī movement. In the late 1930s its founder, Dada Lekhraj, predicted the end of the world from natural catastrophe, civil strife and (apparently) nuclear holocaust. In visions, he saw that these catastrophes would be succeeded by a paradise on earth, whose tiny population would enjoy complete equality in a wholly balanced environment. This remnant would consist of those who heeded the warnings to purify themselves in the face of others' disbelief. Lawrence Babb shows how Lekhraj actually works within the traditional Hindu context, which sees the world periodically ending in calamities, but invests this with special urgency by speeding up the cycle. Thus, the Brahmā Kumārī world time of four *yuga*s lasts only 5000 years, by contrast with the 4,320,000 of the puranic accounts. The 'endlessly repeating cycles of world creation, degeneration, and destruction',[11] which the Brahmā Kumārīs accept, apparently do not detract from the urgency of adopting a *sāttvic* (pure) lifestyle, practising a form of *rāja yoga* and belonging to a movement which has attracted considerable opprobrium for its ideal of female celibacy.

In this section we have tried to show from a variety of perspectives that to contrast a Hindu repetitive cyclical view of time with a Western linear one is too stark. There is not just one Hindu (nor indeed one Western) scheme of time. Even the *yuga* scheme varies in significance in different contexts. It can stress the vastness of time scales in the cosmos, as much as their repetitive nature. Within this *Kaliyuga*, the focus can be sharply on an individual life or on the legitimation of a ruler in an immediate historical situation. Myth, with its purview of millions of years, becomes rooted in ritual on an annual or even weekly basis with, for example, a fast for Santoshī Mā, the recently popular North Indian goddess of contentment whose story is released on video. Speeded up, the cycle pressurizes decisions about lifestyle and equality for members of the Brahmā Kumārī movement. Considered in its awful infinity, it directs the modern Rāmakrishna Mission Advaitin both beyond it to liberation and within it to social service. Finally, as Roger Hooker observes: 'While some contemporary Hindu thinkers appeal to the past in a nostalgic way, others are trying to give positive significance to time and change, and therefore to history' (1989: 74).

Continuity, change and causation

Much has been written on continuity and change in Hinduism, especially on the place of the Veda in this process.[12] Rather than engage in this large question, we shall look at one way in which Hindu traditions have themselves consciously envisaged continuity and the possibilities for change that this has allowed. We shall then briefly consider two forms of causation, one mainly developed in myth and hagiography, the other in philosophical analysis, to see how these compare with historians' accounts of causation.

> Now the line of teachers. The son of Pautimāṣī (received this teaching) from the son of Kātyāyanī; the son of Kātyāyanī from the son of Gautamī ... Yājñavalkya from Uddālaka ... Prajāpati from Brahmā (or Brahman). Brahmā (or Brahman) is the self-existent. Adoration to Brahmā.
>
> (*Bṛhadāraṇyaka Upaniṣad* 6.5.1–4)

So ends the great *Upaniṣad*, with its line of teachers going back to the creator god, or perhaps even to the Ultimate Reality, *brahman*, for the Sanskrit could be read either way. The pupil who receives teaching today does so conscious of the unbroken *paraṃparā*, the succession of teachers who from time immemorial have seen the truth and passed it on unchanged through their teaching tradition (*saṃpradāya*). The concept of *saṃpradāya* is fundamental to many Hindus' sense of religious identity as well as to the legitimacy of a *guru*'s teaching. So the complex arguments about whether the International Society for Krishna Consciousness (the Hare Krishna movement) is a Hindu movement often centre on teaching tradition. Those who wish to legitimate it trace Prabhupāda's lineage back through the Goswāmis to Caitanya (and thence to Viṣṇu). Opponents point out that the succession of teachers was interrupted until the nineteenth century, hence ISKCON's claims are not well-founded.

A sense of identity with one's forerunners from the past is heightened in those traditions where membership is through personal initiation by a *guru* only. So, for example, children of Pushti Mārg members in Britain can only become members themselves when a Mahārāj or deputed *guru* comes from India to perform such ceremonies. 'Pushti Mārg' means 'Path of Grace', and was founded by the vedantin teacher Vallabha (fifteenth century CE) who, of course, traced his teaching back to the *Upaniṣads* themselves.

There is a danger, found in all religions, that a tradition can fossilize if successive teachers see their task as one of mere repetition or simplification. At its best, though, the many different *saṃpradāyas* within Hinduism have produced profound thinkers of great calibre who responded to the challenges of their times and whose influence continues to the present day. It is not surprising that such thinkers have inspired their followers to write of their lives. Hagiographies abound, often reflecting the concerns of a much later age and premises which modern historians might not share. Thus Mādhava's *Śaṃkara Digvijaya* records how the gods approached Śiva at a time when religious practice had degenerated, partly under Buddhism's sway, and begged him to re-establish the vedic religion.

> When the Devas had completed their submission, the great God Siva said: 'Taking a human body . . . I shall establish the Dharma, conquering all the leaders of the perverse paths. I shall produce a commentary on the Brahma Sutras, setting forth the true teaching of the Vedas. I shall do this, taking the form of a great Sannyasin, Sankara by name. . . . All of you . . . should also take birth on earth like Myself and assist Me in My mission'.[13]

It is perhaps as unwise to dismiss such stories as of no historical significance as it is to accept them as literal accounts. The translator is circumspect in granting their mythological content, yet he maintains:

> They are living traditions that transmit a little of their original impact to the generations that have come later, whereas pure historical productions are only like dead specimens . . . preserved in the corridors of Time's museum.[14]

It is not a question of seeking historical evidence in the hagiographies for Śaṃkara's own time. Rather, we should note their engagement with questions which still occupy historians and sociologists: what is it that makes an original thinker – charisma, the needs of the times, the readiness of people to recognize a new 'solution'? If the intervention of the gods seems to create too radical a disjunction from preceding human teaching, consciousness of the *saṃpradāya* may be seen as a counterbalance to this view.

Perhaps the best-known Hindu approach to causation is through the notion of *karman* (literally, action, and originally, ritual action). Although it takes various forms, the common idea is that all actions have results, some of which are immediate, but others long-term, perhaps not maturing until many lives hence. The results of actions then create the conditions for a person's rebirths in a linear development. They do not 'determine' the future, but create the conditions in terms of which human beings live and make choices which in turn affect the future both contingently and remotely. John Brockington notes that 'the concept has at times had a similar function in Hinduism to the idea of history in Western thought, though with the important qualification that it operates at the individual rather than societal level'.[15] It is also different in that, while the historian hopes to use evidence to understand both immediate and more long-term causes, such evidence is unavailable to ordinary mortals at a personal level since the trauma of birth effaces all memory of previous lives. Popularly, a person may well say 'I must have done something terrible to be undergoing this now', but the particular cause is unlocatable. Nonetheless, the karmic principle that all events are due to past and complex causes is one shared by historians, whose interests, if not methods, overlap with the myths and traditional teachings yet again.

History, myth and nationalism

Finally, we shall turn to a modern phenomenon to explore some of the political ramifications of our topic. The factors influencing the growth of Indian nationalism in the late nineteenth and early twentieth centuries are extremely complicated, but concern us in at least two ways. The first is the reaction to Orientalist portrayals of Indian history which led writers like the Bengali Bankim Chandra Chatterjee to search their own heritage to repudiate assertions about Indian lack of military prowess, for example. The second related factor is the inspiration which was provided by both *Mahābhārata* and *Rāmāyaṇa* at this time. With his historical novels, political satire and poem *Bande Mātaram*, which became the anthem of the Swadeshi (nationalist) movement, Bankim was undoubtedly a key figure, but his ideas and influence have been variously interpreted. He tried to use historical methods to show that the *Mahābhārata* represented life in the period between the vedic and Buddhist ages. The *dharmarājya* (rule of righteousness) established by its war, he saw not as a fact of remote history but as a goal to be realized in contemporary India. Importantly, he seems to have envisaged this *dharmarājya* in an open sense which saw love of one's country as the highest of all smaller loves, provided that it did not militate against the selfless, God-directed love of humanity. Other writers, like Bipin Chandra Pal, developed ideas of a specifically Indian form of democracy which would recognize the divine equality of every human being, whether Hindu, Muslim, Buddhist or Christian. More recently, Pandit Nehru's pride in the history of India, embracing the achievements of the Buddhist emperor Asoka and the Muslim ruler Akbar, as well as Harappa and the sacred geography of Hindu India, reflects the inclusive attitudes of those who drew up the constitution of India as a secular state.

In the 1980s and 1990s, this secularism has come under strong pressure for a web of reasons, many associated with weakness in the ruling Congress Party. Once more, an epic, the *Rāmāyaṇa*, colours the debate. In December 1992, the Babri mosque in Ayodhya was destroyed by militant Hindus, the culmination of a long dispute which had been simmering for decades. Ayodhya is the traditional birthplace of Lord Rām, the mosque having been built over the site of a Hindu temple, a claim for which historical evidence is mustered. During the election campaign of 1989, the Vishwa Hindu Parishad (VHP), a highly organized religious group linked with the political opposition party, the BJP (Bharatiya Janata Party), encouraged Hindus from all over India to carry consecrated bricks to Ayodhya to rebuild the Rāmjanmabhoomi (site of Rām's birth). Rajiv Gandhi, the Prime Minister, had earlier supported the laying of a foundation stone, then stopped further work. His assassination on 21 May 1991 perhaps reflected his failure to understand the growing communalism among many Hindus who feel that secularism has favoured Muslims.

Some observers feel that the Hindi *Rāmāyaṇa*, screened on Indian television in 1987–88, contributed to sentiment worked on by the VHP in its overt anti-Muslim stance, which intends to target other mosques built over Hindu temples in future elections. Some more extreme VHP propaganda even suggests that the Taj Mahal was originally a Hindu building. What is notable is the way that history is being made the issue: first, the historicity of Rām; secondly, rights over land and sacred places going back some 500 years. Earlier Western attitudes, which denigrated myth and looked down on aspects of the Hindu past and its lack of records, have surely seeped down, transmuted in reaction in this popular consciousness.

The BJP is supported by many educated middle-class Hindus disillusioned with the Congress Party. Its appeal should not be underestimated. Yet a potter quoted in *India Today* in December 1990 was pragmatic about historical issues: 'We don't know about the past, we don't know if Ram was born in Ayodhya or not or if there was a temple before the masjid [mosque] was built. We know only one thing: because of this controversy our livelihood is in jeopardy' (31 December 1990: 46).

At Dassehra celebrations in Delhi, following the screening of Ramanand Sagar's *Rāmāyaṇa*, Mark Tully watched two Sikhs and three

Hindus circling an effigy of Rāvaṇa together and setting its fireworks alight. For him it was a sign of hope that the epic serialization could unite communities as well as divide them (Tully, 1992: 152). Whichever it does, it will be as a consequence of the sense of identity imbued from the past by the present.

Conclusion

The subject of myth and history in Hinduism is vast. It is only in passing that we have been able to indicate some of the many functions of myth in Hindu traditions: as common cultural reference points, as stories relived through festivals and pilgrimage, as sanctions for rituals, iconography and order in society, as the basis for devotion, meditation and purification, as testimony to those deities experienced in one's own life, as pointers to the Ultimate Reality beyond all human description and conceptualization. We have not been able to discuss the many different approaches used to analyse Hindu myth, for example, the Jungian stance of Heinrich Zimmer in *Myths and Symbols in Indian Art and Civilisation*, the structuralist method of Wendy O'Flaherty in *Śiva: The Erotic Ascetic*, or the narrative analyses in the collection edited by Paula Richman, *Many Rāmāyaṇas*. Nor again have we been able to consider the 'silence' of women in Indian history and the ways in which Hindu women are seeking to reclaim both history and myth today. What we have tried to examine is the relation between myth and history in different Hindu contexts, to challenge the view that these are mutually opposed categories.

' "Indian history" ', says Gonda, is 'an expression by which I mean the process of development of the *humanitas indica*.'[16] If Indian history is this development of what makes India India, the embodying values of Indian civilization, the constitution of a people's sense of identity, then the contribution of Hindu myths and legendary history is a highly significant factor. In particular, the ways in which myths together with rituals are constitutive of social order profoundly affect those within and outside the caste system.

Yet this is a complex issue. For Indian history is by no means synonymous with Hindu traditions, as Nehru tried to show in his letters to his daughter. To predicate modern Indian-ness on acceptance of the great leaders of Indian history, like Lord Rām and Lord Kṛṣṇa (*sic*), as a BJP MP did in a recent speech in Britain, would seem highly problematic for Muslims and Christians, who would reject their divinity, if not their historicity. On the other hand, to dismiss the importance of these epic figures in Indian historical consciousness would be foolish. *Rāmrājya*, the rule of Rāma, need not be interpreted in an exclusivist sense, and indeed has not been by many great Hindu thinkers. Nor is the *Rāmāyaṇa* bound to only one telling: it has Jain and Buddhist versions as well as modern political narrations, as we saw above. Thapar sees cultural strength in these various recensions, which reflect different social aspirations and ideological concerns.

Since these stories were first told, they have always affected Hindus' understanding of past and present. They were, after all, seen as *itihāsa*, accounts of how things were. We have also seen how some scholars are increasingly recognizing the historical value of both *itihāsa* and *purāṇa* for genealogical material and for more or less 'embedded' historical evidence. Yet we have heard the warnings of eminent Indian historians against historicist approaches to such texts, which try to press them into the service of a modern form of history alien to their nature and read them in a literalistic way.

Story is central to Hindu traditions. It is not then surprising that there is a plethora of terms for different types of story, and sophisticated interpretations of story in both classical and modern traditions. 'What is not here is not anywhere.' May the stories be heard and retold.

Notes

1 Rawlinson quoted in 'Historiography' in B. Walker (1968) *The Hindu World*, vol. 1. London: George Allen & Unwin, p. 455.
2 Ibid., p. 456.
3 For more detail on different texts and schools of interpretation, see Chapter 6 in this book.
4 *Mangal Ramayan* as narrated by Ever Revered Sant Sri Morari Bapu. Bombay: Prachin Sanskriti Mandir, 1987.
5 R. Thapar (1986) 'Society and historical consciousness: the Itihāsa-Purāṇa tradition' in S. Bhattacharya and R. Thapar (eds) *Situating Indian History, for Sarvepalli Gopal*. Delhi: Oxford University Press.
6 Walker, op. cit., p. 453.
7 P. Richman (1991) 'E. V. Ramasami's reading of the *Rāmāyaṇa*' in P. Richman (ed.) *Many Rāmāyaṇas: The Diversity of a Narrative Tradition in South Asia*. Berkeley: University of California Press, p. 178.

8 M. Michaelson (1987) 'Domestic Hinduism in a Gujarati trading caste' in R. Burghart (ed.) *Hinduism in Great Britain: The Perpetuation of Religion in an Alien Cultural Milieu*. London: Tavistock Publications, p. 45.
9 C. J. Fuller (1992) *The Camphor Flame: Popular Hinduism and Society in India*. Princeton, NJ: Princeton University Press.
10 R. Puligandla (1988) 'Modern physics and Advaita Vedānta' in S. S. Rama Rao Pappu (ed.) *Perspectives on Vedānta: Essays in Honor of Professor P. T. Raju*. Leiden: E. J. Brill, p. 189.
11 L. A. Babb (1986) *Redemptive Encounters: Three Modern Styles in the Hindu Tradition*. Berkeley: University of California Press, p. 112.
12 J. Gonda (1965) *Change and Continuity in Indian Religion*. The Hague: Mouton & Co; B. K. Smith (1989) *Reflections on Resemblance, Ritual and Religion*. Oxford: Oxford University Press.
13 Madhava-Vidyaranya (1980) *Sankara-Dig-Vijaya: The Traditional Life of Sri Sankaracharya*. 2nd edn, trans. Swami Tapasyananda; Madras: Sri Ramakrishna Math, p. 5.
14 Ibid., p. vii.
15 J. Brockington (1992) *Hinduism and Christianity*. Basingstoke: Macmillan, p. 118.
16 J. Gonda (1965) *Change and Continuity in Indian Religion*. The Hague: Mouton & Co, p. 7.

Further reading

Biardeau, M. (1989) *Hinduism: The Anthropology of a Civilization*, trans. Richard Nice. Delhi: Oxford University Press.

Bowes, P. (1977) *Hindu Intellectual Tradition*. New Delhi: Allied Publishers.

Dimmitt, C. and van Buitenen, J. A. B. (eds and trans.) (1983) *Classical Hindu Mythology: A Reader in the Sanskrit Purāṇas*. Calcutta: Rupa & Co., by arrangement with Temple University Press.

Gupta, S. P. and Ramachandran, K. S. (eds) (1976) *Mahābhārata: Myth and Reality: Differing Views*. Delhi: Agam Prakashan.

Hooker, R. H. (1989) *Themes in Hinduism and Christianity: A Comparative Study*. Frankfurt am Main: Verlag Peter Lang.

Jackson, R. and Killingley, D. (1988) *Approaches to Hinduism*. London: John Murray.

Klostermaier, K. K. (1989) *A Survey of Hinduism*. Albany: State University of New York Press.

Lipner, J. J. (1994) *Hindus: Their Religious Beliefs and Practices*. London: Routledge.

Narayan, K. (1989) *Storytellers, Saints and Scoundrels: Folk Narrative in Hindu Religious Teaching*. Philadelphia: University of Pennsylvania Press.
Narayan, R. K. (1987 reprint) *Gods, Demons and Others*. Delhi: Vision Books.
O'Flaherty, W. D. (trans.) (1975) *Hindu Myths: A Sourcebook Translated from the Sanskrit*. Harmondsworth: Penguin.
O'Flaherty, W. D. (1980) *The Origins of Evil in Hindu Mythology*. Paperback edn; Berkeley: University of California Press.
Shulman, D. D. (1980) *Tamil Temple Myths: Sacrifice and Divine Marriage in the South Indian Śaiva Tradition*. Princeton, NJ: Princeton University Press.
Sontheimer, G. D. and Kulke, H. (eds) (1991) *Hinduism Reconsidered*. Delhi: Mahohar.
Thapar, R. (1966) *A History of India*, vol. 1. Harmondsworth: Penguin.
Timm, J. (ed.) (1992) *Texts in Context: Traditional Hermeneutics in South Asia*. Albany: SUNY Press.
Tully, M. (1992) *No Full Stops in India*. Paperback edn; Harmondsworth: Penguin.

6. Sacred writings

Gavin Flood

The sacred writings of Hinduism constitute a vast body of literature, composed mostly in Sanskrit, but also in other Indian languages, particularly Tamil. The earliest layers of the most authoritative of this literature, the Vedas, stretch back over 3000 years, while compositions by modern holy men and women are also regarded as sacred by their devotees. The category of 'sacred writings' therefore tends to have more fluid boundaries within Hinduism than in most other traditions. This does not mean that Hinduism has not developed categories for understanding its own sacred scriptures; it has, but the lines between these categories are sometimes blurred. Nor does this fluidity of boundaries mean that there are no constraints controlling a particular text, rather that 'controls' operating within a text may be harder to specify; but there can be no 'random' texts. This fluidity of boundaries is seen particularly, though not exclusively, with regard to sacred texts of human authorship, as opposed to the eternal, revealed texts.

It has been recently observed that the Western understanding of sacred scripture in Hinduism, as indeed in Buddhism and Jainism, has been deeply influenced by the text and function of the Bible within Christianity (Timm, 1992: 2). But in contrast to Western religious scriptures, one of the most striking features of the Hindu 'revealed' texts is that they were not put into writing for perhaps as long as a thousand years after their origin. Indeed the oldest text, the *Ṛg-veda*, was only printed as a 'book' in the nineteenth century at the instigation of a European scholar, F. Max Müller, an event which Wilfred Cantwell Smith describes as 'an entrancing instance of nineteenth-century Western cultural imperialism . . . quietly imposing the western sense of scripture' (Cantwell Smith in Levering, 1989: 35).

It needs to be borne in mind, therefore, that the category of 'sacred writings' is a Western one and that the emphasis in Hinduism has always been not on the canonized written word, but on the 'heard' word received through the tradition in an unbroken succession from teacher (*guru*) to disciple. Indeed, to write, as Staal and others have observed, was regarded among some Brahmans as a ritually polluting activity. Staal quotes the *Aitareya Āraṇyaka* (5.5.3) which states that a pupil should not recite the Veda 'if he has eaten flesh, or seen blood, or a dead body, or done what is unlawful ... or had intercourse or written' (Staal, 1989: 371; also quoted by Coburn, 1989: 104). This quotation reminds us that the recitation of the Veda by the Brahmans must be located in the context of brahmanical ritual and a life lived maintaining, and within the boundaries of, Hindu *dharma*, one's social and moral duty concerned with preserving the boundaries of the cosmic, ethical order.

That which is heard

Revealed scripture, 'that which is heard', and its use in a ritual context, is at the heart of 'orthoprax' Hinduism. Indeed, acceptance of the body of texts collectively called the Veda ('knowledge') as authoritative revelation could be said to be a characteristic implied by the term 'Hindu'[1] (notwithstanding views which regard the very term 'Hinduism' as a misnomer). Although these texts have had a seminal influence on Indian philosophical and ritual traditions, most Hindus would not have known their 'Hinduism' through these revealed texts, but rather through ritual traditions and the mythologies of the *smṛti* literature. Bharati makes the point (though without giving a source for his figures) that 'less than five percent of all Hindus ever knew these texts even by name, and much less than one percent knew even parts of their content'.

Śruti, the Hindu revelation, is thought to be the eternal word (*śabda*) or sound, which is not composed or uttered by any human, or even (according to some Hindus) divine, being. This 'word' was 'heard' by the ancient sages (*ṛṣis*) and passed down orally through the generations in the form of the Veda, a vast body of texts composed in vedic Sanskrit, the sacred language of the gods. The Veda comprises four large groups or layers of texts, the *Saṃhitās*, the *Brāhmaṇas*, the *Āraṇyakas* and the *Upaniṣads*. Another way of regarding this scheme is that the term 'Veda' refers only to the collections of the four *Saṃhitās*: the *Ṛg*, *Sāma*, *Yajur* and *Atharva*, each of which has its own *Brāhmaṇas*, *Āraṇyakas* and *Upaniṣads*. These layers represent the rough chronological order of their composition; thus the earliest texts are the hymns of the *Ṛg-veda*, while the latest are the *Upaniṣads*.[2]

Various theological schools are important in the classification of the Veda. Different families of Brahmans, the only class qualified by virtue of their pure social status to learn the Veda, would specialize in learning portions of the text, and the layers of the texts are related to each other through these schools or 'branches' (*śākhā*). A particular Veda will have associated with it a number of branches. For example, the male members of a particular Brahman family might specialize in the *Taittirīya* branch, comprising the *Taittirīya Saṃhitā* of the black *Yajur-veda*, the *Taittirīya Brāhmaṇa*, *Taittirīya Āraṇyaka* and *Taittirīya Upaniṣad*. These 'branches' are the diachronic means whereby the texts are transmitted through the generations. This structure can be portrayed diagrammatically (only the *Taittirīya* branch is recorded here by way of illustration):

Saṃhitā:	*Ṛg*	*Sāma*		*Yajur*	*Atharva*
			white YV	black YV	
'Branch' (*śākhā*)				*Taittirīya*	
Brāhmaṇa				*Taittirīya B.*	
Āraṇyaka				*Taittirīya A.*	
Upaniṣad				*Taittirīya U.*	

The *Saṃhitā* portion of the Veda comprises the *Ṛg*, *Sāma*, *Yajur* and *Atharva* Vedas. The *Ṛg-veda* is a collection (*saṃhitā*) of ten books (*maṇḍalas*) of 1028 hymns made up of 'verses' (*ṛcs*) to various deities. Composed over a period of several hundred years, probably from as early as 1200 BCE, by bardic families, these texts are the most important source of our knowledge of vedic religion. Within these hymns we find the cosmos divided into three broad spheres, the sky (*svar*), the atmosphere (*bhūvas*) and the earth (*bhūr*). Each of these realms was inhabited by certain deities to whom sacrifice was offered, particularly Indra, the warrior god of the atmosphere, Agni the fire god, and Soma the god who is both deity and hallucinogenic plant (possibly a vine or mushroom). Of all the deities in the text, Agni and Soma are particularly important, being the links between heaven and earth, the fire conveying the sacrifice to the gods and the plant soma inspiring the seers (*ṛṣi*) with vision from the gods and inspiration for the composition of their hymns (or, in Hindu terms, for the atunement necessary to receive the word).

The *Sāma-veda* is a book of songs or chants (*sāman*) based on the *Ṛg-veda*, with instructions on their recitation (*gāna*). The *sāman*s are songs or melodies to which different verses (*ṛc*) can be sung. The *Yajur-veda* is a further collection of hymns or short prose formulae (*yajus*) for use in ritual. There are two recensions of the *Yajur-veda*, known as the 'black' (*kṛṣṇa*) and the 'white' (*śukla*), the former being composed of formulae (*yajus*) and prose, the latter being composed entirely of verses or *mantra*s. The white *Yajur-veda* contains one book, the *Vājasaneyi-saṃhitā*, while the black *Yajur-veda* contains three books, the *Taittirīya*, the *Maitrāyaṇī* and the *Kāṭhaka saṃhitā*s, all of which are associated with the elaborate ritual of the sacrifice. Lastly, we have the *Atharva-veda*, a collection of hymns and magical formulae compiled a few centuries after the other Veda, around 900 BCE, though some of the material it contains may well be older than even the *Ṛg* (Brockington, 1981: 23). This collection tends not to have quite as high a status as the other three Vedas, and is concerned not so much with elaborate priestly rituals, but rather with topics such as magical healing and the invoking of otherworldly beings, concerns which reflect a more popular layer of vedic religion.

These texts reflect changing religious attitudes over a long period of time, showing that the ritual of sacrifice becomes much more elaborate and complex in the later tradition. But what is most significant about the Vedas is that from the time of their composition, they have been associated with, and the first three chanted during, ritual. This was, and still is, their primary function. Indeed the vedic *Saṃhitā*s are associated with the three classes of ritual specialists who recite them during the liturgies, namely the *hotṛ*, who recites from the *Ṛg-veda*, the *udgātṛ*, who chants the *Sāma-veda*, and the *adhvaryu*, the ritual director, who recites from the *Yajur-veda*.

The *Brāhmaṇa*s, manuals for the Brahmans, are attached to the books of the Veda (in the narrower sense) within the branches or schools. Thus we have the *Kauṣitaki* and *Aitareya Brāhmaṇa*s attached to the *Ṛg-veda*, the *Taittirīya Brāhmaṇa* to the *Taittirīya Saṃhitā*, and the *Jaiminīya Brāhmaṇa* to the *Sāma-veda* and so on. These prose texts contain rules and elaborate symbolic explanations of vedic ritual, postulating various magical links (*bandha*) between the sacrifice and the cosmos. They are thus interpretations of earlier texts and begin a hermeneutic tradition which runs throughout the history of Indian religions. The *Āraṇyaka*s or 'forest books' are a development of the *Brāhmaṇa*s, speculating upon the symbolism of the sacrifice and representing the emergence of a more contemplative strand in the tradition. Dasgupta illustrates this from the *Bṛhadāraṇyaka*, where 'we find that instead of the actual performance of the horse sacrifice (*aśvamedha*), there are directions for meditating upon the dawn (*Uṣas*) as the head of the horse, the sun as the eye of the horse, the air as its life and so on' (Dasgupta, 1975: 14).

With the *Upaniṣad*s the process of speculation on the meaning of the earlier ritual continues, and the seeds of later philosophical speculation are laid. Indeed, with the *Upaniṣad*s we find a turning away from the ritual sacrifice which characterized the vedic *Saṃhitā*s, and an emphasis placed on inner, mystical experience, spoken of as the 'internalization of the sacrifice'. The more esoteric nature of these texts is implied in the very term *upaniṣad*, which can be translated as 'sitting near', which is suggestive of a disciple sitting at the feet of his master.

Key ideas are articulated in the *Upaniṣad*s that were to become central to Hindu traditions and that, partly due to the nineteenth-century 'Hindu Renaissance', are commonly identified with 'Hinduism': namely the doctrines of the transmigration of the soul due to action (*karma*) and its result, the liberation of the soul from this process through controlling and stilling the mind (*yoga*), and the idea of liberation as experiential knowledge of the identity of the particular soul (*ātman*) with absolute being (*brahman*).

Knowledge (*jñāna*), rather than the ritual action (*karman*) of the earlier Veda, takes precedence, a knowledge which is the means of salvation from the cycle of birth and death (*saṃsāra*). For example, rather than the performance of rituals to feed the deceased in the next, ghostly, world (*preta loka*) to ensure that it passes into the world of the ancestors (*pitṛ loka*) in a body created and nourished by food offerings, the *Upaniṣad*s begin to emphasize the prevention of rebirth through knowing the true state of reality as unitary.[3] The earliest expression of this idea is in the *Bṛhadāraṇyaka Upaniṣad* where the Brahman Uddālaka receives the esoteric teaching from the prince Pravāhaṇa Jaivali (a *Kṣatriya*), never before revealed to a Brahman, that the soul is either reborn through traversing the path of the ancestors (*pitṛ-yāna*) or is liberated through the path of the gods (*deva-yāna*) (6.2.1–16; cf. the *Chāndogya Upaniṣad* 5.3–10). What is important here is not ritual action but knowledge as a necessary condition for liberation, by which beings 'pass into the light' (6.2.15: *te'rcir abhisambhavanti*) and thence to the gods from where there is no rebirth. This liberation is knowledge of the truth (*satyam*), which is knowledge of the identity of the particular soul (*ātman*) with the absolute being (*brahman*) (*Chāndogya* 3.14), an idea central to later Hindu soteriologies.

The *Upaniṣads*, however, are not a homogeneous body of texts. The earliest, such as the *Bṛhadāraṇyaka*, the *Chāndogya*, and the *Taittirīya*, dating from about the eighth century BCE, are closely linked with the earlier *Brāhmaṇas* and contain speculation about the underlying nature of the universe as a single, abstract principle. In a later group of texts, however, including the *Īśa*, the *Śvetāśvatara*, the *Mahānārāyāṇa* and the *Maṇḍukya*, an emphasis on a more personal theistic reality begins to appear. For example, in the *Śvetāśvatara* we find the lord (*Īśa*) as the creator and sustainer of the cosmos and the soul (*ātman*), as in some sense distinct from him, becoming free through knowledge: 'the soul, not being the Lord, is bound due to the condition of being an enjoyer [of the world], (but) having known God, it is freed from all bonds' (1.8: *anīśas cātmā badhyate bhoktṛbhāvāt jñātva devam mucyate sarvapāśaiḥ*). These developments reflect theistic trends within the Hindu tradition which become particularly associated with the deities Śiva and Viṣṇu, who are elevated by their devotees to the status of the absolute. Indeed the term *bhakti* ('devotion'), which was to become so significant in later Hinduism, occurs in the last verse of the *Śvetāśvatara*, and although this verse may be a later interpolation, it is nevertheless significant in that *bhakti* is a doctrine based on sacred revelation, a view which is corroborated by the *Bhagavadgītā*.

Texts with the name *Upaniṣad* continued to be produced throughout the Middle Ages and into the modern period. These texts tend to reflect particular traditions within Hinduism; thus there are Śaiva *Upaniṣads*, Yoga *Upaniṣads* and so on. There is even, as Coburn notes, an Allāh *Upaniṣad* composed in the seventeenth century (Coburn, 1989: 106).

There are implications here for the idea of 'sacred scripture' as inviolable. A class of texts, the *Upaniṣads*, which continue to be composed into the seventeenth century and even later, demonstrates a certain fluidity in the notion of sacred scripture, which leads Coburn to conclude that '*śruti* must be seen as [an] ongoing and experientially based feature of the Hindu religious tradition' (Coburn, 1989: 112).

But even so, it is nevertheless the case that a certain group of the older *Upaniṣads* were taken to be authoritative and commented upon in later philosophical and exegetical traditions, particularly certain phrases, or the 'great sayings' (*mahāvākyas*), within those texts (see below, p. 145). Indeed, while the edges of certain classes of Hindu literature may be blurred, the texts themselves, such as the *Ṛg-veda*, remain intact through the generations.

The Vedas (in the wider sense, including the *Upaniṣads*) are of extreme importance in two areas of Hindu life: in ritual, and in philosophical speculation, which takes the form of the interpretation of the revealed texts. These two routes from the Veda originate in the texts themselves, which contain material (the *mantra* portions) for ritual use as well as exegesis of the ritual (the *brāhmaṇa* portions). Ritual and speculation have thus become the contexts within which the Veda has functioned throughout the history of Hinduism, and within these routes the Veda has functioned, not as a written text, but as an oral and recited text.

Remembering the Veda

One of the most remarkable things about the Veda is that it has been handed down as an oral tradition through the generations with little or no change to its contents. Such accuracy has been due to a system of double-checking by two transmissions, in which each word could be 'checked' by the way it related to the preceding and subsequent words (i.e., by its *sandhi*). The continuous recitation of the Veda, called the *saṃhitāpāṭha*, in which the Sanskrit rules of euphonic combination (*sandhi*) operated, were checked by another system of recitation, the *pādapāṭha*, in which the euphonic combination was broken down and the recitation was made 'word for word'. These two systems were related by various rules (see Staal, 1989: 37–46). To cite an example given by Staal, the sentence from the vedic *Saṃhitās*, 'the immortal goddess has pervaded the wide space, the depths and the heights', is remembered in two recensions, the continuous flow of the *saṃhitā-pāṭha* ('*orv aprā amartyā nivato devy udvataḥ//*') and the word-for-word recitation of the *pādapāṭha*, stripped of euphonic combinations ('*a/ uru/ aprāḥ/ amartyā/ nivataḥ/ devī/ udvataḥ//*') (Staal, 1989: 37).

Apart from these two systems of recitation, the supplementary disciplines (*prātiśākhyas*) of grammar, phonetics and definitions were developed, each vedic tradition having its own *prātiśākhya*, the earliest of which may date from around 1000 BCE. Through these disciplines, which, for example, formulated the rules of euphonic combination, the correct transmission of the Veda could be checked and assured. This practice of using the *prātiśākhya*s to ensure correct transmission is still continued. Indeed, Coward observes that after independence the Indian government established a commission to check the transmission of the Veda through the *prātiśākhya*s (Coward, 1988: 117).

Not only has the Veda been preserved in a tradition of recitation, but also in ritual, where sentences from it may be recited during private morning and evening rites as well as at public festivals (*utsava*). Indeed, the use of the Veda during ritual is its primary function within Hinduism. These chants used during rituals are called *mantra*s. *Mantra*s are 'sacred formulae' taken from the Veda, or, to use Staal's phrase, 'bits and pieces of the Veda put to ritual use' (Staal, 1989: 48). There are also *mantra*s derived from a later body of texts, the *Tantra*s, though these *mantra*s are regarded as polluting by the orthodox. The recitation of *mantra*s may make up a ritual sequence, and may not necessarily bear any relationship to the acts which they accompany other than that they accompany those acts; that is, there is no necessary semantic link between the recitation of the Veda and the ritual act (see Staal, 1989: 191–7). These *mantra*s may be semantically complete or may include sequences of meaningless syllables called *stobha*s (such as *hā bu hā bu hā bu bhā bhaṃ* . . ., cited by Staal, 1989: 50, 200) which are recited at different times during a ritual by different priests.

Staal (1989) argues that, as can be seen in their ritual use, *mantra*s do not share semantic properties with 'language', though they do share syntactic and phonological properties. That is, in ritual it is not the meaning of *mantra*s which is important, indeed their meaning is often impossible to establish, but rather their correct recitation in the right place by the right person. The function of the text in ritual is thus not its meanings but primarily its uses. What the particular phrases or sentences in a ritual mean is secondary to their place in the ritual sequence and their correct recitation. Indeed, this view was rigorously propounded by the Mīmāṃsā school of philosophy, which regarded the Veda as a series of injunctions – instructions on the ritual act.

The meaning of the texts, particularly the *Ṛg-veda*, might not be understood even by the reciter, for they are in an archaic form of

Sanskrit, more terse than the language of the later literature. Meanings are variable and open to different interpretations by different generations, but the recitational sequence of the text, its structure and place in ritual are invariant to a striking degree: the *Ṛg-veda* has functioned in an almost identical way in a ritual context for nearly 3000 years.

Each of the layers of the Veda is connected through the 'branches'. These branches are further related to another group of texts, the ritual *sūtra*s, concerned with ritual practice. There are three groups of these texts, the *Śrauta-sūtra*s, *Gṛhya-sūtra*s, and *Dharma-sūtra*s. The *Śrauta-sūtras*[4] are concerned with major non-obligatory rituals detailed in the *śruti* literature, each *sūtra* growing out of a particular branch of the tradition. Thus, for example, the *Baudhāyana Śrauta-sūtra*, *Vādhūla SS* and *Āpastambha SS* all belong to the *Taittirīya Saṃhitā*. The *Gṛhya-* and *Dharma-sūtra*s, on the other hand, are concerned with domestic rites, rites of passage such as marriage, birth and funerary rites, and law and social relationships pertaining to the high-caste or twice-born householder. Developing from these texts are the *dharma-śāstra*s, the most famous of which is the *Manusmṛti* or *Laws of Manu*.[5]

Interpreting the Veda

There is no formal, centralized authority in Hinduism akin, say, to the Catholic Church, but, in the main, different communities of Brahmans, the highest *varṇa*, have perpetuated the traditions and been the interpreters of it. While the sacred texts have been read and interpreted from different perspectives by different social classes in India, it is the Brahmans who have conveyed the traditions of Sanskrit learning and culture. A number of orthodox interpretations of the Veda developed (as opposed to the heterodox views of the materialists, Buddhists and Jains). A route from the *Brāhmaṇa* literature can therefore be traced which emphasized the interpretation of the texts rather than the performance of rituals, and which developed into the great Sanskrit tradition of philosophical commentary and sub-commentary by different schools (*darśana*s). This hermeneutical tradition shows, on the one hand, that the meanings of the Veda are plural and, on the other, that the text itself is regarded by the traditions as eternal and unchanging; what has been discovered through interpretation is not a new meaning but the original or 'true' meaning.

What is significant about these schools is that they are not only metaphysical systems, but also methods of interpretation. The vehicle of philosophical inquiry is almost always dialogue through a commentary on an authoritative text – the *śruti* literature or some *smṛti* literature, most notably the *Bhagavadgītā* and the *Brahma-sūtra*s. There has been an emphasis in Western scholarship on understanding the abstract philosophical systems of the schools, but it is now becoming recognized that Indian philosophy is inextricably linked to exegesis and strategies of interpretation. For example, the monistic metaphysics of the philosopher Śaṃkara, in contrast to the theism of Rāmānuja, can be shown to arise partly out of the interpretative strategies they employ; or at least their interpretative strategies are bound up with their metaphysics. Mumme even suggests that 'from an Indian perspective, an orthodox metaphysical system may be only a by-product of a proper hermeneutical approach to scripture'. She goes on: 'It is certainly true that creative philosophical systems in Indian thought cannot gain the stamp of orthodoxy without equally creative interpretative approaches to scripture' (Mumme, 1992: 70).

THE MĪMĀṂSĀ

The distinction between the meanings and interpretations of a sacred text on the one hand, and its function on the other, is reflected in the division of the Veda itself by later philosophical schools, specifically the Pūrva and Uttara Mīmāṃsā, into the sections on ritual action (*karmakaṇḍa*) and sections on knowledge (*jñānakaṇḍa*), or into *mantra* and *brāhmaṇa* portions of the texts: those sections concerned with ritual injunctions and those concerned with the interpretations of meanings. These philosophical schools were acutely aware of problems concerning the nature of a sacred text's authority, with what the sentences and phrases of these texts referred to, and what their primary function was.

The Pūrva Mīmāṃsā[6] provided a basis for the interpretation of vedic texts. It argued that the earlier portions of the Veda – the *Saṃhitā*s, *Brāhmaṇa*s, and *Āraṇyaka*s – are primary, being concerned with injunctions (*vidhi*) about correct and incorrect ritual and social behaviour; while the *Upaniṣad*s are secondary, being concerned with the interpretation of injunctive statements. The function of the Veda is to command appropriate activity or to restrain people from prohibited actions (*niṣeda*). The Veda is about imperatives and no word has meaning unless it has reference to some action, either an action which must be performed without a particular reward, such as ritual and social duty, or action which will result in happiness in the next world or riches in this. So the interpretations or sentences of the *Upaniṣads*, if taken out of context, are by themselves meaningless; their only function is to shed light on the meaning of the vedic injunctions.

The Pūrva Mīmāṃsā has a distinctive understanding of *śruti*. For this school, *śruti* is the revealed word (*śabda*) which is discovered, as it were, or 'seen', by the sages (*ṛṣis*). This revelation is eternal, and the relationships between its words and their meanings are constant. The words of revelation do not acquire their meaning through convention (only personal names do this), but, rather, meaning is an inherent power which the words of the Veda possess. Thus the Veda is inherently meaningful; it is self-revealed and self-illumined, though its meanings may be obscured by human consciousness. The inherent meaning of the sacred texts transcends the human condition in so far as it predates and will post-date human reality. In itself the Veda is the primary source of all knowledge (*pramāṇa*) and shines independently of finite, human error which obscures its pristine validity. The task of philosophical inquiry is the retrieval of this original meaning (though there was, of course, wide disagreement as to what this was).

There is no need in this system, therefore, for a God who sustains the cosmos and who is the author of this revelation. Although the Mīmāṃsā accepted the plurality of vedic deities, it comes to regard them only as names which serve in the process of the sacrifice; their ontology is simply unimportant. The more impersonal the Veda is, the clearer its message and the more forceful its injunctions when stripped of any personal, limited will. Indeed, the Veda is the prime source of knowledge because a human, personal source, which is subject to error and deceit, cannot be the source of a cognition of that which is eternal and transpersonal. As Śabara says, humans cannot make valid statements about transpersonal things, for they are 'like statements on colour by persons born blind' (Pereira, 1991: 87). We need the Veda to tell us of the transcendent truth of *dharma*, which, by definition, is beyond human perception and known only through revelation.

The only recourse for knowledge of the transpersonal, or knowledge of *dharma*, is through the eternal Veda. While ordinary, worldly experience is sufficient for most aspects of life, a knowledge of transcendence can only come through a trans-human revelation. But more important than knowledge of the Veda is action (*kriyā*) enjoined by the Veda, whether its purpose (*artha*) is clearly understood or not. In the everyday world, an action is considered to be complete once the result is seen. On the contrary, with regard to vedic actions, the result may not be seen, but the action should nevertheless be regarded as complete, simply because it has been done exactly according to the text (*Mīmāṃsā-sūtra* 11.1.28). Revelation, therefore, constantly points to the transcendence which is itself. What is important is for the Veda's injunctions to be performed for their own sake, or rather because they are so enjoined by the text. Although there is a payoff in heaven for the performer of the injunctions, this is not of primary importance. Rather, remembering the Veda and fulfilling its injunctions is its own transcendent purpose. Jaimini writes:

> The hymns (*sāmans*) are sung for the purpose of learning [the singing]; in fact they take different forms with different verses; for the purpose served by them is beyond the ordinary (*alaukiko*) because it is enjoined.[7]

The purpose of learning to sing the hymns is the singing of the hymns, which, because it is an injunction, is transcendent and therefore needs no other justification.

Reciting the text of the Veda and performing its rituals are therefore sacred, self-fulfilling actions in accordance with the eternal *dharma*. The Mīmāṃsā is the brahmanical philosophy *par excellence*, and although most Brahmans would not now claim to be Mīmāṃsākas, many of the ideas it expressed are maintained by contemporary Brahmans. The Veda is learned because it is sacred tradition; vedic rituals are performed because the Veda says they should be performed; a Brahman learns the tradition because it is his *dharma* to do so.

THE VEDĀNTA

In contrast to the Pūrva Mīmāṃsā, the second important brahmanical, orthodox and orthoprax philosophy, the Uttara Mīmāṃsā or Vedānta,[8] regarded *śruti* as important not so much because it enjoined action, but rather because it revealed knowledge (*jñāna*). This tradition was therefore more concerned with interpreting the 'knowledge sections' (*jñānakaṇḍa*) of the Veda, namely the *Upaniṣads*, rather than the 'sections on ritual action' (*karmakaṇḍa*). As the Pūrva Mīmāṃsā develops from the *Mīmāṃsā-sūtra* of Jaimini, so the Vedānta schools develop from the *Brahma-* or *Vedānta-sūtra* of Bādarāyaṇa (around the second century CE), a text upon which commentaries were written by all the major schools of Hindu thought. Indeed, the Vedānta reveres a 'triple canon' (*prasthara-traya*) of texts, the *Upaniṣads*, the *Bhagavad-gītā* and the *Brahma-sūtra*, taking them as its authority, even though these last two are not, strictly speaking, *śruti*. Indeed, to begin a philosophical school or to seriously disagree with an opponent, a theologian needed to write a commentary on the *Brahma-sūtra*.

The most famous exponent of the Non-dualistic (*advaita*) branch of Vedānta was Śaṃkara (788–820 CE), who, while assuming a study of Pūrva Mīmāṃsā as a starting point, diverged widely from that school's understanding of sacred scripture.

For Śaṃkara, the sacred texts have two concerns, *dharma* and *brahman*: Hindu duty or law, and knowledge of absolute being. While maintaining that all of *śruti* is grounded in, and emerges from, the absolute (*brahman*), the earliest portions of the Veda (namely the *karmakaṇḍa*) are primarily concerned with *dharma* and ritual injunction (*vidhi*), while the later portions (namely the *Upaniṣads* or *jñānakaṇḍa*) are primarily concerned with knowledge of the absolute and the freedom (*mokṣa*) from the cycle of reincarnation, gained as a result of that knowledge. Śaṃkara therefore rejects the Mīmāṃsāka claim for the primacy of action. Performing *dharma* is, of course, important, but what is more important is the eradication of ignorance through renunciation (*saṃnyāsa*) and knowledge of the absolute.

What reveals this knowledge is, primarily, sacred scripture. As with the Mīmāṃsā, for Śaṃkara verbal testimony (*śabda*), which primarily refers to the Hindu revelation, is the source of knowledge about *brahman*, revelation's origin. Śaṃkara's high opinion of scripture is illustrated in his commentary on the *Brahma-sūtra*. For example, he writes:

> Brahman is the *yoni* (i.e., the material and efficient cause) of great scriptures like the Ṛg-veda etc. which are supplemented by other scriptures that are themselves sources (of various kinds) of knowledge, which reveal all things like a lamp, and which are almost omniscient. For scriptures like the Ṛg-veda, possessed of all good qualities as they are, cannot possibly emerge from any source other than an all-knowing One. . . . It goes without saying that that Great Being has absolute omniscience and omnipotence, since from him emerge the Ṛg-veda etc. – divided into many branches and

constituting the source of classification into gods, animals, men, castes, stages of life etc. and the source for all kinds of knowledge. . . .

(*Brahma-sūtra-bhāṣya* (BSB) 1.1.3, trans. Swami Gambhirananda, 1977, Advaita Ashrama, Delhi)

We see here that for Śaṃkara the Veda is not authorless and eternal, as for the Mīmāṃsā, but rather that it emanates, along with all other branches of knowledge incorporated in the supplementary vedic texts (the *Vedāṅgas*), from the absolute source of all.

Thus, rather than being an end in itself, the Veda is a means of knowing *brahman*. Each object of knowledge (*prameya*) has an appropriate means whereby it can be known (*pramāṇa*) and sacred scripture is the appropriate means whereby we know *brahman* as the 'object' of its knowledge. Such knowledge, for Śaṃkara, brings liberation, though such an inquiry into the absolute (*brahmajijñāsa*) cannot strictly speaking be commenced, for *brahman* is not a 'thing' in the common sense of an object of cognition distinct from a subject (see BSB 1.1.1).

The importance of scripture for Śaṃkara cannot be underestimated. Knowledge of *brahman*, which in the strictest sense is unknowable, can come only through 'the word': *brahman*, which is without qualities (*nirguṇa*), cannot be known through the senses, which can only grasp objects appropriate to their own sphere, or through mere reasoning (BSB 1.1.2). Indeed, even meditation and ritual cannot yield up knowledge of *brahman*, for *brahman* is uncaused and so cannot be attained through causes and conditions. But although in one sense *brahman* is unknowable, it is nevertheless 'revealed' through the word which emanates from it, and can be existentially apprehended 'as the content of the subject "I"' (BSB p. 3). That *brahman* is the content of the subject 'I' – the irreducibility of the subjective – is revealed particularly in the 'great sayings' (*mahāvākyas*) of the *Upaniṣads* and *Bhagavadgītā*: 'I am the absolute' (*aham brahmāsmi*), 'this self is the absolute' (*ayam ātmā brahma*), 'all this is indeed the absolute' (*sarvam khalu idam brahma*) and 'you are that' (*tat tvam asi*).

These statements were interpreted in a purely monistic sense by Śaṃkara's unremitting non-dualism, but there were other schools of Advaita Vedānta which understood these sentences in a less uncompromising way, a way which is perhaps more central to the general tendency of Hindu thought. Most significant of these is the

Viśiṣṭādvaita or qualified non-dualism, made famous by Rāmānuja (*c.* 1017–1137). Rāmānuja interpreted the sacred scriptures not to mean, as Śaṃkara did, that the everyday world was unreal or illusory (*māyā*), but rather that it is a mode of expression of the absolute. He thus rejects Śaṃkara's interpretative strategy of dividing scripture into a lower and higher level of truth and relegating all statements implying dualism to the former. All parts of the Veda are of equal value for Rāmānuja, for there are no grounds internal to the Veda for maintaining the supremacy of some statements over others or for taking such statements out of their total context.

For Rāmānuja the Veda was the word of the Lord who was united with his creation, yet still maintained his transcendence. (This philosophy is therefore a 'qualified non-dualism', *viśiṣṭādvaita*.) Yet it was not the *śruti* texts themselves which provided the main authority for Rāmānuja, but rather the *Bhagavadgītā* and Bādarāyaṇa's *Brahmasūtra*. Not only did he regard these texts as authoritative, inheriting as he did an expanded Hindu notion of sacred scripture, but he and the Śrī Vaiṣṇava tradition, of whom he was the hierarch, also revered texts of the 'tantric' Vaiṣṇava tradition of the Pāñcarātra and Tamil songs of the Āḻvārs, the seventh-century devotees (*bhaktas*) of Viṣṇu.

Indeed, the *Tiruvaimoḻī* of Nammāḻvār, a collection of his 'sweet Tamil songs', was known as the Tamil Veda and treated with as much authority as the Sanskrit scriptures. This text was, and is, believed to contain great spiritual knowledge, and is recited by the Śrī Vaiṣṇavas during daily rituals and in its entirety at weddings, funerals and other occasions (Carman and Narayanan, 1989). Rāmānuja never actually composed a commentary on this text, though his disciple and cousin Piḷḷān did, in Maṇipravāla, a hybrid of Tamil and Sanskrit. Other commentaries followed after this into the thirteenth century.

What is significant here is that the sacred text is no longer confined to Sanskrit, but a respectable orthodox tradition has widened the boundaries of the sacred to include a text in a Dravidian language. Indeed, the *Tiruvaimoḻī* was thought to have sacred power akin to the Veda and could be taught only to a suitable disciple in the process of transmission from teacher to pupil (*ōrāṇ-vaḻi*). In contrast, however, to the Sanskrit Veda, which was restricted to twice-born males, this text could be heard by all castes, including *śūdras*, and by both genders.

We see here, then, the expansion of the idea of a sacred, revealed scripture which is accessible to a wider community of people in a language more easily understood. Of course the Tamil texts would not be accepted as authoritative by highly orthodox Brahmans from outside the Śrī Vaiṣṇava community, but we see here a strong sense which prevails in much of Hinduism, that 'revelation' is not something in the distant past but a continuing tradition, and indeed the line between revelation and compositions of human authorship is sometimes quite thin.

That which is remembered

So far we have examined the idea of revelation and seen how there are two paths which lead from it, the primary path of ritual in which the Veda functions liturgically, and the path of interpretation where it functions as an authoritative basis or source of knowledge upon which, or around which, metaphysical systems such as the Pūrva Mīmāṃsā and Vedānta can be built. We have also seen how there can be the expansion of the idea of the sacred text in some communities to include works which are not written in Sanskrit and which are not ancient. We shall return to this theme of revelation presently in discussing a different class of text often contrasted with the Veda, namely the *tantra*, which again raises questions of authority and authenticity. But first it is necessary to survey briefly a vast body of literature of human authorship, 'that which is remembered' (*smṛti*), for it is this literature which is most significant at a popular level within Hinduism, and which has captured and filled the Hindu imagination.

Within this category are classed the *śāstra*s, associated with various branches of the Veda (see above, pp. 134–6), the epic literature (*itihāsa*), i.e., the *Rāmāyaṇa* and *Mahābhārata*, the compendiums of mythology, ritual, yoga and doctrine called the *Purāṇa*s, and the *āgama*s and *tantra*s which are, however, regarded by their followers as being equal in status to the Veda.

THE EPICS

The *Rāmāyaṇa*,[9] traditionally composed by Vālmīki, is more concise than the *Mahābhārata*, which it predates. The story, briefly, concerns the banishment into the forest of Prince Rāma, who is an incarnation of Viṣṇu, along with his wife Sītā and brother Lakṣmaṇa, as a consequence of his stepmother's wishes. Here they live the life of hermits until the demon Rāvaṇa, from Śrī Laṅka, abducts Sītā. With the help of a monkey army of the king Sugrīva, headed by the monkey-general Hanumān, Sītā is rescued and Rāvaṇa defeated.

The importance of this epic lies particularly in the messages it presents concerning correct behaviour and duty (*dharma*). Rāma and Sītā are models of moral rectitude. Rāma demonstrates filial piety by exiling himself because his father has so asked him, even though both know such an exile is unjust, and Sītā is the ideal wife, accepting her fate when she is banished into the forest towards the end of the story because people are suspicious of her purity, even though Rāma knows she is innocent. Sītā and Rāma are the ideal married couple, each embodying the expected virtues of the husband and wife and demonstrating the constant Hindu idea that social duty and obligation are far more important than personal desires.

The *Mahābhārata* and the *Purāṇa*s are thought by many Hindus to have been composed by Vyāsa, a Brahman seer who appears in the *Mahābhārata* and is thought to be an incarnation of the deity Viṣṇu-Nārāyaṇa. Vyāsa taught the epic poem to his pupil who then recited it during the snake sacrifice of King Janamejaya, from whence the poem was passed down orally through the generations. The *Mahābhārata*[10] is an encyclopedic work which was begun probably in the fifth or fourth century BCE, and which was complete by about the fourth century CE. It contains a wealth of mythological, ritual and philosophical material, woven around the story of an internecine war between the five Pāṇḍavas and their cousins, the Kauravas.

The *Mahābhārata* was added to over the years, particularly by a Brahman clan (*gotra*), the Bhārgavas, and it contains many stories embedded within the larger framework. These may have originally existed independently. Perhaps the most famous of these embedded episodes, after the *Bhagavadgītā*, is the story of Nala and Damayantī. Nala, 'a tiger among men', is King of Niṣadha, while Damayantī, 'a mind-agitating' beauty, is the daughter of King Bhīma. They fall in love by hearing of each other's qualities, and eventually Damayantī chooses Nala for a husband at her *svayamvara*, the free choice of a husband allowed to Kṣatriya girls. Nala, however, comes to grief by gambling away all he has (reflecting Yudhiṣṭhira's behaviour) and wanders in the forest. Eventually he wins everything back and lives happily with Damayantī.

Although the Nala episode reflects the narrative structure of the larger story, it is probable that we have here an example of the Sanskritization of a folk tale. Indeed, the story of Nala is still found as an oral tradition in northern India, and rather than these being derived from the Sanskrit version, it is more probable that the North Indian folk tales and the epic version are both derived from an older, oral tradition.[11] This happens throughout the epic, and many episodes contained within it may have been folk tales viewed through a Vaiṣṇava lens.

Both epics are important in telling us about the kind of religious and social changes occurring in India during the periods of their composition. These texts paint a picture of life in north and north-east India during the last half of the last millennium BCE, depicting a number of small kingdoms, a hierarchical social structure and groups of ascetics living in the forests seeking release (*mokṣa*) through yoga and asceticism (*tapas*). The gods Brahmā (not the impersonal force, *brahman*, of the *Upaniṣads*) and Indra are important in the text, and the text also reflects the rise to prominence of Śiva and, particularly, Viṣṇu.

The epics have been at the centre of the Hindu religious imagination, functioning to reinforce ideals of behaviour, interaction and social duty (*dharma*) of both householders and renouncers, and also reflecting the Hindu love of poetry and a good story. These texts would have been known not through the written word, but through being told by bards around the villages, and by being acted out and danced. In contemporary India the stories are still a living tradition and have captured the minds of millions of Hindus by being serialized though the medium of television, the television set becoming a shrine during their transmission. Indeed, the televised epics may well have been instrumental in the recent increase of support for political Hindu movements such as the Bhāratīya Jana Saṅgh.

THE *BHAGAVADGĪTĀ*

The *Bhagavadgītā* is located within Book 6 of the *Mahābhārata*. A text originating with the Vaiṣṇava Bhagavata cult, it became a pan-Hindu authority, being commented upon by the main Vedānta thinkers, Śaṃkara, Rāmānuja and Madhva, and also by some important Śaiva thinkers such as Rāmakaṇṭha and Abhinavagupta, though undoubtedly the Vaiṣṇavas have been much more interested in this text than the Śaivas. One is even tempted to think that Abhinavagupta wrote his *Bhagavadgītā-saṃgraha*, not out of a deep respect for the text, but rather to align his monistic Śaiva tradition with more orthodox ways of thinking. Although technically *smṛti*, the *Gītā* has been treated as though it were *śruti*. Indeed, the commentators do not seem to be very concerned with this problem. The text even calls itself the *Bhagavadgītā-upaniṣad*, which Coburn says, with justification, substantiates his claim that the classification of Hindu scriptures needs to be re-examined (Coburn, 1989: 126, n. 63).

The *Gītā* is a text expressing two central concerns of Hinduism, the need to perform one's duty (*dharma*) and the need to attain liberation (*mokṣa*) from the cycle of birth and death (*saṃsāra*) through detachment and love (*bhakti*) for God (Viṣṇu/Kṛṣṇa). It begins with Arjuna, one of the Pāndu brothers, being driven in a chariot by Kṛṣṇa, an incarnation of Viṣṇu, between the two armies on the eve of the great battle. Arjuna expresses a deep moral concern to Kṛṣṇa about the war, how he does not want to fight, for it means destroying the lives of so many of his relations (1.28–46).

Kṛṣṇa attempts to allay Arjuna's apprehensions by giving three reasons why he should fight in the battle. First, he tells Arjuna that to fight is the manly thing to do (2.2–3), but Arjuna is not convinced by this argument. Kṛṣṇa then presents a deeper reason as to why Arjuna should not flinch from the battle, namely that soul (*ātman*) is eternal and passes at death from one body to another (2.13); the eternal soul, being 'unborn, eternal, everlasting and ancient' (*ajo nityaḥ śāśvato 'yaṃ purāṇo*), cannot die, neither can it kill (2.19–20). The existential understanding of this eternal soul and its dependence upon the absolute is, of course, liberation. But of more immediate concern is the third and most important reason for Arjuna to fight, namely that it is his duty, his *svadharma*, as a member of the warrior class (2.31). Indeed, not to fight would be to transgress his warrior's duty and would therefore be a 'sin' (*pāpa*) (2.33).

Attempting to bring together the two realms of *dharma* and *mokṣa*, the text unfolds a teaching of detachment and devotion. One can be in the world, performing one's worldly duties, but should be detached from it, dedicating the fruits of one's action (*karmaphalam*) to Kṛṣṇa in order to attain peace (2.11; 5.10–12). Undoubtedly the text's highest ideal is liberation through devotion (*bhakti*) to the theistic reality of Kṛṣṇa (18.55–7), who, as is revealed in chapter 11, is the supreme absolute who creates all universes, and in whom all universes are consumed (11.15–31).

Many influences have fed into the *Gītā*, and it is a great reservoir of ideas which can seem contradictory. Indeed, the openness of the text is seen in the commentarial tradition which developed from it. Śaṃkara saw the text as propounding non-dualism (*advaita*) of the soul and absolute, while other theistic traditions read the text in purely theistic terms, maintaining a clear distinction between the soul and the absolute. One such interpretational divergence is illustrated by Patricia Mumme with regard to verse 18.66, the so-called *caramaśloka*. The verse reads: 'Having relinquished all dharmas, resort to me alone as refuge. I will save you from all sins; do not fear' (*sarvadharmān parityaja / mām ekaṃ śaraṇaṃ vraja ahaṃ tvāṃ sarvapāpebhyo / mokṣayiṣyāmi mā śucaḥ*) (Mumme, 1992: 69).

A hundred or so years after Rāmānuja's death, the Śrī Vaiṣṇava community had split into the Teṉkalai, the 'southern culture', and Vaṭakalai, the 'northern culture', schools. The former placed emphasis on the Tamil scriptures and the idea of surrender to God's grace as the only means of liberation, the latter emphasized the Sanskrit sources of their tradition, i.e., the Vedas, and effort as playing a part in the process of salvation (Carman and Narayanan, 1989: 187–90). Accordingly, the Teṉkalai teachers understood the *caramaśloka* to be saying that there are two distinct paths, that of *bhakti-yoga* and that of surrender (*prapatti*); surrender being the superior, esoteric 'path' in which the devotee is wholly dependent on God's (Viṣṇu's) grace. Vedānta Deśika (1269–1370), by contrast, the main theologian of the Vaṭakalai school, maintained that the verse referred to two groups of people. On the one hand there are twice-born males who are liberated through the performance of ritual devotion (i.e., *bhakti-yoga*), while on the other hand there are all the others, for whom surrender (*prapatti*) is appropriate. Thus the verse 'having relinquished all dharmas' does not mean that there is a superior path to *dharma*, which means here the performance of devotional ritual, but refers to those who cannot perform ritual because they are not twice-born (Mumme, 1992: 78).

This verse serves to illustrate the 'openness' of the *Gītā*, and is an example of the way in which it has functioned almost as revealed scripture in the hermeneutic traditions of Hinduism. However, it has enjoyed a wide popular appeal among the Hindu urban classes only since the Hindu Renaissance, which began in the nineteenth century. The text also functioned to stir nationalist aspirations before Indian independence, drawing as it does on the more martial elements of the Hindu tradition. The struggle against colonialism was seen as the struggle of righteousness (*dharma*) against unrighteousness (*adharma*). Part of the *Gītā*'s popular appeal may also be due to what Bharati has called the 'pizza-effect', namely that the *Gītā* has been exported to the West, particularly through 'new religions' such as Transcendental Meditation and the Hare Krishna movement, and then imported, as it were, back into India. Indeed, the founding *guru*s of these two movements, Maharishi Mahesh Yogi and Bhaktivedanta Swami Prabhupada, have both written commentaries on the text, one from an advaitin perspective, the other from a devotional, theistic perspective.

While the *Gītā* has undoubtedly been very influential at the level of philosophy and in modern, urban Hinduism, it does not play such an important role for rural Hindus, for whom, rather than the Kṛṣṇa of the *Gītā*, it is the stories of the erotic, youthful Kṛṣṇa of the *Bhagavata Purāṇa* which have been the source of amusement and wonder.

THE *PURĀṆAS*

The *Purāṇas*[12] are a vast corpus, covering a wide range of material, often derived from the *Upaniṣads*, the *Brāhmaṇas* and epics. They include mythologies of the Hindu deities and incarnations (*avatāras*) of Viṣṇu, the origins of the cosmos and of humanity, law codes, ritual, pilgrimage and so on. Traditionally there are eighteen major and eighteen minor (*upa*)*purāṇas* which overlap in content and present different versions of the same myths. This largely depends upon sectarian affiliation, as many *purāṇas* promote a particular deity, such as Viṣṇu or Śiva, over others. Indeed, local stories and traditions were incorporated into the puranic tradition in the process known as Sanskritization: the absorption by the 'great tradition' of local, low-caste, 'little traditions'. This process of control was done by orthodox Brahmans, the Smārtas (those who followed *smṛti*).

The dating of these texts is very problematic, partly because they were composed over a long period of time and freely borrow material from each other. Indeed, these are very uncircumscribed texts, and they have always been transmitted without clearly defined boundaries, so much so that the notion of establishing critical editions is at least problematic. So while, as some scholars have argued, the search for an 'original' text in the case of the *Purāṇas* may be a waste of time,[13] we can nevertheless establish a rough chronology, with, for example, the

Brahmāṇḍa, composed from about 350 to 950 CE, the *Viṣṇu* about 450 CE and the *Bhagavata* in about 950 CE (O'Flaherty, 1988: 5).

Popular Hinduism has been conveyed mostly through the medium of these texts, which were performed by reciters going around the villages, for, of course, the written text would be accessible only to the literate. Indeed, there were public readings of the *Purāṇas*, for, unlike the Veda, there were no restrictions on who could hear them; they were open to all, even to the lowest class (*śūdra*) and to women. Perhaps the most popular and authoritative *Purāṇa* among the Vaiṣṇavas has been the *Bhagavata-Purāṇa*. This text depicted Kṛṣṇa's play (*līlā*) with the cowgirls (*gopīs*), and promoted the idea of the longing devotion of separation (*viraha-bhakti*) from the Lord as the means to salvation. These stories have captivated the minds of generations of Hindus, inspiring theological speculation, dance and iconographic representations of Kṛṣṇa and the *gopīs*. Indeed, rather than the monism of the *Upaniṣads*, it is the devotionalism (*bhakti*) of texts such as the *Bhagavata* which pervades popular, rural Hinduism.

THE *ĀGAMAS* AND *TANTRAS*

While the *śruti* literature and *smṛti* texts (the *Dharma-śāstras*, the epics including the *Bhagavadgītā* and the *Purāṇas*) have functioned as the authoritative source for orthodox Hindu society (particularly for Vaiṣṇavas), all mainstream schools of Śaivism revere a different group of texts. These are the *tantras* and *āgamas*, dating mostly from about the seventh to eleventh centuries CE.

The *tantras* and *āgamas* are a vast body of literature which generally take the form of a dialogue between Śiva and his consort (Śakti), dealing with ritual, the divine nature of the body, the female energy (*śakti*) of god, cosmology (particularly speculation on the cosmos as an emanation of energy as divine sound), and the construction of ritual formulae or *mantras*. Theoretically the *tantras* contain four sections (*pādas*), on knowledge (*jñāna*), yoga, ritual (*kriyā*) and behaviour (*caryā*), though most are not clearly divided in this way and there is much overlap in contents.

A Hindu who follows the ritual prescriptions and behaviour enjoined by the *tantras* is a *tāntrika*, in contrast to a person who follows only the vedic prescriptions, a *vaidika*. A *tāntrika* has undergone initiation (*dīkṣā*) by a *guru* into a particular school and would regard the *tantras* as a more powerful revelation than the Veda, providing an effective soteriology in the present age of darkness (*Kali-yuga*). Indeed, the tantric householder would not reject the vedic rites, but would perform his tantric rites in addition, maintaining that this was a more rapid path for one desirous of liberation (*mumukṣu*). A popular dictum has even maintained that one should be a *vaidika* in one's social practice, externally a Śaiva, but internally a *tāntrika*. There was also an initiation into an alternative path for those who desired magical powers and pleasure in heavenly abodes (*bubukṣu*).

The classification of these texts is a complex matter, for, as Sanderson has shown, later developments absorbed the revelations of their predecessors in an initiation hierarchy.[14] That is, the later developments regarded their revelation and ritual initiation as containing, yet superseding, the earlier revelations. One way of looking at the *tantras* would be to divide them into 'monistic', or 'northern' *tantras*, the authoritative source of 'Kashmir' Śaivism, and 'dualistic', or 'southern' *tantras*, the source of Śaiva Siddhānta. Very generally speaking, the 'northern' texts tend to be called *tantras* while the Siddhānta texts tend to be called *āgamas*. There was also a tantric Vaiṣṇava tradition, the Pāñcarātra, whose texts, called *saṃhitās*, closely resemble the Śaiva *tantras* in many respects. These texts were revered by the Śrī Vaiṣṇavas, and Rāmānuja defended their orthodoxy (see above, p. 146; and Carman and Narayanan, 1989: 181).

Quite different from the more respectable, vedically aligned Pāñcarātra, we have, at the opposite end of the tantric spectrum, the Śākta *tantras*. These were produced by groups of cremation-ground ascetics, worshipping ferocious female deities such as Kālī or one of her manifestations. These terrible (*ghora*) female deities needed to be placated by substances which were anathema to the orthodox, namely non-vegetarian offerings, alcohol and sexual fluids. In later *tantras* these offerings became known as the 'five *ms*': wine (*madya*), flesh (*māṃsa*), fish (*matsya*), parched grain (*mudrā*) and (caste-free) sexual intercourse (*maithuna*). These substances could, for some deities, be substituted by harmless, symbolic substances such as milk and ghee etc., as was done by the more orthodox Goddess-worshipping tradition, the Śrī Vidyā, which became associated with the Śaṃkara Brahman tradition of South India.

Mention should also be made of the vast body of Buddhist *tantras*. These are mostly preserved in Tibetan, and their form is akin to the Śaiva texts which influenced them. There is also Jain tantric literature.

Examining the 'intertextuality' of these Hindu, Buddhist and Jain sources (as well as the tantric material in Tamil) is a major task which needs to be done.

While the metaphysics of the *tantra*s themselves is sometimes ambiguous, the *tantra*s of the north, the authority of Kashmir Śaivism, have been interpreted by that school through the lens of a monistic metaphysics in which there is only the reality of pure consciousness (*saṃvit*), identified with Śiva, of which the cosmos is an appearance. Śaiva Siddhānta, the older system, by contrast, maintained that there is an eternal distinction between the Lord (*pati*), souls (*paśu*s) and matter (*pāśa*). Some of the *tantra*s, such as the *Svacchanda*, have been interpreted in both ways by these schools.

Both Kashmir Śaivism and Śaiva Siddhānta had thriving commentarial traditions. Kashmir Śaivism, whose main exponent was Abhinavagupta (*c.* 975–1025), revered not only the revelations of the *tantra*s but also the independent revelation of Vāsugupta (*c.* 875–925), who in a dream was told by Śiva that on the Mahā Deva mountain he would find a secret (*rahasya*) text inscribed upon a stone for the benefit of the world. This text is the *Śiva-sūtra*, which generated a tradition of commentarial literature and intertextual dialogue. But over and above philosophy, the importance of the *tantra*s and *āgama*s lies in their use as ritual manuals and as objects of recitation. For example, the *āgama*s of the South Indian Śaiva Siddhānta are still used today in personal, daily ritual and in temple rites. In the sense that the *tantra*s are liturgical manuals, there is a strong continuity with the vedic tradition, though the deities and the *mantra*s used in ritual would be different and, indeed, regarded as polluting to the orthodox, especially if the focus of the rites is one of the terrible deities of the harder, 'left-hand' traditions.

Although not technically *śruti*, the *tantra*s and their associated literature, such as the *Śiva-sūtra*, have been revered by initiated *tāntrika*s and by the wider Śaiva communities of Kashmir, Nepal and South India. With the *tantra*s, we have another Hindu instance which demonstrates the ongoing nature of revelation within the Hindu traditions, outside of orthodox, vedic boundaries. While the orthodox Brahmans would never accept the *tantra*s or their related literature as 'canonical', these texts have been accepted by a significant body of the Hindu tradition, which would claim equal right to the term 'Hindu'.

THE VERNACULAR TRADITIONS

Not only the *tantra*s and *āgama*s, but also poetry in vernacular languages is authoritative for some of the Śaiva traditions. In a way akin to the Tamil poetry of the Āḻvārs for the Śrī Vaiṣṇavas, the southern school of Śaiva Siddhānta honoured, along with the *āgama*s, the Tamil poetry of the Śaiva poet-saints, the Nāyaṉārs. Another Śaiva school, the Liṅgayats or Vīraśaivas, established in Mysore, similarly revere the Kannada poetry of their founders, including the powerful poetry of a female initiate, Mahadevyakka (Ramanujan, 1973: 111).

In addition to the Tamil poetry of the Āḻvārs, the Nāyaṉārs, and the Kannada poetry of the Liṅgayats in the south, there is also Bengali and Hindi devotional poetry (O'Flaherty, 1988: 138–87). The Hindi poetry of the north is of great significance in the development of Indian religious traditions. A distinction can be made here between poetry which eulogized the Lord who possessed qualities (*saguṇa*), usually Kṛṣṇa and Rāma embodied in a temple image, and praise of a formless, transcendent Lord without qualities (*nirguṇa*). Generally, these poets were low-caste and criticized orthodox forms of worship in favour of devotion to the transcendent Lord, through repeating his divine names and apprehending the name (*nām*) or sound (*śabda*) of God in meditation through the grace of the *guru*.

Tulsi Das's (*d.* 1623) *Rāmcaritmānas*, a Hindi version of the *Rāmāyaṇa*, was a very influential work which eulogizes the saving power of God's infinite name. Among the most famous poets in the tradition of 'good people' or *sant*s is Kabir (fifteenth century). Nominally a Muslim of the weaver caste, his poetry is terse and disparaging of traditional soteriologies, emphasizing, rather, devotion to the formless absolute through repeating his name:

> I have searched all the Vedas,
> the Puranas, the Smriti –
> Salvation lies in none.
> Kabir says, 'So I repeat Ram's name –
> he erases birth and death'.[15]

With the Sant poetry we have a reinterpretation of the traditional Hindu idea of the revealed word. Rather than a group of received scriptures (*śruti*), the word becomes a transcendent reality, whose power goes beyond the traditional understandings of the heard scripture, becoming a means of transformation and salvation.

The devotional poetry of the Sant tradition is very popular in North India and much of it is collected in the holy book of the Sikhs, the *Ādi Granth*. This poetry is sung with great feeling at various festivals and during the community meetings (*satsang*s) of contemporary *gurū*s (such as those of the Rādhā Soami tradition), functioning to express popular devotional sentiments and a soteriology without the necessity of caste qualification, elaborate ritual or stringent *yoga*.

In a curtailed survey such as this it is impossible to cover all genres, aspects and functions of sacred texts in Hinduism. We have seen that the heard, rather than the written, word plays a central part in Hindu traditions, as the conveyor of those traditions through time and as the pointer to how people should live their lives in accordance with the higher power of *dharma*. Revelation is not static, but while there is a central corpus of unchanging texts, the Veda, passed down orally through the generations, there is also a fluidity and acceptance of new texts. Revelation is not something in the far distant past but a constant and present possibility. The Hindu traditions have always reassessed themselves, introducing new ideas, though rooting them in the past, and occasionally even rejecting the old models. The received word has functioned to constrain behaviour into certain forms, and whether complied with, modified or rejected, it has been at the heart of the development of the amalgam of regional traditions, doctrines and behaviour which the term 'Hinduism' has come to designate.

Notes

1 A. Bharati (1982) *Hindu Views and Ways and the Hindu–Muslim Interface*. Santa Barbara: Ross Erikson, pp. 2–3.

2 The complete corpus of vedic literature has not yet been translated into European languages, and translations which are available are often inaccessible. Some of the translations are as follows. The standard translation of the *Ṛg-veda* is by Karl F. Geldner (1951) *Der Rig-veda, aus dem Sanskrit ins Deutsche übersetzt und mit einen laufenden Kommentar versehen*. 4 vols, Harvard Oriental Series 33–35; Cambridge: Harvard University Press. In English there is H. H. Wilson (1850–88) *Rig-Veda-Sanhita: A Collection of Ancient Hindu Hymns*. 6 vols; London. W. D. O'Flaherty (1981) has published a very readable translation of selected hymns in *The Rig Veda*. Harmondsworth: Penguin. W. D. Whitney (1905) produced a translation of the *Atharva-veda* (revised by C. Lanman). 2 vols, Harvard Oriental Series 7, 8; Cambridge (repr. Delhi,

1962). M. Bloomfield (1897) also translated some of the text in *Hymns of the Atharva Veda*. Sacred Books of the East 42; Oxford (repr. Delhi, 1964). R. T. H. Griffith (1899) produced *The Hymns of the Yajur-Veda*. Benares. For the *Brāhmaṇa*s we have J. Eggeling (1882–1900) *The Śatapaṭha Brāhmaṇa According to the Text of the Mādhyandina School*. 5 vols, Sacred Books of the East 12, 26, 41, 43, 44; Oxford (repr. Delhi, 1963); and W. Caland (1955) *The Pañcaviṃśa-Brāhmaṇa*. Biblioteca Indica (repr. Delhi, 1982). For the *Āraṇyakas* see A. B. Keith (1908) *The Śāṅkhāyana Āraṇyaka*. London: Royal Asiatic Society; and (1909) *The Aitareya Āraṇyaka*. Oxford: Clarendon Press. English translations of the *Upaniṣads* are a little more accessible. Here we have Hume (1971) *Thirteen Principal Upanishads*. New York: Oxford University Press; and S. Radhakrishnan (1953) *The Principal Upanishads*. London: Allen & Unwin.

3 J. Bowker (1991) *The Meanings of Death*. Cambridge: Cambridge University Press, pp. 148–67.

4 For an English translation see J. M. van Gelder (1961–63) *The Mānava Śrauta-sūtra Belonging to the Maitrāyaṇī Saṃhitā*. 2 vols; New Delhi (repr. Delhi, 1985).

5 English translation by W. D. O'Flaherty (1992) *The Laws of Manu*. Harmondsworth: Penguin.

6 The Pūrva Mīmāṃsā or 'Primary Investigation' is a 'realistic' school of philosophy dating from about the second century BCE with the *Mīmāṃsā-sūtra* of Jaimini. It was concerned with vedic ritual, the purposes of the eternal Veda as injunctions to correct action and the avoidance of wrong action, and the invisible force (*apūrva*) which gives rise to the future result of a ritual act. Śabara wrote a commentary on this text (which in turn was commented upon by Prabhākara and Kumārila). These provide the basis of two sub-schools which have some disagreements concerning the nature of verbal testimony and error: see Dasgupta (1975), pp. 367–405; Francis Clooney (1990) *Thinking Ritually*. Vienna: De Nobili.

7 *Mīmāṃsā-sūtra* 7.2.15 translated by Clooney, op. cit., p. 134.

8 The Pūrva Mīmāṃsā was so called because it concentrated on the earlier (*pūrva*) parts of the Veda which it regarded as injunctions, whereas the Uttara Mīmāṃsā emphasized the later (*uttara*) parts of the Veda, namely the *Upaniṣads*.

9 English translations by R. Goldman and S. J. Sutherland (1984) *The Rāmāyaṇa of Vālmīki*, vol. 1, and S. I. Pollock (1986) *The Rāmāyaṇa of Vālmīki*, vol. 2. Princeton: Princeton University Press. A complete translation exists by Hari Prashad Shastri (1952–59) *The Rāmāyaṇa of Vālmīki*. 3 vols; London: Shanti Sadan.

10 A good, though unfortunately incomplete, English translation is by J. A. B. van Buitenen (1973–78) *The Mahābhārata*, vols 1–3. Chicago: University of Chicago Press.
11 See van Buitenen, op. cit., vol. 2, pp. 184–5.
12 For translations of the *Purāṇa*s see C. Dimmitt and J. A. B. van Buitenen (1978) *Classical Hindu Mythology: A Reader in the Sanskrit Purānas*. Philadelphia: Temple University Press; W. D. O'Flaherty (1975) *Hindu Myths*. Baltimore: Penguin.
13 Madeleine Biardeau observes: 'The approach of historical philology will never be suitable for an oral tradition, which has no essential reference to its historical origin': 'Some more considerations about textual criticism', *Purāṇa* 10(2) (1968), pp. 115–23.
14 A. Sanderson (1988) 'Śaivism and the tantric traditions' in S. Sutherland, L. Houlden, P. Clarke and F. Hardy (eds) *The World's Religions*. London: Routledge, pp. 660–704.
15 Nirmal Dass (1991) *Songs of Kabir From the Adi Granth*. Albany: SUNY, p. 128.

Further reading

Brockington, J. L. (1981) *The Sacred Thread*. Edinburgh: Edinburgh University Press.

Carman, J. and Narayanan, V. (1989) *The Tamil Veda*. Chicago: University of Chicago Press.

Coburn, T. B. (1989) ' "Scripture" in India: towards a typology of the word in Hindu life' in Levering (1989).

Coward, H. (1988) *Sacred Word and Sacred Text*. New York: Orbis Books.

Dasgupta, S. N. (1975) *A History of Indian Philosophy*, vol. 1. Delhi: MLBD.

Gonda, J. (1975) *Vedic Literature*. Wiesbaden: Otto Harrassowitz.

Gonda, J. (1977) *Medieval Religious Literature in Sanskrit*. Wiesbaden: Otto Harrassowitz.

Levering, M. (ed.) (1989) *Rethinking Scripture*. Albany: SUNY.

Mumme, P. (1992) 'Haunted by Śaṅkara's ghost: the Śrī Vaiṣṇava interpretation of *Bhagavad Gītā* 18.66' in Timm (1992).

O'Flaherty, W. D. (ed.) (1988) *Textual Sources for the Study of Hinduism*. Manchester: Manchester University Press.

O'Flaherty, W. D. (ed.) (1993) *Purana Perennis: Reciprocity and Transformation in Hindu and Jaina Texts*. Albany: SUNY Press.

Olivelle, P. (1996) *Upaniṣads*. Oxford and New York: Oxford University Press.

Pereira, J. (1991) *Hindu Theology: A Reader*. Delhi: Motilal Banarsidass.

Ramanujan, A. K. (1973) *Speaking of Śiva*. Harmondsworth: Penguin.
Staal, F. (1989) *Rules Without Meaning*. New York: Peter Lang.
Timm, J. R. (ed.) (1992) *Texts in Context: Traditional Hermeneutics in South Asia*. Albany: SUNY.

7. Picturing God

Sharada Sugirtharajah

The Hindu tradition is replete with a wide variety of images of the Divine. The Supreme is seen as a personal God, as a transcendent Being, as immanent within each person as *Antaryāmin* ('inner Controller'), and in all creation. Images of the Divine as lord, king, judge, master, father, mother, husband, friend, beloved and as creator, preserver and destroyer of evil, find expression in scriptures, mythology, art, iconography, music, dance and worship. The Divine is also described in terms of its plethora of attributes, such as love, wisdom, knowledge, beauty, power, and also in abstract categories such as pure consciousness, pure Being.

Monistic and theistic images of the Divine

BRAHMAN

Ultimate Reality is conceptualized in many different ways in the Hindu tradition. The Sanskrit term *brahman*, which is used for the Ultimate Reality, is seen as the one eternal, all-pervading and all-transcending principle of the universe and all creation (*Śvetāśvatara Upaniṣad* 6.11). There seems to be more than one linguistic derivation of the term. In the Veda it denotes the cosmic or sacred power contained in the vedic chants, and the priest who chanted the sacred verses was called Brahman (a member of the priestly class). In the *Upaniṣads* the term *brahman* comes to refer to the impersonal transcendental principle, the first cause of the universe. Hindu monists see *brahman* as being identical with the inner self or *ātman*, the spirit dwelling within us. For Hindu theists, *ātman* is only partially identical with *brahman*.

Brahman is described as *Sat-cit-ānanda* (Truth, Consciousness and Bliss). It is conceived as both one and many, form and formless, immanent and transcendent, male and female, benign and terrible – not so much opposites as complementary aspects of the One Being (*Śvetāśvatara Upaniṣad* 4.1–3).

Brahman is perceived and experienced as both *saguṇa* (with qualities, personal) and *nirguṇa* (without qualities, non-personal). The image of the Divine as a personal god is central to the theistic tradition, whereas the image of an impersonal Absolute is central to the monistic tradition. While the former affirms the infinite attributes of the Absolute, the latter does not deny such qualities in a preliminary way, but sees *brahman* as being beyond all thought and speculation. Both positive and negative categories are used to affirm the reality of the Supreme. The Absolute is affirmed as *iti iti*, meaning that all this is *brahman* – emphasizing the immanental dimension (*Chāndogya Upaniṣad* 3.14.1) – and *neti neti*, implying that *brahman* is 'not this, not that' – emphasizing that *brahman* is more than what we perceive and experience (*Bṛhadāraṇyaka Upaniṣad* 4.5.15). Both conceptions of the Divine are equally valid, though there has been a tendency to exalt one over the other.

In the *Ṛg-veda* there is a trend towards monotheism – all the different vedic gods are seen as manifestations of the One Reality. The *Upaniṣads* affirm both the personal and non-personal dimensions of the Supreme, with the latter being predominant, but the epics, the *Purāṇas* and the *Bhagavadgītā* (secondary scriptures) focus on the personal dimension of the Supreme in the form of *avatāras*, 'descents' of Viṣṇu (one of the vedic gods) into humanity in various animal, semi-human and human forms, at times of crisis to conquer evil and restore harmony (see 'Viṣṇu', pp. 170–2 below). Some Śaiva texts speak about the *avatāras* of Śiva but these have not played a central role in Śaiva thought.

The Absolute in its formless aspect is far removed from the experience of most people, but the experience of the Absolute in its personal aspect/form is within the reach of all. The Supreme is conceived of as having many attributes, functions, forms, manifestations and names but, at the same time, oneness is seen as the basis of all multiplicity. The Hindu concepts of *Trimūrti* and *avatāra* illustrate the point.

THE DIVINE AS *TRIMŪRTI*

In the epics, the transcendent Being becomes a personal, living God. Images of the Divine, such as creator, sustainer and destroyer of evil, are dominant in the epic literature. The One Reality is seen as having three different but complementary aspects or functions – that of Brahmā who creates, that of Viṣṇu who preserves, and that of Śiva who destroys evil. In the *Upaniṣads*, *brahman* is the cause of the endless cyclic process of creation, preservation, and destruction of evil, but in the epics it is attributed to the three gods of the Hindu Triad. Although each of these gods is assigned a specific role, their functions are not mutually exclusive; they overlap with one another. Though Śiva is primarily the destroyer of evil, he is also seen as Śiva Trimūrti – manifesting the triple aspects of creation, preservation and destruction of evil. Viṣṇu, too, represents all the three functions, though his primary role is the preservation of *dharma*. Though Brahmā is the creator, he is shown in popular iconography as emerging forth from a lotus flower which grows out of Viṣṇu's navel (see Brahmā, Viṣṇu and Śiva below). Each of these gods has a consort who is worshipped in her own right (see 'Feminine images of the Divine', pp. 188ff. below).

AVATĀRA, 'DESCENT' OF THE DIVINE

Although the Ultimate Reality is seen as formless (*nirākāra*), and beyond all thought and speculation, it is seen as assuming forms. The idea of oneness as the basis of the multiplicity of forms is illustrated through the concept of *avatāra*, which literally means 'descent' of the Divine into the world. The Divine takes different forms whenever there is a decline of righteousness, in order to restore harmony and peace (*Bhagavadgītā* 4.7). The significance of the *avatāra* is twofold: the descent of the Divine into the world, and the rise of humanity to a divine consciousness. This concept is particularly applied to Viṣṇu, who has taken various forms to conquer evil. Of all the *avatāras* of Viṣṇu, Rāma and Kṛṣṇa are the most popular and have become the object of devotion and worship. The plurality of forms of the Divine does not diminish the oneness of the Divine; rather it enhances it. As Sri Aurobindo states:

> The Divine Being is not incapable of taking innumerable
> forms because He is beyond all form in His essence,
> nor by assuming them does He lose His divinity,
> but pours out rather in them the delight
> of His being and the glories of His godhead;
> this gold does not cease to be gold because it shapes itself
> into all kinds of ornaments . . .
>
> (Sri Aurobindo, 1955: 765)

In contrast, a monist Hindu philosopher like Śaṃkara may accord only a secondary status to the various forms; they are seen as being relatively real – as having an empirical appearance of reality which is finally negated when one experiences the formless *brahman* or Absolute. But both theist and monist Hindus acknowledge the different approaches to the Divine, although each may look upon their conception as having greater validity.

MANY NAMES OF THE DIVINE

In Hindu worship the Supreme is affirmed through names and forms. The idea of giving many names to the One Reality finds expression in the *Ṛg-veda*, where names of vedic deities such as Indra, Mitra, Varuṇa and Agni refer to the Divine. 'Truth is one but the sages call it by manifold names' (1.164.46). Each of the gods and goddesses has more than one name, each signifying one of the various attributes of the deity. Chanting the name of one's chosen deity (*iṣṭa devatā*) and worshipping God in embodied form are seen as strengthening the personal bond between God and the worshipper. For example, Viṣṇu is known by names such as Nārāyaṇa, Hari and Padmanābha, and Kṛṣṇa is known by names such as Madhusūdana, Gopāla and Janārdana (see Viṣṇu, Kṛṣṇa and other gods).

There are masculine and feminine forms of addressing the Divine. Expressions such as *Paramātman* (the Supreme Self), *Parameśvara* (the Supreme Lord), *Īśvara* (Personal Lord), *Bhagavān* (God), indicate different ways of addressing the Divine. Feminine forms of address such as *Devī* (Goddess) or *Mahādevī* (the Great Goddess) are used in prayer, meditation and worship. Village deities are addressed as *amman*, mother (see 'Village deities', p. 199 below).

ICONIC IMAGES OF THE DIVINE

The variety of names and forms of the Divine is affirmed in worship, dance, music, art, iconography, literature, mythology, folklore and philosophy. In Hindu worship, images play a central role. The Sanskrit word that is commonly used for an iconic image is *mūrti*, but *mūrti* is more than an iconic representation of the deity; it is an embodiment or form of the Divine itself. It suggests more than what one can readily perceive and experience. The infinite attributes and aspects of the Divine, which may appear contradictory to the uninitiated beholder, are reflected, for instance, in the four-armed dancing Śiva with a third eye in the middle of his forehead; Gaṇeśa, the elephant-headed deity with four arms; Subramaṇya with six faces; and Kālī with a garland of skulls around her neck and dancing on her husband Śiva.

The Divine is represented in a variety of ways: fully human (e.g., Rāma); half-human and half-animal (e.g., Gaṇeśa and the Narasiṃha *avatāra* of Viṣṇu); half-male and half-female (e.g., Śiva as Ardhanār-īśvara). All are shown holding various emblems in their hands, symbolizing their power and authority. They are depicted in standing, sitting or dancing positions, with their hands held in *abhaya mudrā* (protective gesture). They are usually shown with their mounts. Animals and birds are associated with various deities as their vehicles, *vāhanas*. For instance, a bull is seen with Śiva, an elephant with Lakṣmī, a swan with Sarasvatī, a peacock with Subramaṇya, a garuḍa with Viṣṇu, a cow with Kṛṣṇa.

Iconographical representations of various gods and goddesses adorn the temple towers (*gopurams*) and walls within the temples of India. Some of the North and South Indian temples are known for their splendid sculptural representations of the deities and of stories from the epics and the *Purāṇas*. The *sanctum sanctorum* (*garba gṛha*), womb of the temple, houses the images, made of stone, metal or wood, to whom worship is offered. Domestic shrines may contain a variety of images made of brass or copper and framed calendar pictures. Even a roadside tea or coffee shop will have a picture of a deity. In the workplace, whether it be school, factory or hotel, one can see calendar pictures of the deities. Most Indian film producers include an invocation to a deity before the actual film is shown. Most drivers of cars, buses, trucks and other vehicles will have pictures of their chosen deities, to whom they offer incense and pray for safe travel. Images made of clay are used on festival occasions, after which they are ceremoniously immersed in a river (see 'Feminine images of the Divine', pp. 188ff. below).

ANICONIC IMAGES OF THE DIVINE

Images such as *liṅga* (Śiva) and *śālagrāma* (Viṣṇu), which do not have any anthropomorphic shape or form, are also the focus of worship in the Hindu tradition. As Diana Eck points out, 'the aniconic images are those symbolic forms which, although they refer to a deity, do not attempt any anthropomorphic form or any representational likeness' (Eck, 1985: 32). The aniconic symbol of Śiva, the *liṅga*, has a central place in Śaiva worship. The word *liṅga* means both 'sign' and 'phallus'; it has various levels of meanings, such as procreation and fertility (see Śiva). Śaiva homes may have a small stone image of the Śiva *liṅga* and small smooth polished stones known as *bāṇaliṅgas* in their *pūjā* (worship) room. Vaiṣṇavas may have small rounded river-worn ammonite stones, *śālagrāmas*, symbolizing Viṣṇu. Other aniconic representations, such as geometrical diagrams called *yantras* and *maṇḍalas*, which function as sacred symbols, are used in tantric worship and meditation. Wayside shrines may have a symbol such as a spear or a stone representing a particular deity. Even a tree or a particular spot is invested with religious significance as all forms of life are seen as sacred. The manifold aspects of nature such as rivers, mountains, trees, plants and flowers are seen as embodiments of divinity. For example, Śiva is associated with the sacred river Ganges; *tulsī* (basil) leaves are offered to Viṣṇu in worship, and *bilva* (wood-apple tree) leaves to Śiva. Of the trees, pipal and banyan are considered particularly sacred.

VEDIC IMAGES OF THE DIVINE

The vedic tradition has a variety of aniconic images, affirming the presence of the Divine in all creation – the sun, moon, sky, fire, storm and various other manifestations of nature. Most of the gods of the vedic pantheon are personifications of nature, such as Sūrya the sun god, Indra the storm-god, Agni the fire-god, Vāyu the wind god and Uṣā the goddess of dawn. The central focus of the vedic tradition was not the image but *yagña* or fire sacrifices (see Agni below) which were offered to the gods, and hymns were chanted during the performance of the ceremony.

THE DIVINE AS *ŚABDA-BRAHMAN*

In the vedic ritual tradition the emphasis was not on visual representation of the gods, but sound (*śabda*). Accurate chanting of hymns and *mantra*s during the performance of sacrificial rituals was important. It is for this reason that the Veda (*śruti*, 'hearing') was transmitted orally and preserved in the form of sound before it came to be written down. Of all sounds, *Auṁ* (OṀ) is the most sacred sound – the primordial sound from which all other sounds have emerged. Therefore the Divine is also seen as *Śabda-brahman* ('the *brahman*-sound, revealed aspect of *brahman*'). In meditation, prayer and worship, sound plays an important part.

THE DIVINE AS AGNI

Agni, the fire-god, is one of the important vedic deities to whom a great number of hymns are addressed. He is described as a friend and companion. He symbolizes warmth, protection and purification. He figures as the messenger of gods and mediator between the gods and humanity. Vedic worship centred on Agni, the divine minister of sacrifice who received sacrificial offerings and carried them to the gods and thus sanctified them.

Although Agni as fire is an aniconic image, he is represented in sculpture as a three-legged deity riding on a ram. The three legs stand for three sacred fires: marriage, ceremonial and sacrificial. He is depicted with one or two faces and seven hands. The two faces symbolize two fires, solar and terrestrial. The seven hands may indicate the all-pervasive quality of Agni. From his mouth emerge flames which receive the sacrificial offerings.

Agni is of central importance in the religious practices of the Arya Samaj, a modern Hindu reform movement founded by Swami Dayananda Sarasvati (who believed in the absolute authority of the Veda and aimed at purifying Hinduism from within). Followers of this sect do not use images in their worship. They perform *havan* or *homa* (fire-offering) instead of *pūjā*. Fire continues to play a central role in most

Hindu ceremonies, particularly marriage and death. For both the sanctification of marriage and the purification of death, Agni is essential.

THE DIVINE AS SŪRYA

Sūrya, the sun god, is seen as dispeller of darkness, both physical and spiritual. He is the source not only of light and warmth, but also of knowledge. In time, other solar divinities, such as Vivasvat and Savitṛ, were merged with Sūrya, and he has many other names which affirm his various attributes. In the *Ṛg-veda* he figures riding across the sky in a golden chariot drawn by splendid horses. Sūrya is represented in this form in the sun temple in Koṇārak, Orissa, where worship is offered to him. He may be depicted standing on a lotus pedestal and holding two lotuses, with a halo round his head. In South Indian representations he is barefooted, whereas the North Indian images show him wearing knee-high boots.

The *Gāyatrī mantra* in the *Ṛg-veda* (3.62.10), in honour of the sun god, is the most sacred *mantra* of the Veda and is repeated by orthodox Brahmans each day at sunrise and sunset. The officiating priest whispers this *mantra* in the ear of the initiate at the sacred thread ceremony, and this marks the beginning of new birth:

> *tat savitur vareṇyaṃ*
> *bhargo devasaya dhīmahi*
> *dhiyo yo naḥ pracodayāt*
>
> ('We meditate upon the glorious splendour of the Vivifier divine. May he himself illumine our minds!').
>
> (Panikkar, 1989: 38)

This *mantra* is uttered in almost all Hindu rites and ceremonies. There are many sacred verses in honour of Sūrya, whose blessings are invoked. *Sūrya-namaskāra* (prostrations to the sun god) are performed in the morning by some Hindus and are seen as promoting the physical and spiritual well-being of those who perform them.

In South Indian temples, worship offered to Sūrya, along with other planets such as Mars, Jupiter and Mercury, known as *Navagraha*(s) (nine planets), is common. Hindus light a *diva* (small clay lamp) and place it before the shrine. It is commonly believed that the position of the planets can have adverse effects on people and therefore they are worshipped.

It is said that Sūrya's wife, Samjñā, had to leave him because she could not bear the intense blazing light of her husband. Leaving behind her shadow (*chhāyā*), she departed for the colder regions in the north. The desperate Sūrya went in search of her and found her. The architect of the gods, Viśvakarma, expressed his desire to refashion Sūrya and urged him to accept his proposal. Viśvakarma created a magnificent and luminous form of Sūrya but his legs remained untouched.

Masculine images of the Divine

The Divine as creator: Brahmā

Brahmā was originally an important member of the Hindu *Trimūrti* or Triad. Brahmā is the creator and lord of the world and all creatures. In popular art and iconography Brahmā is usually shown with four heads (sometimes five; the fifth was burnt off by Śiva's third eye) and four arms, indicating that he is the creator – the cause and source of all creation. The four heads are also seen as representing the four Vedas (sacred scriptures), the four *varṇa*s (classes), the four *āśrama*s (stages of life) and the four *yuga*s (epochs of time). In his hands he is seen holding the sacred scriptures (as the author of sacred knowledge), a string of prayer beads (representing time), a ladle (a sacrificial spoon), and a water jug (symbolizing the water from which all creation has evolved). Brahmā's bearded face shows him as a venerable sage and god of wisdom. He is usually depicted wearing a white garment and his mount is a goose (*haṃsa*), a symbol of discrimination and creative power.

In the Veda Brahmā figures as the creator, the lord of sacrifice and father of gods. In the *Purāṇa*s he is conceived of as having sprung from the golden cosmic egg. In mythology he is subordinated to Viṣṇu and Śiva, whose help he often seeks. He is represented as emerging from a lotus which sprang out of Viṣṇu's navel.

Although he is the creator, Brahmā occupies a less prominent place when it comes to worship. Unlike Viṣṇu and Śiva he has no devotees. He figures in temple sculptures but there is perhaps only one temple in India dedicated to Brahmā, at Puskara in Rajasthan.

The Divine as preserver and sustainer: Viṣṇu

Viṣṇu, the preserver and sustainer of the world, is the second member of the *Trimūrti*. He is conceived of as the cosmic god, Nārāyaṇa, 'moving in the waters', pervading the whole universe. He is often shown in iconography seated or reclining on a seven-headed snake called Śeṣa, or Ananta ('the Endless'), floating in the middle of an ocean, signifying a state of complete absorption before creation begins. In this representation he is also known as Ananta-śāyana ('who sleeps on the serpent Ananta'), and is seen with his consort Lakṣmī massaging his feet with devotion and Brahmā (creator) seated in a lotus emerging from his navel. Viṣṇu in this reclining posture is worshipped in the Southern Indian Vaiṣṇava temple at Srirangam.

Viṣṇu is also shown in standing posture. The symbols he carries in his four hands are of enormous significance. The white conch shell (*śaṅkha*) signifies the primeval sound of creation and victory over the demons, the rotating wheel (*cakra*) which he uses to confront and conquer adverse forces shows him as a sustainer of the world and represents the cycle of time, the golden mace (*kaumodakī*) is a symbol of his royal power and authority, and the lotus flower (*padma*) symbolizes purity, perfection and the unfolding of forms (also associated with other gods and goddesses). The Vaiṣṇava sign of three vertical lines is worn in the centre of the forehead by the followers of Viṣṇu. Viṣṇu's *vahana*, or vehicle, is Garuḍa, an enormous bird, partly human and partly eagle. Garuḍa, the king of the birds, is seen as the destroyer of evil and is one of the manifestations of Viṣṇu himself (see 'Lakṣmī', pp. 191–4 below).

Viṣṇu is also represented in the form of a *śālagrāma*, a river-worn ammonite shell which is spiral or rounded in shape, which is seen as a 'natural form' (*svarūpa*) of Viṣṇu. It is said that Lord Viṣṇu appeared in the form of *śālagrāma* stones on the Gaṇḍakī river bed in answer to the prayer of the river goddess, Gaṅgā, who desired that Viṣṇu be born in her womb. Viṣṇu is worshipped in this form along with his other *avatāra*s, especially Rāma and Kṛṣṇa.

Viṣṇu has a thousand names (*sahasra-nāma*), each of which affirms one of his attributes. It is a common practice among Hindus to chant the manifold names of their chosen deities. Chanting the thousand names of Viṣṇu is seen as purifying and awakening one's spiritual consciousness. In Vaiṣṇava and other temples, chanting is done in the early hours of the morning.

Viṣṇu, as his names suggest, is one who pervades and sustains the world. As Nārāyaṇa, he is associated with water; as Hari, with saving activity; and as Padmanābha, with creation. As Nīlameghaśyamā, the blue sky, he signifies the all-pervasive nature of being.

Viṣṇu's love and compassion are manifested in his *avatāra*s ('descents' into the world whenever righteousness declines, to restore harmony and peace – *dharma*). Of the three gods of the Hindu Triad, Viṣṇu alone assumes various forms – animal, semi-human and human – to conquer evil. According to the *Bhāgavata Purāṇa*, Viṣṇu's *avatāra*s are twenty-two, but the standard list is ten. The myths surrounding these *avatāra*s are many. Viṣṇu incarnated himself as a fish (*matsya*) to save Manu, the first ancestor, from a flood; as a tortoise (*kūrma*) to support a mountain on his back so that the gods and demons could churn the ocean to retrieve the lost divine treasure, the nectar of immortality, *amṛta*; as a boar (*vārāha*) to raise on his tusks the earth, which had been pushed down into the depths of ocean by a demon; as a man-lion (*narasiṃha*) to destroy the demon king Hiraṇyakaṣipu (who could not be killed by either a man or a beast) who inflicted untold suffering on his son Prahlāda, an ardent devotee of Viṣṇu; as a dwarf (*vāmana*) to restore the harmony of the earth (which was threatened by King Bali; when Bali granted Viṣṇu's request to take the space covered by his three steps, the dwarfish *avatāra* assumed a gigantic form and took three steps – two covering the earth and the third being placed on Bali). As Paraśurāma, Viṣṇu appears as a militant Brahman who destroys the *kṣatriya*s; as Rāma, the seventh incarnation of Viṣṇu, he restores the ideal of *kṣatriya* (warrior) and justice. Viṣṇu in the form of Rāma figures as the ideal prince, ruler, husband, son. Viṣṇu in the form of Kṛṣṇa is perhaps the most complete expression of God's humanity and divinity. The Buddha, who opposed brahmanical orthodoxy and ritualism, is the ninth *avatāra* and the tenth, Kalkin, is yet to come. The anthropomorphic and other images of Viṣṇu are usually represented on the walls of a Vaiṣṇava temple. The saving activity of Viṣṇu through his ten *avatāra*s (*Daśāvatāra*) is given a significant place in the South Indian classical dance, *Bharatanatyam*.

In Viṣṇu, one finds the most complete expression of a loving and compassionate god. In the *Ṛg-veda* he is a minor god, but he becomes an important member of the Triad in the epics and the *Purāṇa*s. In the *Padma Purāṇa* Viṣṇu represents all the triple aspects (creation, preservation and destruction of evil), although his primary function is the preservation of the divine order.

RĀMA AS SUSTAINER OF *DHARMA*

Rāmacandra, or Rāma, the seventh incarnation of Viṣṇu, is the subject of the epic, the *Rāmāyaṇa*. In some iconographical representations he is shown standing with a bow (*śārṅga*) in his left hand. The bow symbolizes valour and strength. Rāma succeeded at a contest in breaking the bow of Śiva given to Sītā's father, King Janaka, and thereby won the hand of Sītā. In popular art and temples Rāma is usually shown with his wife Sītā, his brother, Lakṣmaṇa, and the monkey-god, Hanumān.

Rāma emerges as a son obedient to his father (going willingly into exile), as a husband devoted to his wife Sītā, as a valiant prince who rescues Sītā from the hands of the demon king Rāvaṇa, and as an ideal ruler. The purpose of Rāma *avatāra* was to establish *dharma*, justice and peace in society. Gandhi used the concept of *Rāma Rājya* (kingdom of justice on earth) in his non-violent struggles against all forms of oppression and injustice.

Rāma's wife, Sītā, figures as a devoted and faithful wife who follows him into the forest. Both Rāma and Sītā are seen as ideal partners in marriage, embodying all the ideal qualities of manhood and womanhood. The Hindu festival *Daśarā* (also known as *Navarātri* and *Durgā-pūjā*) is associated with the victory of Rāma over the demon Rāvaṇa. It is said that Rāma prayed to the goddess Durgā before embarking on his expedition to defeat Rāvaṇa. On this day effigies of Rāvaṇa are burned and the story of the *Rāmāyaṇa* is enacted on the stage. Some Hindus associate *Diwālī* with the return of Rāma and Sītā to their kingdom Ayodhyā, to be crowned as king and queen after vanquishing Rāvaṇa. The festival of *Rāma Navamī* commemorates the birth of Rāma and is celebrated by Hindus in most parts of India, especially by Vaiṣṇavas.

In personal devotions, meditations and prayers, names of gods and goddesses are used as *mantra* (sacred word) to attain peace. Gandhi believed in the efficacy of the Rām *mantra*.

HANUMĀN AS AN IDEAL DEVOTEE

Hanumān, the monkey-god, the friend and devotee of Rāma and Sītā, figures in the *Rāmāyaṇa*. In popular representations he is shown kneeling at the feet of Rāma, showing his devotion and love. Another popular representation shows Hanumān flying through the air, carrying a mountain containing medicinal herbs to cure Rāma's brother who was wounded in the battle against Rāvaṇa. He helps Rāma to recover his wife Sītā from Rāvaṇa's captivity. Being the son of the wind god, he leaps into the air, travels swiftly and performs extraordinary feats to vanquish Rāvaṇa. He is known for his agility, strength, valour, steadfastness and devotion to Rāma. The relationship between Rāma and Hanumān is one of mutual affection. The epic has scenes where Rāma demonstrates his love for his devotee by embracing him. In some representations Hanumān is shown tearing open his chest with both his hands, revealing Rāma and Sītā. This picture shows Hanumān's devotion to Rāma, as well as the idea that God resides in our hearts. Hanumān is worshipped in his own right, and his *mantra* is said to help one overcome fear of any kind. The birthday of Hanumān (*Hanumān Jayanti*) is celebrated especially in Delhi and in certain parts of South India.

Kṛṣṇa

Kṛṣṇa, the eighth *avatāra*, is considered the most complete incarnation of Viṣṇu. Kṛṣṇa is pictured as divine child, friend, beloved, teacher, master and so on. *Smṛti* literature (the *Mahābhārata*, the *Bhagavad-gītā* and the *Bhāgavata Purāṇa*) offers splendid insights into the many-faceted personality of Kṛṣṇa. There is only passing reference to the name Kṛṣṇa in the *Ṛg-veda* and the *Upaniṣads*. It is in the epic *Mahābhārata* that Kṛṣṇa assumes a central role as a god in his own right.

Kṛṣṇa means 'the dark one' or 'black'. The colour is seen as indicating his non-Aryan origins. In popular pictures he is blue – the colour of the sky and oceans – symbolizing the endless and infinite nature of the Supreme.

KṚṢṆA AS DIVINE CHILD

Kṛṣṇa figures as a mischievous but enchanting child. His early youth and adult years are the subject of classical and popular music, dance, art and literature. His miraculous birth and early years are recorded in the *Purāṇas*. As divine child he evokes maternal love in mothers, who find it emotionally and spiritually satisfying to worship Kṛṣṇa in that form. This kind of relationship between God and his devotee is known as *vatsalya bhava*. In popular pictures he may be shown eating butter or stealing it, along with his friends. He may also be seen in a crawling position or holding a sweet cake in one of his hands. On Kṛṣṇa's birthday, a picture or an image of the infant Kṛṣṇa becomes the focus of devotion and worship. Sometimes a bronze or silver image of Kṛṣṇa in a swing may be used. That the idea of God as divine child appeals to the Hindu mind is evident from the way Kṛṣṇa's *janamaśtamī* (birthday) is celebrated by Hindus in their homes and temples, especially at Mathura (the birthplace of Kṛṣṇa) and Vrindavan (where Kṛṣṇa is said to have spent his early years). Tiny footprints of baby Kṛṣṇa are drawn with white or coloured powder all along the hallway leading to the *pūjā* (worship) room.

Hindus are fond of listening to stories about Kṛṣṇa's childhood or watching them being enacted on the stage. One of the most delightful and awe-inspiring stories is about Kṛṣṇa eating clay. Kṛṣṇa's friends report it to his foster-mother Yaśodā. Kṛṣṇa convinces his mother that he has not eaten clay and opens his mouth to show that he is not up to any mischief. Yaśodā sees the whole universe in Kṛṣṇa's mouth and herself with Kṛṣṇa on her knee. Yaśodā is as awe-struck as Arjuna is in the *Bhagavadgītā* when Kṛṣṇa reveals his cosmic form, *viśvarūpa* (see 'Kṛṣṇa as the Immanent and Transcendent God', pp. 177–8 below).

The image of divine child helps one to approach God with the freedom and spontaneity of a child. A mother's love for her child is uninhibited and the child is not bound by social norms or conventions; it responds to its mother's love in a spontaneous manner. Kṛṣṇa in the form of an infant and a child invites devotees to abandon all formality and approach him openly.

KṚṢṆA AS A YOUNG COWHERD

In the *Purāṇas* Kṛṣṇa emerges as cowherd (Kṛṣṇa Gopāla), playing melodious music on his flute and thus ravishing the hearts of the *gopīs* (cowherd girls); even peacocks are said to dance to his music. He is sometimes shown standing beside a cow, playing the flute and surrounded by birds and animals. In this form he is also known as Veṇugopāla ('cowherd with flute'). Popular and miniature paintings portray Kṛṣṇa in his pastoral setting, and his childhood and boyhood days offer an endless variety of images. Kṛṣṇa dancing on the poisonous snake Kāliya shows him as a conqueror of evil. The snake has poisoned the holy river Yamunā with its venom, making the water lethal and unfit for consumption. He fights with the snake, in whose coils he becomes enmeshed, but frees himself, takes hold of the tail of the snake and stands on its hood and dances. He does not kill the snake but pushes it into the ocean where it can harm no one.

Another popular image of Kṛṣṇa Gopāla shows Kṛṣṇa lifting the mountain Govardhana (near Mathura) with one hand and sheltering the inhabitants from angry thunderstorms, severe winds and rain unleashed by the god Indra. In both these representations Kṛṣṇa is seen as a protector and sustainer.

KṚṢṆA AS BELOVED

Kṛṣṇa is also seen as the eternal beloved, inspiring intense devotion and the longing of the soul to merge with him. In popular iconography and Rajput miniature paintings, Kṛṣṇa is seen dancing with the *gopīs*, who long to be united with him. Kṛṣṇa's dance with the *gopīs* is known as *Rāsalīlā*. *Rāsa*, in this context, refers to 'emotional delight' and *līlā* to 'play' or 'sport'. Kṛṣṇa's sport with the *gopīs* symbolizes the soul's deep yearning to be united with the Divine (Kṛṣṇa). He multiplies himself innumerable times to make himself accessible to each of the *gopīs*; each is led to believe that she alone is dancing with Kṛṣṇa.

Kṛṣṇa is usually shown with his favourite *gopī*, Rādhā, playing on a swing. Kṛṣṇa is also depicted sitting on a high branch of a tree, having stolen the garments of the *gopīs* while they are bathing; they have come to him to fetch their clothes. This highly erotic scene is interpreted as meaning that one has to be spiritually naked, to abandon all shame and honour in the presence of the Divine.

In the *bhakti* tradition, the image of the Divine as beloved has a central place. The senses are not rejected but turned towards the Divine to experience mystical love, as in the amorous *Rāsalīlā* dance where Kṛṣṇa makes himself available to each of his devotees. Even male devotees need to suspend their masculinity to relate to Kṛṣṇa as their eternal beloved. Bengali *bhakti* poets such as Jayadeva (twelfth century) and Chandi Das (fifteenth century) were inspired by the divine–human love expressed in the relationship between Kṛṣṇa and

Rādhā, and their poetry is replete with such images of passionate love. The South Indian devotional hymns of Āḷvārs are known for their intense fervour. The hymns of the Āḷvār saint Andal, who looked upon herself as one of the *gopīs*, express her intense devotion to Kṛṣṇa. They are sung by women, especially young girls who look forward to happy marriages.

It is not uncommon to find the concept of God as the husband and the devotee as bride (*mathura bhava*). This is best exemplified in the relationship of the sixteenth-century Rajput saint Mirabai to Kṛṣṇa. Her intense spiritual yearning and love for Kṛṣṇa come alive in her devotional songs.

> Come to my house, O Krishna,
> Thy coming will bring peace.
> Great will be my joy if I meet Thee,
> And all my desires will be fulfilled.
> Thou and I are one,
> Like the sun and its heat.
> Mira's heart cares for nothing else,
> I want only the beautiful Shyām.
>
> (Alston, 1980: 80)

KṚṢṆA AS FRIEND, TEACHER AND LIBERATOR

While in the *Purāṇas* Kṛṣṇa emerges as a delightful and energetic youth, in the *Mahābhārata* he assumes the stature of an epic hero. In the *Bhagavadgītā*, which is part of the *Mahābhārata*, Kṛṣṇa figures as a divine teacher and friend to Arjuna in the guise of a charioteer. Kṛṣṇa takes the side of the Pāṇḍavas, who were unfairly cheated in a game of dice by their cousins, the Kauravas. In his dialogue with Arjuna, Kṛṣṇa addresses him as a friend and instils confidence in the warrior Arjuna who is reluctant to fight against his cousins. As a *guru*, or spiritual teacher, he shows the path that is appropriate for Arjuna but does not force it upon him. The opening chapter of the *Bhagavadgītā* offers us a visual image of the divine–human encounter – Kṛṣṇa and Arjuna in a chariot in the middle of a battlefield. The iconographic representation of this scene has become popular since the last century, when the *Bhagavadgītā* was used (to encourage selfless commitment to the cause of freedom) during the struggle for Indian independence.

Kṛṣṇa's role as a gracious lord and liberator is pronounced in the *Bhagavadgītā*. One of his names is Janāradana, meaning liberator. Kṛṣṇa tells Arjuna:

> Even if a man of the most vile conduct worships me with undistracted devotion, he must be reckoned as righteous for he has rightly resolved.
>
> (*Bhagavadgītā* 9.30)

> And whoever, at the time of death, gives up his body and departs, thinking of Me alone, he comes to My Status (of being); of that there is no doubt.
>
> (*Bhagavadgītā* 8.5)[1]

KṚṢṆA AS THE IMMANENT AND TRANSCENDENT GOD

The *Bhagavadgītā* affirms the immanent and transcendent dimensions of Kṛṣṇa. The tenth chapter gives a vivid picture of Kṛṣṇa as both the eternal and personal Lord. Although 'unborn', the Supreme is seen as the source of all forms. Kṛṣṇa tells Arjuna that he is the beginning and end of the entire universe and that the world is strung on him like pearls on a string (7.7). He is the nucleus of all things, both animate and inanimate. Things of beauty, strength and spiritual power have sprung from a fragment of his splendour (10.41):

> [I am] the goal, the upholder, the lord, the witness, the abode, the refuge and the friend. [I am] the origin and the dissolution, the ground, the resting place and the imperishable seed.
>
> (*Bhagavadgītā* 9.18)

> There is no end to My divine manifestations . . . What has been declared by Me is only illustrative of My infinite glory.
>
> (*Bhagavadgītā* 10.40)

The eleventh chapter of the *Bhagavadgītā* presents us with a glorious and terrifying cosmic form or *viśvarūpa* of Viṣṇu. The immanence and transcendence of Kṛṣṇa are revealed to Arjuna, who seeks to know the truth. Kṛṣṇa discloses his infinite forms, with innumerable mouths, arms, thighs, feet, bellies – all blazing with glory. Kṛṣṇa emerges as the

Supreme Person, who is both divine and human. Arjuna, who grasps this truth, utters:

> I behold Thee with Thy crown, mace and discus,
> glowing everywhere as a mass of light, hard to
> discern, (dazzling) on all sides with the radiance
> of the flaming fire and sun, incomparable.
>
> Thou art the Imperishable, the Supreme to be realized.
> Thou art the ultimate resting-place of the universe;
> Thou art the undying guardian of the eternal law.
> Thou art the Primal Person, I think.
>
> (*Bhagavadgītā* 11.17 and 18)

Kṛṣṇa in the form of Jagannāth ('Lord of the Universe') is the focus of worship in Puri, Orissa. The large wooden images of Jagannāth, his sister, Subdharā, and brother, Balarāma, are taken out yearly in a grand ceremonial procession in three beautifully decorated *raths*, chariots, on the festival of *Rathayātrā*. This festival is also celebrated in a grand manner by the International Society for Krishna Consciousness (also known as Hare Krishna).

The Kṛṣṇa temple at Guruvayur in the south-western state of Kerala is also one of the major pilgrim centres. It is known for the healing powers of Kṛṣṇa, and even today many visit the temple to seek the grace of the lord of Guruvayur. The central shrine contains the image of Kṛṣṇa standing with a crown and four arms: holding a conch, a *cakra*, a club and a lotus, symbols often shown in images of Viṣṇu. The temple is open to Hindus of all castes, and many Hindus wish to be married in the Guruvayur temple.

Śiva

If Viṣṇu has many *avatāras*, Śiva has many aspects, and is more complex than Viṣṇu. Śiva's origins go back to the pre-Aryan period. The images of Śiva as father-god, lord of animals and ascetic are seen to be pre-vedic. One of the Harappan seals depicts a three-faced deity seated cross-legged and deep in meditation, surrounded by animals. This yogic figure corresponds with the later conceptions of Śiva as Mahāyogin (the great ascetic), as Pāśupati (lord of the beasts), and as having three eyes and a trident. Śiva is identified with the Rudra of the

Veda, who is both a destructive and a beneficent deity. The vedic storm-god Rudra has developed into a great god, Śiva, merging with pre-vedic god-concepts.

ŚIVA AS *TRIMŪRTI*

Śiva seems to hold together all opposites, tensions and contradictions in a variety of ways. Although he is primarily the destroyer of evil, he is also portrayed in the three-fold form, *Trimūrti*, as creator, preserver and destroyer of evil. The Mahādeva image in the Elephanta Caves in Bombay shows Śiva representing these triple aspects. The three faces also represent the masculine and feminine aspects – the face to the left shows Śiva in his terrifying aspect (*bhairava*) and the face to the right shows his gentler nature. The silent and serene face in the centre harmonizes the two aspects of terror and love – the Supreme that transcends all contradictions.

The elaboration of this concept of *Trimūrti* is seen as an attempt to harmonize Vaiṣṇavism and Śaivism. Vaiṣṇavas look upon Viṣṇu as the supreme god and Śiva as an emanation or creation of Viṣṇu, while Śaivas regard Śiva as the high god and Viṣṇu as an emanation of Śiva. They were occasionally at loggerheads over this issue, but generally Vaiṣṇavas and Śaivas have lived together without friction, acknowledging that both Viṣṇu and Śiva are manifestations of the same Divine Being. Another significant attempt at such a synthesis is seen in the representation of Śiva as Harihara, Hari being a title of Viṣṇu and Hara of Śiva. In Sangameshvara temple in Mysore, Śiva is depicted in sculpture as Harihara. The holy city of Hardwar is associated with both Śiva and Viṣṇu. The holy river Ganges flows through the hair of Śiva and the feet of Viṣṇu, so it is sacred to both Śaivas and Vaiṣṇavas.

ŚIVA AS NAṬARĀJA

Śiva has many names and one of the best-known is Naṭarāja, the Lord of the Dance. In this aspect Śiva is associated with the arts. Exponents of Indian classical dance look upon him as the supreme dancer who revealed the rules of the sacred dance to men and women. As Lord of the Dance, Śiva symbolizes the cosmic energy that flows through and sustains the world and the universe. The eternal dance involves the destruction of evil, which brings about new creation. In this form he performs all the three functions – creation, preservation and destruction of evil. Unlike the ascetic Śiva, whose hair is collected in a top-knot, the dancing Śiva has his hair loose. It symbolizes power, strength and energy. While the ascetic Śiva conserves his energy, the dancing Śiva releases it – and both for the good of the world. All apparent tensions are held in a harmonious unison.

The four-armed dancing Śiva in the renowned South Indian temple at Cidambaram holds a drum and a fire-ball in two of his hands (Figure 7.1). The drum symbolizes rhythm and sound – both are associated with creation. Sound is associated with ether, one of the five elements of the universe (the others being air, fire, water and earth). The fire-ball and the circle of flames around Śiva symbolize the destruction of the world. He is the symbol of life and death and the renewal of life. The hand in an upright gesture, *abhaya mudrā*, signifies grace and protection, and the one pointing to his feet signifies that liberation is open to all those who seek refuge in him. He has one foot on a demon, symbolizing the triumph over evil, ignorance or ego. The dynamic movements of his body stand in sharp contrast to his serene yogic face.

An invocatory hymn in praise of Lord Naṭarāja precedes any South Indian classical dance. All fine arts, including dance, have a spiritual dimension to them. *Devadāsī*s ('servants of God') were married to the gods, and they sought union with God through dance. Even today a devoted dancer sees her dance as a spiritual journey leading to the Divine.

ŚIVA AS *YOGI* AND *GṚHASTHA*

Śiva figures as a great *yogi* (ascetic) and a *gṛhastha* (householder). He symbolizes both renunciation and affirmation of life. Both as ascetic and householder he is the source of life. The ascetic Śiva is represented seated in a yogic posture (cross-legged) on a tiger-skin, with prayer beads and a mendicant's bowl. The third eye in the middle of his forehead is interpreted as the eye of wisdom and enlightenment. The snake around his neck shows his association with death and his power to retain sexual energy. He holds in his left hand a trident (symbol of power) which represents the triple aspects of Śiva as creator, preserver

Figure 7.1 Śiva as Naṭarāja, Lord of the Dance (by Kathy Wedell)

and destroyer. His right hand is held in *abhaya mudrā* (upright position), assuring protection. The three horizontal marks in the middle of his forehead also indicate the three functions of Śiva. Śaivas may wear this mark on their foreheads. His long matted hair, raised up in a top-knot with a crescent moon on it (symbol of creation) and water flowing from it, brings out the dual nature of Śiva: serenity and dynamism. Śiva retains and releases his energy for the benefit of the world. Sometimes a small figure of the goddess Gaṅgā is seen on his top-knot, showing Śiva's close association with the river Ganges. In order to reduce the forceful impact of the flow of the river Ganges upon the earth, Śiva allows the river to flow smoothly through his hair, thus fertilizing the earth. The river Ganges is *śakti*, or the feminine aspect of Śiva.

In the South Indian Mīnākṣī temple in Madurai, Śiva is known as Sundraeśvara and his consort is Mīnākṣī. In popular art Śiva is seen with his wife Pārvatī and their children Gaṇeśa and Kārttikeya (also known as Skanda or Murugan). Śiva nourishes and sustains the world, both as a householder (*gṛhastha*) and as an ascetic (*saṃnyāsin*), these two stages being the second and fourth in the pattern of Hindu life.

ŚIVA AS DAKṢIṆĀMŪRTI

As a universal *guru* or spiritual teacher Śiva is known as Dakṣiṇāmūrti. As expounder of sacred knowledge he is known as Jñāna Dakṣiṇāmūrti (*jñāna* means 'knowledge', *dakṣiṇa*, south, and *mūrti*, image of the deity). He is depicted seated facing south, his right foot resting on a demon (symbolizing ignorance), and his left foot on his right thigh and his right hand in a *mudrā* (gesture) of explanation. Śiva's various other names, such as Vīṇādhara Dakṣiṇāmūrti (teacher of music), Yoga Dakṣiṇāmūrti (teacher and master of *yoga*), show him as the patron of all the arts.

ŚIVA AS MASCULINE AND FEMININE

Śiva is also depicted iconographically as *Ardhanāri* (half-female and half-male), symbolizing the union of the feminine and masculine. One of the myths in the *Śiva Purāṇa* tells that Śiva assumed this form to help Brahmā complete the task of creation. Brahmā created a number of males to begin the work of creation but his mission was unsuccessful. Hearing his prayers, Śiva appeared in the androgynous form of Ardhanārīśvara. On seeing Śiva in this form, Brahmā realized that without the creation of the female, he could not complete his task. Without the activating power of the feminine principle (*śakti*) creation will remain incomplete. This myth conveys the upanisadic idea of the divine being both male and female (*Bṛhādaraṇyaka Upaniṣad* 1.4.3).

In Śaiva temples Śiva is worshipped in the form of *liṅga* (a phallic symbol) in association with *yoni* (womb). It is cylindrical in shape with a rounded top rising out of a horizontal base, the *yoni*. This symbol lends itself to a variety of interpretations. It is seen as symbolizing the union and co-existence of the male and female principles. The *liṅga* represents creativity at all levels: biological, psychological, spiritual and cosmic. In some of the temple sculptures, the *liṅga* is depicted with the face of Śiva (*Mukhaliṅga*) or four faces (*Caturmukha*) – and the fifth face represented by the *liṅga*. The five-faced *liṅga* represents the five elements of the universe.

Liṅga is the most important symbol of Śiva and the main object of Śaiva worship. The holy city of Kāśī, meaning 'luminous' or 'shining' (also known as Banaras or Varanasi), is dotted with *liṅga*s and numerous shrines to Śiva. The city itself is seen as a *liṅga* of light. It is said that Śiva's *liṅga*, a fiery column of light, arose from the nether-worlds, piercing the earth and sky at Kāśī. Here the Divine has manifested itself in the form of *liṅga*, so the city is seen as the very embodiment of Śiva himself. To die in Kāśī is seen as being sanctified and purified of all sins.[2]

On the festival of *Śivarātri*, Hindus fast and sing hymns in praise of Śiva. Śaiva temples all over India are crowded with devotees who come to offer their devotions and have a *darśan* (view or glimpse) of Śiva and receive *prasāda* (blessed food).

Śiva's mount, the sacred bull Nandi, is found in Śaiva temples, usually at the entrance, facing the shrine. It is Śiva in his animal form, symbolizing fertility.

The veneration of the *liṅga* was common among non-Aryan peoples and later became the most important form of worship among the Śaivas.

Gaṇeśa

GAṆEŚA AS REMOVER OF OBSTACLES

Gaṇeśa is one of the most popular Hindu deities worshipped all over India. He is represented as a pot-bellied deity with four (or more) arms and the head of an elephant, but with a single tusk, and accompanied by a mouse (see Figure 7.2). The elephant-head is seen as signifying macrocosm, and his body, microcosm. In other words, the half-

Figure 7.2 Gaṇeśa as remover of obstacles (by Usha Azad)

elephant and half-human form of Gaṇeśa stands for the cosmic and human dimensions of existence. His large belly is seen as containing within it the entire created world. It also signifies prosperity.

Gaṇeśa may be shown in various postures: sitting, standing or dancing. In some iconographical representations he may be shown with two tusks (one whole and one broken), and holding in his hands a goad, noose, rosary and the broken tusk. The unbroken tusk symbolizes the unmanifest Truth and the broken one represents the manifest world. Both the abstract and manifest world are two aspects of the One Reality. The noose indicates the need to restrain desires and passions, the goad is a symbol of authority and the rosary is associated with Śaiva meditation and mendicants. In some representations Gaṇeśa may be shown holding a sweetmeat in one of his hands, indicating his fondness for sweets, and his right hand is usually in *abhaya mudrā*, assuring protection. The swastika is a symbol also associated with Gaṇeśa; it represents good luck. His large fan-like ears signify his willingness to listen to problems. The elephant trunk symbolizes Gaṇeśa's role as remover of obstacles, and his mount, a mouse, is seen as performing the task of removing obstacles by drilling holes and finding its way to its destination. Both the elephant and the mouse, in different ways, remove obstacles on the way. On the other hand, the mouse is also an obstacle to our undertakings. Gaṇeśa's task is to create and remove obstacles. His association with the mouse shows that he cares for even the most ordinary creatures.

Gaṇeśa is also represented as the master of the arts. He is depicted in a graceful dancing pose. In this form he is called Nṛttagaṇapati (dancing Gaṇeśa). He is also worshipped in aniconic forms such as *yantra*s (geometrical diagrams), *liṅga*s and *kalaśa*s (pots of water).

Gaṇeśa is sometimes shown with his two wives, Siddhi and Ṛddhi. Siddhi symbolizes success and Ṛddhi prosperity. Gaṇeśa is known by many names but most commonly called Piḷḷaiyār ('the son or the young elephant') or Gaṇapati ('lord of the group'), especially in South India. Some of his names give a visual picture of the deity. He is called Gajānana ('elephant-faced'), Ekadanta ('single tusked'), Lambodara ('pot-bellied'), Vighneśvara ('lord of obstacles'), Vināyaka ('leader'). He is also known as lord of learning or wisdom. The Gāṇapatyas sect (in South and Western India) look upon him as their supreme deity and offer special devotions to him.

As Gaṇeśa is the remover of obstacles, his blessings are invoked before embarking on any new venture, whether it be buying a house, applying for a job or going on a journey. Most Śaiva temples in India have shrines to Gaṇeśa. Both rural and urban India have countless shrines to Gaṇeśa. Sometimes he is comfortably seated under a banyan tree. Most students pay a visit to his shrine just before exams to pray for success, and offer coconuts to Gaṇeśa on passing their exams.

GAṆEŚA AS GUARDIAN DEITY

There are many legends associated with the birth and beheading of Gaṇeśa. According to one of them, Pārvatī created Gaṇeśa from the scurf of her body. She asked him to guard the house while she had her bath. In the meantime, Śiva arrived but was refused entry into the house by Gaṇeśa. A quarrel ensued between the two and Śiva cut off Gaṇeśa's head. Pārvatī was annoyed and demanded that her son should be brought back to life. Śiva replaced Gaṇeśa's lost head with the head of an elephant with a single tusk, as this was the first one his attendants chanced upon, and made Gaṇeśa the lord of his attendants. Gaṇeśa's role as a guardian deity and remover of obstacles is further enhanced by his newly acquired elephant-head which has close associations with the elephant symbolism in Indian culture. Elephants are associated with Hindu deities and guard the door of temples, and lead religious and royal processions.

The festival of *Gaṇeśa Caturthī* celebrates the birth of Gaṇeśa and is popular in most parts of India, particularly in western, central and southern India. Small and large clay images of Gaṇeśa are made for the festival and worship is offered to them. This festival is celebrated in a grand style in and around Bombay. Large clay images of Gaṇeśa are carried out in a ceremonial procession through the crowded streets and eventually to the seashore in Bombay and immersed in the sea.

Skanda as Devasenāpati, Subramaṇya and Ṣaṇmukha

Skanda, the second son of Śiva and Pārvatī, is a complete contrast to his brother, Gaṇeśa. He is young and handsome. He is usually depicted (see Figure 7.3) with two (or four) hands, holding a sword and a spear, symbolizing his triumph over the demons. In other words, it signifies the destruction of ignorance. He may be shown standing by, or seated on, a peacock, in whose legs a snake lies entangled. The snake

Figure 7.3 Skanda and his vehicle, the peacock (by Usha Azad)

symbolizes time and the peacock the transcendence of time and all dualities. The peacock also signifies the beauty and splendour of all creation. Skanda is sometimes seen with his two consorts, Vallī and Devasenā.

Skanda figures as Devasenāpati, the god of war and a military commander. He was born in order to destroy the demon Tārakā. He is more popular in South India than in the North. He is known as Subramaṇya ('one who tends the spiritual growth of the aspirants') and more popularly as Murugan in the South. He is also known as Kumāra (Prince). Most temples to Murugan in South India are situated on a hill-top. The Murugan temple in Palani in South India is a well-known pilgrimage place. The Skanda Vale ashram in rural Wales is a place of spiritual retreat and worship and has become an important pilgrimage centre for Hindus in the United Kingdom.

It is said that Skanda was brought up by six divine mothers of the star Kṛttika (Pleiades), and therefore came to be called Ṣaṇmukha (six-faced) and Kārttikeya. In this form he is shown with six faces and twelve arms. The six faces of this deity symbolize six divine attributes and six seats of spiritual consciousness. The twelve hands indicate his power and capacity to accomplish all kinds of tasks.

Feminine images of the Divine

The Divine is perceived and experienced as both male and female. The *Upaniṣads* affirm the masculine and feminine dimensions of the Divine and the spiritual equality of both male and female. The feminine Divine is seen as *śakti* or energy (see p. 189) and is of central importance in tantric tradition. Feminine images of the Divine such as virgin (*kumārī*), consort, mother, daughter, warrior, sustainer, and as both love and terror, are represented in worship, art, literature and iconography. The female counterparts of the male gods Brahmā, Viṣṇu and Śiva are Sarasvatī, Lakṣmī and Pārvatī (and her other forms, Durgā and Kālī), who are associated with wisdom, wealth and power respectively, and are worshipped in their own right.

THE DIVINE AS VIRGIN

The image of the Divine as a virgin, or *kanyā kumārī*, is represented in a South Indian temple in Kanya Kumari (formerly Cape Comorin). Although Kanyā Kumārī is unmarried, she is said to answer the prayers of those who wish to be married. She is an embodiment of *śakti*, or divine energy, and her virgin status signifies her creative power.

THE DIVINE AS *ŚAKTI*

The many goddesses are seen as many aspects or manifestations of the one supreme principle or energy known as *śakti*, the feminine power, usually addressed as Devī (Goddess) or Mahādevī (the Great Goddess) – the ground and centre of all creation and existence. The well-known text *Devi-māhātmya* ('The Exaltation of the Goddess'), of the sixth century CE, affirms the primacy of the feminine power or *śakti*. *Śakti* is known by various names. She is linked to the masculine as *śakti*, or power inherent in it, without which the male principle is incomplete. Without the activating power of *śakti*, Śiva is said to be incomplete. In her gracious form she is Mahālakṣmī and Mahāsarasvatī, and in her terrible form she is Mahākālī. As Mahāsarasvatī she is the goddess of supreme knowledge, as Mahālakṣmī she is the goddess of supreme love and grace and as Mahākālī she is the goddess of supreme strength who conquers evil and is the embodiment and reconciliation of all apparent opposites. In both her benign and terrible forms she offers comfort and solace.

Sarasvatī as bestower of knowledge and wisdom

Sarasvatī, the consort of Brahmā, is the goddess of wisdom and fine arts. She is usually depicted with four arms, holding a stringed musical instrument called a *vīnā* with two hands (symbol of the arts), and manuscripts (symbol of wisdom and learning), and a string of prayer beads (see Figure 7.4). Her vehicle, a swan, symbolizes spiritual perfection and transcendence. Sometimes she is seen with a peacock, or standing or seated on a lotus flower (symbol of purity), which also symbolizes the transcending of all imperfections. She is usually draped in a white sari and her face is calm and benign, signifying the quality of *sattva guṇa* (goodness and purity). Although Brahmā is associated with sacred rituals and knowledge, it is Sarasvatī who plays an active role in imparting wisdom and perfecting every mode of expression. She symbolizes all forms of artistic and intellectual knowledge and expression.

Sarasvatī is popular among all classes of people and is worshipped on her special day by students, teachers, scholars and others. Most Hindus perform Sarasvatī-*pūjā* in their homes during the festival of *Navarātri*. Sacred books, academic texts and musical instruments are

Figure 7.4 Sarasvatī, goddess of wisdom and fine arts (by Usha Azad)

placed before the image of the goddess and her blessings are sought for the growth of knowledge and wisdom.

As well as through stories and festivals, Hindu children learn about their tradition through dance and music. There is no strict demarcation between the sacred and secular areas of life and activity. Dance, music, knowledge, wealth are very much intertwined with the sacred dimension of life. Lord Naṭarāja is the patron of dance and all forms of art (see 'Śiva', pp. 179–80 above), and Indian classical music is seen as having its origin in one of the sacred texts of the primary scriptures, *Sāma-veda*, which was chanted during the vedic fire-sacrifice (*yagna*) ceremony. Music plays an important part in worship, and on religious occasions women are expected to chant or sing devotional hymns. Most Hindus start the day listening to devotional music. Audio-cassettes of Sanskrit *sloka*s, sacred verses in praise of various deities and their attributes, are easily available and they are also played on special occasions such as Sarasvatī- or Durgā-*pūjā*, when the goddesses are honoured in a special way.

The goddess Sarasvatī was originally associated with a river in the Vedas, and with the goddess of speech, Vāc. Later, she came to be associated with wisdom, learning and all forms of creative art. As the goddess of creative speech or sound, Sarasvatī embodies the power of the sacred *śabda* (sound). The conception of the Divine in the form of sound (*Śabda-brahman*), from which all creation proceeds, finds expression in Hindu sacred literature and in some iconographical representations, especially in the dance of Śiva who holds a drum in one of his hands, symbolizing the origin of sound.

There are many accounts of Sarasvatī's origin. It is said that Brahmā divided himself into two halves – male and female – in order to create the world but fell in love with the female half and she became his consort. In some myths Sarasvatī's origin is associated with Viṣṇu and Kṛṣṇa.

Lakṣmī

LAKṢMĪ AS GODDESS OF WEALTH AND PROSPERITY

The goddess Lakṣmī (consort of Viṣṇu) symbolizes wealth, prosperity and good luck. In popular iconographical pictures Lakṣmī is shown with four arms (see Figure 7.5). In two of her hands she holds a lotus flower (symbolizing purity), her right hand is held in an upright gesture (*abhaya mudrā*), symbolizing assurance, and from her lower left hand fall gold coins, symbolizing wealth and prosperity. As Gaja-Lakṣmī, she is depicted standing on a lotus flower, which is her main symbol, with a white elephant (*gaja*) on each side, representing royalty. She is shown holding a lotus flower, a fruit, a pot of *amṛta* or nectar and a

Figure 7.5 Lakṣmī, goddess of wealth, prosperity and good luck (by Usha Azad)

conch shell (*śaṅkha*), symbolizing protection and liberation.

In mythology Lakṣmī is said to have emerged from the primeval ocean with a radiant lotus in her hand, along with the other divine treasures which the gods were trying to rescue. Śiva desired Lakṣmī as his wife, but since he had already taken possession of the crescent-moon, she became the consort of Viṣṇu. It is said that Śiva's disappointment at the loss distracted him and led him to hold in his throat the poison emitted by the serpent so that he came to be called Nīlakaṇṭha, the 'Blue-necked One'.

Earlier associated with kingly power and royal authority, Lakṣmī is known as *śrī* ('beauty' and good fortune) and worshipped along with Viṣṇu. The couple symbolize marital harmony, prosperity and stability. She is shown seated on Viṣṇu's right thigh, with his left arm around her waist and her right arm around Viṣṇu's neck.

Lakṣmī is worshipped on various occasions during the year. Women perform Vara Lakṣmī-*pūjā* in the month of August. In this form she offers boons and assures prosperity and long life. The Hindu festival *Diwālī* is particularly associated with the worship of Lakṣmī. For Gujarati Hindus *Diwālī* is the beginning of the New Year and the financial year. Business men and women place their account books before the image of Lakṣmī and have their books blessed by the priest. The pursuit of wealth (*artha*, one of the four aims of Hindu life) is seen as legitimate as long as one acquires it by proper means and for useful purposes, such as providing for the needs of family, society and community.

Lakṣmī plays an important role in Śrī Vaiṣṇava philosophy and devotion. She figures as an intercessor between Viṣṇu and his devotees. She has a central place in the Vaiṣṇava Pāñcarātra school of philosophy. She is associated with the cosmic functions of Brahmā, Viṣṇu and Śiva. As the female counterpart of Viṣṇu she is linked with the creation and evolution of the universe. When worshipped on her own, Lakṣmī is regarded as 'Lokamātā', mother of the world.

LAKṢMĪ AS DEVOTED WIFE

Lakṣmī is sometimes shown with two arms when she is seen with Viṣṇu, massaging his feet with devotion. In popular iconography Lakṣmī is often shown with Viṣṇu, riding on Garuḍa, the divine eagle in whose claws a snake lies entangled. Both the animals are representations of Viṣṇu and Lakṣmī – symbols of opposite forces harmonized in Viṣṇu. The eagle, which symbolizes the sky and the sun, is at constant war with the snake, which symbolizes the watery element (the source of life). Unless a balance of opposites is maintained, the harmony of the world and the universe is believed to be at risk.

Lakṣmī figures as the consort of Viṣṇu in each of his incarnations. When Viṣṇu took the form of Vāmana, the dwarf *avatāra*, Lakṣmī emerged from the waters, gliding on the flower of a lotus, and hence came to be called Padmā (lotus) or Kamalā. When Viṣṇu assumed the form of Paraśurāma, Lakṣmī came down to the earth as his wife, Dharanī. When Viṣṇu appeared as Rāma, Lakṣmī was Sītā and when he came as Kṛṣṇa, she appeared as his favourite *gopi* Rādhā and as his wife, Rukmiṇī.

The feminine Divine as Mahādevī

The many feminine forms of the Divine are seen as embodiments of the Great Goddess (Mahādevī), who is manifest in all creation as *śakti* or divine energy. Mahādevī has many names, forms and attributes and has a central role in some myths. She is known as Umā (knowledge), Satī (virtuous wife), Haimavatī (the daughter of Himavan, god of the Himalayas), Pārvatī ('from the mountains'), Durgā ('inaccessible') and Kālī ('black' and 'time'), originally associated with the vedic fire-god Agni.

SATĪ AS VIRTUOUS WIFE

Each of the names throws light on her various functions. As Satī, she attracts Śiva into marriage by her devotion and ascetic practices, and marries him against her father's wishes. To save the honour of her husband (who was not invited to the sacrificial ceremony), she burns herself on the sacrificial fire. The grief-stricken Śiva carries Satī in his arms. In order to end Śiva's grief, which causes cosmic imbalance, Viṣṇu removes Satī's body from Śiva's arms by slicing it until nothing is left. The various places where the pieces of Satī's corpse fell become sacred. The grief-stricken Śiva retreats to the mountains, though in some myths he goes in search of Satī. He eventually finds her in the form of *yoni* and he takes the form of the *liṅga* and enters into her and thus the two remain united forever. The underlying theme of Satī's myths shows the tension between, and reconciliation of, asceticism and love. Satī, in the form of *yoni*, attracts the ascetic Śiva from his seclusion and thus makes him accessible to the world in the form of *liṅga*.

The goddess Satī is also associated with the practice of *satī*, widows immolating themselves on the funeral pyre of their husbands. However, it is not clear whether the death of the goddess is seen as a mythological model for *satī* (Kinsley, 1987: 40).

Pārvatī as spiritual partner

As with Satī, Pārvatī's main role in mythology is to draw the ascetic Śiva into marriage so that his stored-up energy is released for the benefit of the world. She even goes to the extent of performing severe austerities (*tapas*) to win the hand of Śiva and thus make him fulfil the role of a householder. Śiva is impressed by her ability to do *tapas* to win him, and thus considers her a worthy partner. The tension between the householder ideal and the ascetic ideal is the underlying theme of myths concerning Śiva and Pārvatī. The reconciliation between the two finds expression in mythology and iconographical representations of Pārvatī and Śiva. The Śiva–Śakti dance, Śiva as Ardhānarīśvara (half-man and half-woman), and *liṅga* and *yoni* are some of the best examples.

The marriage of Śiva to Pārvatī is the subject of popular iconography. They are shown walking round the sacred fire, Agni, and receiving blessings from Brahmā, Viṣṇu and Indra. Śiva marries Pārvatī in his ascetic garb (clad in a tiger skin). In popular art they are depicted as a happy couple with their two children Gaṇeśa and Skanda. In the *Purāṇa*s they are shown seated upon the mountain Kailāsa, engrossed in either love-making or philosophical debate. In the southern school of Śaiva Siddhānta, Pārvatī figures as Śiva's 'embodied grace'. Pārvatī and Śiva are also depicted dancing together and this dance is called *Umā-tāṇḍava*. *Tāṇḍava* is a vigorous type of dance associated with Śiva who performs the cosmic dance of creation and destruction of evil.

Durgā

DURGĀ AS WARRIOR AND SUSTAINER

Durgā, the fierce form of Pārvatī, figures as a warrior and mother goddess. She is the feminine energy or power, *śakti*, of Śiva. In iconographical representations Durgā is depicted with eight or ten arms, each holding a weapon given by the male gods (symbolizing divine power), riding a tiger or lion, *siṃha* (symbolizing power and authority), and in the act of destroying the demon who was invulnerable to all enemies except a woman. She is also known as Daśabhujā ('the ten-handed One') and Siṃhavāhinī ('the one who rides the lion').

She is both fierce (as her name suggests) and beautiful, and is usually dressed in red.

The gentle Pārvatī assumes the form of a warrior goddess to slay the buffalo demon Mahiṣāsura, who threatened the balance of the world. From then on she came to be called Durgā. She destroys Mahiṣāsura, who attacks her unsuccessfully by changing his form quickly into a lion, elephant, etc. In this form Durgā is known as Mahiṣāsura-mardinī, the slayer of Mahiṣāsura. She acts independently on the battlefield to vanquish the demon. She does not seek the support of the male gods who created her. Instead she fights with the help of female assistants whom she creates from herself.

During the festival of Durgā-*pūjā* in Bengal, beautiful clay images of the warrior goddess are housed in temporary shrines built for the purpose and at the end of the festival the images are taken on a truck to be immersed in the river Hooghly.

The worship of Durgā as a warrior goddess was common among kings and rulers who sought success in battle. The Hindu festival *Daśarā* (also known as *Navarātri*) is associated with Durgā, to whom Rāma prayed for victory in his battle against Rāvaṇa, who had abducted his wife Sītā. The success of the Pāṇḍava brothers in their fight against the Kauravas in the *Mahābhārata* is also associated with Durgā. Arjuna, one of the five Pāṇḍava brothers, sings a hymn in praise of Durgā's military valour, seeking her help in overcoming their opponents.

Durgā departs from traditional norms of womanly behaviour. Her place seems to be not so much in the home as on the battlefield. She, like Kālī, is associated with blood, death and destruction of evil. Durgā, originally associated with the tribal non-Aryan peoples who offered her animal sacrifices, assumes a central role in medieval and later Hinduism. Durgā plays a similar role to that of Viṣṇu, as sustainer and preserver of *dharma*. She intervenes when order and harmony are threatened and restores peace.

DURGĀ AS MOTHER AND DAUGHTER

Although Durgā is often portrayed as an independent deity, she assumes a domestic role in her later history. She is motherly and is fondly called Ambā (mother) or Durgā Ma. In this role she is associated with Pārvatī, who represents the domestic ideal (marriage and family). In popular pictures she is shown as the mother of Gaṇeśa and Kārttikeya, Lakṣmī and Sarasvatī.

In Bengal, the Durgā-*pūjā* has a special significance. Durgā figures in the role of a daughter returning to her family during the festival (as is the custom) and departing to her husband's home after the festival. The festival re-enacts the joy of parents who eagerly look forward to their daughters' arrival and their sadness at their departure. The festival is also associated with agriculture and fertility of the crops. In the North Indian tradition, Durgā's role as mother and daughter is far more pronounced than in the South Indian tradition, where she is depicted as a fiercely independent deity whose sexuality is said to be dangerous.

The feminine Divine as love and terror: Kālī

KĀLĪ AS CONQUEROR OF EVIL

Śiva's *śakti* in terrifying form is Kālī. She is the goddess of destruction of evil but at the same time she initiates new creation. Kālī is depicted with four arms (sometimes ten) holding in three hands a sword, a trident, and the severed head of a demon, while the fourth one offers protection to her devotees. She is seen wearing a garland of skulls around her neck, almost naked except for a belt made of the severed hands of the demons, and dancing on the prostrate body of her husband Śiva. She is dark blue (*shyma*) or sometimes black (*kālī*), as her name indicates, and *kālī* also means 'time'. Her hair is dishevelled and her tongue, dripping with blood, hangs out.

In mythology, Kālī kills the demon Raktavīja who had been granted the boon of being born several times and of becoming more powerful each time a drop of his blood was shed. In fact, Kālī drinks the blood that gushes forth from his wound to the last drop, to conquer evil. She becomes bloodthirsty and goes about killing all the demons. Realizing that this frenzied cosmic dance of destruction would threaten the universal balance, Śiva throws himself down at the feet of Kālī to calm her fury. When Kālī discovers that she is dancing on her husband, she stands aghast with her mouth wide open and her long red tongue jutting out. In this pose she is known as Dakṣiṇakālī ('south facing'). In the South Indian tradition, however, both of them perform the vigorous *Tāṇḍava* dance in which Kālī is subdued. This myth has also been interpreted in more philosophical categories. The passive Śiva under the feet of Kālī and the dynamic activity of Kālī are seen as two different but complementary aspects of the Absolute. Kālī's fierce nature is also evident in her other forms as Caṇḍi ('the fierce') and Bhairavī ('the terrible'). Here Kālī is the female counterpart of Śiva as Bhairava.

Kālī is both attractive and repulsive. In her terrible and ghastly form she is associated with the battlefield or the cremation ground. She is very popular among tribal peoples and others, who offer her blood offerings. She takes life to feed herself and at the same time gives life. Like Śiva, she is the embodiment and reconciliation of apparent contradictions. Kālī plays a central role in Tantrism and popular worship. She is seen as the principal divine energy or force, *śakti*, from whom all else unfolds. She challenges conventional patriarchal standards and traditional norms of purity and pollution. While Pārvatī's role is to attract the ascetic Śiva into the world of domesticity, marriage and love, Kālī's role, on the contrary, is to drag Śiva into vigorous activity – annihilating forces of evil and ignorance and initiating new birth. It is not surprising that contemporary Hindu women look to Kālī as their model. The publishing house Kali in Delhi was set up by two women. They chose the name Kali because she stands for the destruction of ignorance.

KĀLĪ AS MOTHER

In Bengal, Kālī is worshipped as the Divine Mother, and the festival of *Diwālī* is associated with her. Although bloodthirsty and far removed from conventional norms of behaviour, Kālī also assumes a maternal role. She is associated with death but at the same time she is the source of all life. Great Bengali saints of the last two centuries, such as Ramprasad and Sri Ramakrishna and his disciple Vivekananda, were ardent devotees of Kālī and looked upon her as mother. They longed to have her *darśan*, to see her face to face (see below, p. 200). Vivekananda's disciple, Margaret Noble (Sister Nivedita), an Irishwoman, speaks fondly of Kālī in her book *Kālī the Mother*. At the end of her book is a poem on Kālī written by Swami Vivekananda.

> For Terror is thy name,
> Death is Thy Breath,

And every shaking step
Destroys a world for e'er.
Thou 'Time' the All-Destroyer!
Then come, O Mother, Come!

Who can misery love,
Dance in destruction's dance,
And hug the form of Death, –
To him the Mother comes.

(Nivedita, 1983: 111)

The image of the Divine as mother is far more dominant than other feminine images at the popular level. Pre-Aryan beliefs seem, to a great extent, to have been centred on feminine imagery, and female divinities rose to prominence again in post-vedic and classical times. The sacred river Ganges is also personified as mother (Gaṅgā Ma). A holy dip in her waters is seen as purifying one of all impurities. As mother, she nourishes and sustains those who come seeking her. *Mokṣa*, or salvation, is granted by her. The image of mother goddess became far more pronounced during the Indian struggle for independence, especially in Bengal. Kālī was seen as Bengal personified. Legend has it that while Śiva was carrying the dismembered body of Satī, the toe of her right foot fell on earth near the river Ganges, where a temple to Kālī was built. It came to be known as the Kālīghāt temple, and Calcutta derives its name from a neighbouring village, Kalikata. In some parts of India Kālī is symbolized by a black or dark-blue stone.

Village deities as both malevolent and benevolent

The village deities, *grāma devatā*s, are predominantly female and they are perceived as both malevolent and benevolent. Villagers are less directly concerned with the deities of the Hindu pantheon than with the *grāma devatā*s, who are far more involved in the day-to-day life of the villagers. They bring death, disease and famine, and at the same time protect villagers from them. The village goddess in the form of mother is known as *amman* in South India. There are many *amman*s such as Kanaka Durgamman and Māriyamman (bringer of smallpox). The fiercer goddesses, called *śakti*s, have no specific temples or image. It is doubtful whether they have any links with Durgā or Kālī who, as *śakti*s of Śiva, manifest the energy of the male gods.

Darśan of the Divine

Hindus go to a temple to have a *darśan*, glimpse or vision, of the deity. The word means 'seeing'. Hindus consider it a blessing to behold the image of the deity beautifully adorned with ornaments and flowers and to witness the *āratī*-light being waved before the deity. This 'seeing' is auspicious and brings the blessings of the deity to the beholder.

For most Hindus the image is more than a symbol. Once the image of the deity is consecrated in a temple, in a rite called *prāṇa-pratiṣṭhā* ('putting in the breath'), it becomes sacred. The officiating priest implores the deity to come and dwell in the image. From then onwards, the image becomes the living presence of the deity. The Divine is seen as making itself accessible through the image to its worshippers. This communion between the deity and the worshipper is of supreme importance to most Hindus. Worship involves seeing, touching, offering fruits, flowers and incense to the deity, and this helps the worshippers to develop a close relationship with their chosen deities. A deep yearning for the divine finds expression in *bhakti*, devotional literature. In worship *saguṇa brahman* (with attributes) is the object of devotion.

For Hindu monists the images have only a symbolic value. They are no more than aids to meditation and worship. They aim at experiencing *nirguṇa brahman* (without attributes), who is beyond all thought and speculation. The monist Hindu, who sees *brahman* as non-personal, and the theist Hindu, who sees *brahman* as personal, are seeing the same reality but in different ways, and are emphasizing the two different but complementary aspects of *brahman*. The conceptions and experiences of *brahman* as utterly transcendent and as personal lord and creator are seen as equally valid. The paths of *karma-yoga* (selfless action), *bhakti-yoga* (love and devotion) or *jñāna-yoga* (knowledge and contemplation) merge with one another without losing their distinctiveness. Together they lead to an integral vision and experience of the Divine as both matter and spirit, form and formlessness, male and female, love and terror, immanent and transcendent, finite and infinite.

Notes

1 All quotations from the *Bhagavadgītā* are taken from S. Radhakrishnan (1971) *The Bhagavadgītā*. First Indian reprint; Bombay: George Allen & Unwin. For other scriptural references see R. C. Zaehner (trans.) (1966) *Hindu Scriptures*. London: J. M. Dent.

2 See D. L. Eck (1982) *Banāras, City of Light*. New York: Alfred A. Knopf.

Further reading

Alston, A. J. (trans.) (1980) *The Devotional Poems of Mīrabāi*. Delhi: Motilal Banarsidass.

Aurobindo, Sri (1955) *The Life Divine*, vol. III. Pondicherry (India): Sri Aurobindo Ashram.

Coomaraswamy, A. K. (1982) *The Dance of Śiva*. 2nd edn; New Delhi: Munshiram Manoharlal.

Coomaraswamy, A. K. and Sister Nivedita (1967) *Myths of the Hindus and Buddhists*. New York: Dover.

Courtright, P. B. (1985) *Gaṇeśa: Lord of Obstacles, Lord of Beginnings*. New York: Oxford University Press.

Eck, D. L. (1985) *Darśan: Seeing the Divine Image in India*. 2nd revised and enlarged edn; Chambersburg: Anima Books.

Gupte, R. S. (1980) *Iconography of the Hindus, Buddhists, and Jains*. 2nd edn; Bombay: D. B. Taraporevala.

Harshananda, Swami (1981) *Hindu Gods and Goddesses*. Mysore: Sri Ramakrishna Ashrama.

Ions, V. (1967) *Indian Mythology*. London: Paul Hamlyn.

Kinsley, D. (1987) *Hindu Goddesses: Visions of the Divine Feminine in the Hindu Religious Tradition*. Delhi: Motilal Banarsidass.

Mookerjee, A. (1988) *Kālī: The Feminine Force*. London: Thames and Hudson.

Moore, A. C. (1977) *Iconography of Religions: An Introduction*. London: SCM Press.

Nivedita, Sister (1983) *Kālī the Mother*. 2nd edn; Mayavati, Himalayas: Advaita Ashrama.

O'Flaherty, W. D. (1981) *Śiva: The Erotic Ascetic*. London: Oxford University Press (first published in 1973 under the title *Asceticism and Eroticism in the Mythology of Śiva*).

Padoux, A. (1990) *L'Image divine: culte et méditation dans l'hindouisme*. Paris: Centre National de la Recherche Scientifique.

Panikkar, R. (1989) *The Vedic Experience: Mantramañjarī*. 2nd edn; Pondicherry: All India Books.
Pintchman, T. (1994) *The Rise of the Goddess in the Hindu Tradition*. Albany: SUNY Press.
Stutley, M. (1985) *The Illustrated Dictionary of Hindu Iconography*. London: Routledge and Kegan Paul.

8. Worship

Anuradha Roma Choudhury

The concept of worship in Hinduism is as varied as the many facets of the religion itself. Hinduism cannot even be called a religion in the formal Western sense. It does not have any one founder and does not have any one Holy Book of instructions. It grew gradually over a period of about 5000 years absorbing and assimilating all the religious, philosophical, ethical and cultural movements of India. Consequently, there is no one ideal of worship. Different schools of philosophical thought prescribe different forms of rituals or no rituals at all. People belonging to different strata of society also interpret worship in different ways. There is no one term for worship in Hinduism. It can be *yajña*, *homa*, *upāsanā*, *sādhanā*, *bhajanā*, *archanā*, *ārādhanā*, etc. The closest general term for worship, as understood in the West, would be *pūjā*. Then again, *pūjā* can mean more than just ritual worship. It means adoration, honour, respect, devotion, obeisance and much more. *Pūjā* actually means honour in expressions like *vidvān sarvatra pūjyate* ('a learned man is worshipped everywhere', *Chānakyanīti* VIII.20). To a Hindu child, his or her parents are *pūjanīya* (to be respected). It can also mean dedication. Artists or musicians in India often say that pursuing art or music is their life-long *pūjā* to achieve the desired goal.

However, dealing primarily with ritual worship, one has to go back to the earliest period of vedic worship. The world's earliest surviving literature, the Veda[1] (*c.* 1500 BCE), contains hymns praising the all-powerful gods who, more often than not, are the personified elements of nature. The vedic priests around a sacrificial fire chanted hymns with precise intonations. Offerings of milk, clarified butter (*ghṛta*) and *soma-rasa* (an intoxicating drink made from soma plant) were made to the friendly god Agni (fire). Through Agni, the intermediary, gods received the gifts offered by the humans and bestowed blessings on them in return. The objectives of worship in the vedic period were either to appease the wrath of the fearsome gods, the giant forces of nature generating awe and bewilderment in primitive people (e.g., lightning, thunderstorm), or to please the benevolent gods (e.g., rain, fire) for favours of wealth in the form of crops, cattle and children.

The sacrificial worship of the vedic period is known as the *yajña*.[2] Of the four Vedas, the *Yajur-veda* deals specifically with the ritualistic formulae of the *yajña*s. It describes in prose the procedural details of the actual performance of various *yajña*s. Both the words *yajus(r)* and *yajña* are derived from the same root, *yaj*, which means 'to worship'. The purpose of the *Yajur-veda* is to give the hymns of the preceding *Ṛg-veda* an applied form in ritual worship.

The ideology behind the sacrificial worship probably owes its origin to the *Puruṣa Sūkta* (the Hymn of Man) of the *Ṛg-veda*, describing the great sacrifice of the primal man (*puruṣa*) at the beginning of time. As the universe emerged from an enormous sacrifice, constant repetitions of that original sacrifice seemed necessary to maintain the universe in good working order. The rituals performed by high-caste Aryans in the remote Indo-European past are still performed by some orthodox Brahman families. The purpose of the *yajña*s, however, has changed with time. They began as methods of pleasing gods with offerings of obedience and allegiance to them, but gradually came to be looked upon as ways of practising renunciation and penance.

In the course of time the sacrificial worship of the vedic Aryans was replaced by *pūjā*, worship of the deities or gods with images. The scene of worship changed from the sacrificial ground to the places of pilgrimage and ritual bathing. 'Instead of altars there grew up temples with their special deities' (Sen, 1973: 58). It is plausible that in a varied country like India, diverse races and tribes with different ways and objects of worship contributed to the evolution of formalized worship. Some Hindus still worship rivers, specific trees and animals.

The *bhakti* (devotion) cult that grew up with image-worship had its roots in southern India, known as Dravidian country, and points to a non-Aryan origin. As the early vedic sacrificial worship gradually blended in with the non-Aryan ways of worship, each of these cults found a place in Hinduism and influenced it from within. In the transition, even the all-powerful vedic gods were either diminished in stature in competition with the non-Aryan gods or were amalgamated with some of them. For example, the most powerful vedic god Indra lost his importance in later Hinduism and the vedic storm-god Rudra became identified with the non-Aryan Śiva, the god of destruction.

Image-worship

In vedic worship, though many gods were accepted, there was no reference to idols or images. The fact that the Indus Valley civilization (*c.* 2000 BCE) had many images shows that image-worship may have existed in India before the Aryan invasion and thus may be a non-Aryan contribution to present day Hinduism.

Image-worship (*mūrti-pūjā*) is not idolatry. Hindus do not believe that the image itself is Viṣṇu or Śiva, but accept it as a symbol of the deity. They pray not to the image, but to the deity personified by the image. Though Hindus believe in one formless Absolute God (*brahman*), their prayers are strengthened if there is a tangible object of devotion in front of them. The difficulty of comprehending an abstract Absolute entity as God necessitates a symbolic representation in a concrete form, a *mūrti* (literally, 'crystallization'), so that the mind can concentrate upon it. A simple stone may serve the purpose just as well as an elaborately sculptured statue with all the specific features prescribed by the Hindu manuals (*śāstras*) on sculpture.

Symbolism

Hindus who worship a simple stone or a particular plant are venerating something greater, beyond that stone or plant. The stone is often kept in a little shrine, washed, smeared with sandalwood paste and decorated with flowers. Hindus know that the stone itself is not God but is the symbol of God at that moment. It may not be so to others, but to them that does not matter.

The logic of Hindu thinking is as follows. If one really has faith in God being omnipresent, one has to believe that God can be found in anything and everything. Then, all one needs to do is to focus God in *a* thing, be it a stone, a flower or something else. When the scriptures say 'God is omnipresent, omnipotent and omniscient', it sounds so vague and abstract that most people dare not even try to comprehend God. It is too general and too impersonal a statement. But when one focuses, say, on a flower, mentally imposing God on to it, it is possible to meditate on a God who is close at hand at that instant. Neither the colour of the flower nor the number of its petals is in focus at that moment, but God is. This simple act makes concentration much easier and meditation more intense. Thus to a Hindu, anything at all can be an object of meditation once it is chosen as a symbol of God.

However, mention must be made here of a particular symbolic object of worship that is greatly revered by the Hindus. It is the emblem of Śiva in the *liṅga* (phallus) form that symbolizes his vast generative energy. A *Śiva-liṅga*, often made of stone, is complete with the phallus standing on a platform representing the *yoni* (vulva) of his consort Śakti. The generative process in nature through the union of male and female, *puruṣa* and *prakṛti*, passive and dynamic, negative and positive forces, is recognized and worshipped by the Hindus in a *Śiva-liṅga* form. Though it is often described in the West as a primitive fertility symbol and thereby given a sexual connotation, to the majority of the Śiva devotees in India it does not imply any erotic element in his rites. As pointed out by Cavendish (1980: 24), 'the symbol has been a conventional image of the god for so long that most of his devotees do not realise that it has any sexual significance'. In this context one should remember that in Hinduism the conjugal sex-act is venerated as the essential and continuing process of procreation in nature and therefore there is no concept of 'original sin'. Most male deities are balanced by their female counterparts and accordingly worshipped together, and often their offspring are included as well; for example, Viṣṇu with Lakṣmī, Śiva with Pārvatī/Durgā and their two sons Kārttikeya and Gaṇeśa.

Another form of symbolism existing in objects of worship is found in the physical features of the images of deities. The multiple limbs of the images and a third eye are often added to signify the multifarious as well as superhuman attributes of deities. Individual deities have their own characteristic features. For example, Viṣṇu has four arms with hands holding separate implements, each of which represents an activity or aspect of Viṣṇu's identity. Similarly, the ten arms of Durgā, a mother figure of the Hindu pantheon, and the divine weapons they carry, represent her power of destroying all evils and of protecting the creation. Her third eye represents the all-seeing aspect of the divinity (*divya-dṛṣṭi*).

Apart from objects of worship there are several other spheres of Hindu meditative activity where symbolism plays an important role.

MANTRA

A *mantra* in Hindu worship may be a short phrase, a word, or even a sound-syllable, that is uttered repeatedly in meditation to fix concentration. It is an aid for the human mind (which is incessantly rushing from one thought to another) to cut out superfluous thoughts and concentrate on one preferred thought. What the symbolic object of worship does tangibly, the *mantra* does audibly. *Mantra*s have their specific sound values and sound effects. The correct pronunciation is all-important. In the practice of vedic *mantra*s, it is said, the vibration generated by correct intonation is beneficial not only to the reciter but also to the listeners. Therefore *mantra*s are to be chanted audibly. The pitch, the tonal quality and the length of the sounds are of crucial significance. If a *mantra* were not uttered accurately, it would prove ineffectual and would do more harm than good. That is why it is not considered right to read *mantra*s from the written script (*likhita-pāṭhaka*). A *mantra* should be learnt by ear from the oral chanting of a teacher (*guru*) and then memorized in the proper manner. To achieve this, one has to have initiation (*dīkṣā*) from a *guru* who is experienced enough to prescribe the appropriate *mantra*, judging the recipient's temperament and spiritual capabilities. Thus a *mantra* is often considered to be so sacred and personalized a code that it is to be cherished or guarded with secrecy, otherwise it may lose its potency.

Though there are different *mantra*s prescribed by *guru*s for individuals of different mental make-up, there is one *mantra* that all Hindus hold in great reverence. That is 'OM' or 'AUM', known as *Oṁkāra* or *Praṇava*. The *Oṁkāra* is considered to be the seed or essence of the cosmic sound that pervades the whole universe. In the *Upaniṣad*s there are expressions like *Nāda-Brahma* and *Śabdam Brahma* which show that sound (*nāda/śabda*) is elevated to the level of *brahman* itself (cf. 'The Word was God' in the Bible, John 1:1). 'OM', being the symbolic sacred sound, is always uttered at the beginning and the end of all Hindu religious readings and rituals.

The term *mantra* literally means 'that which liberates oneself by focusing one's mind on it' (*mananāt trāyate iti mantraḥ*). In that sense a particular *mantra* called *Gāyatrī* (*Ṛg-veda* III.62.10) is considered by the Hindus as the most liberating of all. It is the most renowned prayer of all the Vedas. The *Gāyatrī* is a *mantra* that glorifies the Sun (*Savitṛ*), symbolizing the power of light that illumines the earth, the sky and the heaven, and that seeks illumination of the human mind with higher intelligence (*dhī*), i.e., spiritual enlightenment. It is recited daily at sunrise and sunset, usually at the time of the ritual bath. In other scriptures *Gāyatrī* is held in high esteem, as *Manu* declares (*Manu-saṁhitā* II.102) that the chanting of *Gāyatrī* at dawn dispels the guilt of the previous night and the evening chant destroys the sins committed during the day, thus emphasizing the purifying power of the *mantra* itself.

YANTRA

A *yantra* can be described as a symbolic pattern which helps a meditative worshipper to concentrate on the object of worship. *Mantra* and *yantra* complement each other and are used in conjunction in an act of worship. Just as *mantra* is an aid to concentration in sound-form, so *yantra* is an aid in visual form.

'A *yantra* is very often referred to as an energy pattern or a power-diagram' (Mookerjee and Khanna, 1977: 54). It is a pure geometric formation without any iconographic representation. Often these geometric patterns are centred on a single point, upon which meditative concentration is to be fixed. During meditation, by visualizing a chosen geometric figure, one can overcome all surfacing superfluous thoughts and be in control of the psyche. Like the sound-element of a *mantra*, the 'patternness' (Rawson, 1988: 64) of a *yantra* is vital for its meditative force. The artistic *yantra*s are often made with coloured powders sprinkled on the floor in front of the image of the deity to be worshipped. However, *yantra*s can be made of many different materials such as stone, rock-crystal, etc. The ground plans of most Hindu temples are themselves *yantra*s. The *yantra*s play a very important role in the *Tantra*[3] tradition.

YOGA

As *mantra* channels one's mind by controlling the psyche, *yoga* disciplines the body to be in tune with the mind. Body and mind work together to achieve a unified goal by being complementary to each other. The term *yoga* means 'union', signifying the union of body and mind; and at a higher level it connotes the union of the individual soul with the Universal or Absolute Soul. *Yoga* can have several meanings, depending upon the context. It has the same connotation as 'yoke' in English, meaning togetherness. In mathematical terms *yoga* means the sum of addition.

Concentration is needed to achieve anything, and to master concentration, a Hindu thinks; physical and mental controls have to work together. The yogic exercises, well known in the West now, are not an end in themselves but a means to an end: the achievement of a healthy, responsive body attuned to a steady determined mind. For a Hindu, *yoga* is not important merely as a physical technique for body-building, but for the state of consciousness it generates during the exercises. A true *yogī* is not only a healthier but also a more composed person.

In the context of worship, yogic postures play an important role. The best-known posture, *padmāsana* (the lotus position), sitting cross-legged on a flat floor with erect spine, helps the worshipper to have a steady supportive body to uphold the meditative mind. Indian sculpture is full of figurines of *yogī*s and the Buddha in meditative *padmāsana* postures. In tantric worship, yogic postures play a vital role. Specific postures have specific significance and experiences, and one has to follow the steps with the strictest accuracy. According to *Tantra*, the human body has six psychic centres (*chakra*s) along its spine. Through the correct practice (*sādhanā*) of *yoga*, the *chakra*s open one by one, leading to the progressive arousal of dormant energy (called *kuṇḍalinī*) from the lowest physical level to the highest psychic plane.

Various modes of worship

Hindus in general do not distinguish between religion and philosophy. To them the two are overlapping, if not synonymous. That is why worship, which is solely a part of religion in other traditions, is a many-faceted feature in Hinduism, where it changes its modes in accordance with each individual philosophy. The ultimate goal of each mode of worship (*sādhanā*) is to achieve enlightenment or liberation (*mukti*/*mokṣa*[4]).

Ritual worship is not the only form of worship in Hinduism, and may not suit everybody. As Hinduism does not recognize any single way of reaching God, the concept of religious worship may vary from person to person or sect to sect, and with it vary the details of religious assumptions. 'One may try to reach God through work (*karma*), or meditation and knowledge (*jñāna*), or simply through devotion (*bhakti*). All are equally valid' (Sen, 1973: 39). In *Bhagavadgītā* (one of the best-known Hindu scriptures) Kṛṣṇa, the God incarnate, declares: 'In whatever way men worship Me, in the same way do I fulfil their desires; it is My path men tread, in all ways' (IV.11). The different ways that people view God, some even apparently conflicting, show the infinite aspects of the same Supreme. One individual's level of understanding may be different from that of another, and Hinduism gives every individual the freedom to choose his or her own way of worship. Swami Vivekananda (1963: 76, 78) explains:

> A religion, to satisfy the largest proportion of mankind, must be able to supply food for all these various types of minds ... And this religion is attained by what we, in India, call *Yoga* – union. To the worker, it is union between men and the whole of humanity; to the mystic, between his Lower and Higher Self; to the lover, union between himself and the God of love; and to the philosopher, it is the union of *all* existence.

A person who follows any of these ways of union (*yoga*) is called a *yogī*. A *karma-yogī* worships through his work, a *rāja-yogī* through power of mind, a *bhakti-yogī* through love and devotion, and a *jñāna-yogī* through knowledge and intellect.

KARMA-YOGA: THE PATH OF ENLIGHTENMENT THROUGH WORK

In a society there are always people whose minds do not dwell on thoughts alone but who find a way of consolidating their thoughts with tangible work. *Karma-yoga* explains why such a person should work for work's sake, without attachment or caring for rewards. Attachment breeds expectation, expectation brings disappointment and disappointment causes pain. If one works because one likes to work and does not care for anything in return, then one can avoid the chain of disappointment and misery. In *Bhagavadgītā* (II.47) Kṛṣṇa advises an undecided Arjuna to follow the path of action (*karma*): 'Thy right is to work only; but never to the fruits thereof. Be thou not the producer of the fruits of (thy) actions; neither let thy attachment be towards inaction' (Swami Swarupananda, 1982: 57).

RĀJA-YOGA: THE PATH OF ENLIGHTENMENT THROUGH CONTROL OF THE MIND

This is the psychological way of enlightenment. Concentration is the keyword in *rāja-yoga*. But proper concentration is very hard to achieve. As soon as one tries to calm oneself and concentrate upon an object of knowledge, thousands of distracting thoughts rush into one's mind. *Rāja-yoga* teaches how to overcome the limitations of the mind with a firm and steady concentration. As this is the basic requirement of all branches of yoga, *rāja-yoga* is called the king (*rāja*) among the *yoga*s.

BHAKTI-YOGA: THE PATH OF UNION WITH A PERSONAL GOD THROUGH DEVOTION OR LOVE

This path of *yoga* is for people of an emotional nature who find image-worship satisfying. They 'do not care for abstract definitions of the truth. God to them is something tangible, the only thing that is real; . . . *Bhakti-yoga* teaches them how to love, without any ulterior motives, loving God and loving the good because it is good to do so' (Swami Vivekananda, 1963: 85). Their love of God at times culminates in exuberance of all kinds such as elaborate rituals, decorations, beautiful buildings and so on.

The *bhakti-yogī*s have a very rich tradition of mythology, poetry, songs and ballads. Group singing of devotional songs (*kīrtana*s or *bhajana*s) is an important part of their worship of the loving God. In a singing session, tears of overwhelming emotion are a common sight in a gathering of the *bhakta*s (devotees). The poet saints such as Jayadeva, Mira and Ramaprasada, whose devotional songs win the hearts of millions of Hindus, have been venerated through the ages as great *bhakta*s. Ramakrishna Paramahamsa, the unassuming saint of the last century, was a *bhakta* of Kālī. The Hare Krishna cult, well known in the West, is an offshoot of the *bhakti* movement, and members of the group are *bhakta*s of Hari and Kṛṣṇa. In a gathering of *bhakta*s it is not uncommon to hear a devotee sing in praise of Śiva while celebrating the birth of Kṛṣṇa or Rāma (both are incarnations of Viṣṇu), and devotees of Kālī join in with the singing. This is because *bhakti* overcomes all barriers, whether intellectual or sectarian.

JÑĀNA-YOGA: THE PATH OF ENLIGHTENMENT THROUGH KNOWLEDGE OR INTELLECTUAL PURSUIT

This is the path for the philosophers and thinkers, who never accept faith or belief as a substitute for their personal realization of the highest truth. A daily routine of rituals is not for them, nor is devotional singing. Reasoning and logic are their searchlights. Their intellect wants to unravel the mysteries of existence and experience the Truth and eventually become one with the Universal Being (*brahman*). The quest is for the realization of the inner self (*ātman*) and for identifying it with the Universal Self (*paramātman*). The ultimate in this form of worship leads to *saṃnyāsa* (renunciation of the world). The person, a *saṃnyāsīn* or ascetic, is lost to society at large. Certain sects of ascetics aspire to achieve spiritual height by ignoring physical comfort or even torturing the body in different strenuous ways.

None of these four modes of worship (*sādhanā*) is considered less important than the others. Different ways are right for individuals with different propensities and levels of spiritual capability. The variation in spiritual levels in people is taken into consideration when Kṛṣṇa advises Arjuna, his disciple, on how to worship ideally (*Bhagavadgītā* XII.8–11):

> Fix your mind on Me only, place your intellect in Me, [then] you shall no doubt live in Me hereafter.
>
> If you are unable to fix your mind steadily on Me, then by *abhyāsa-yoga* [repetitive practice of withdrawing the mind from material objects] do seek to reach Me.
>
> If you are unable to practise *abhyāsa* even, be intent on doing actions for Me. Even by doing actions for My sake, you shall attain perfection.
>
> If you are unable to do even this, then taking refuge in Me, abandon the fruit of all action.

The above quotation shows that there are gradations in the modes of worship. The discipline of the rituals is very important at the beginning to bring one's mind homeward, as it were, from the rushing world's material affairs. One engaged in mere rituals, even without knowing the significance of it all, will gradually calm down through the sheer regularity of performing the rituals. This will set the scene for religious thoughts. One day this person may not need the aid of rituals any more and may become a *jñāna-yogī*. In this way an earlier step lays the foundation for the next step. Each stage or way of worship is valid for the person who finds it worth pursuing. The most important common element in all of them, however, is sincerity (*śraddhā*). In *Bhagavadgītā* (VII.21 and XII.2) Kṛṣṇa states:

> Whatsoever form any devotee seeks to worship with *Śraddhā* – that *Śraddhā* of his do I make unwavering ... Those who, fixing their mind on Me, worship Me, ever-steadfast, and endowed with supreme *Śraddhā*, they in My opinion are the best versed in Yoga.
>
> (Swami Swarupananda, 1982: 174 and 277)

Relationship of the worshipper with the worshipped

The concept of an Absolute Creative Source from which the whole creation materialized is the basis of Hindu theology. This Absolute entity, called *brahman*, cannot be described, is beyond all attributes (*guṇātīta*), does not have shape or form (*nirākāra*) and does not have a gender (*liṅgātīta*). *Brahman* can be expressed by negation only (i.e., what it is not). The *Upaniṣads*, the *Bhagavadgītā* and other scriptures have tried in various ways to establish a relationship of this unknowable (*ajñeya*) *brahman* with the creation at large: it is the Supreme Soul (*paramātmā*) from which the individual souls of all creatures (*jīvātmā*) come, and into which they are absorbed. To achieve spiritual liberation (*mokṣa*) one has to realize the identity of one's individual soul with the universal *brahman*, and so on. Yet the concept of *brahman* is too abstract and too impersonal for ordinary people to comprehend. Only a *jñāna-yogī* (see above) can endeavour to achieve such a height and declare 'I am He' (*so'ham*) or announce 'You are That' (*tat tvam asi*). For others, a more personal, a more intimate God is needed, a God whom one can pray to and look up to in moments of need or grief, whom one can thank when something good happens, who looks after one's personal well-being. The majority of Hindus are familiar with this concept of a personal God. One's personal God can be male or female: *Īśvara* or *Bhagavān* is prayed to as a father figure, and *Īśvarī* or *Bhagavatī* as the mother.

Though the father-figure portraiture is quite common, to most Hindus the ideal of a protective mother is very close to their heart. The powerful mother-cult (worshipping of Śakti/Kālī/Durgā as a mother) seems to be a non-Aryan contribution to Hinduism, as there is no prominent mother-figure in vedic literature.

God is worshipped not only as a parent but in all sorts of human relationships. The various deities worshipped by individuals represent various relations. Kṛṣṇa (a male deity), the God of love, is never worshipped as a father but as a friend (*sakhā/bandhu*) or a lover (*priya*) or even as a child (*bāla*). Arjuna addresses him (in the *Bhagavadgītā*) as a friend, Mira (a sixteenth-century saint) and most female devotees consider him as a lover, and some even choose to worship him as a child (*bāla-Kṛṣṇa*). Durgā, though primarily worshipped as a protective mother inspiring reverence, is also looked upon as a daughter evoking affection in the minds of the devotees. This is particularly true in Bengal, the eastern region where *Durgā-pūjā* is the most important religious festival. The four-day festival is like the long-awaited annual homecoming of a married daughter. Thus in Hinduism all human feelings, emotions and relations are established with deities, not just reverence and obeisance.

Choice of deities

Since Hindus believe that the various deities are merely various aspects of the one and only God, individuals have the freedom to choose their own deity to suit their individual need for a personal God. In spite of the fact that there are many distinct deities, at a given moment any of them can be worshipped as though he or she were the supreme deity, encompassing the attributes of all the rest. That is why, in a Hindu family, it is possible to find a mother worshipping child-Kṛṣṇa, a father Śiva, a son Kālī and a daughter Lakṣmī, with the images of all these deities placed in the same family shrine side by side without provoking rivalry. However, more often than not children follow the family tradition and get used to the discipline of worshipping the deity of their parents' choice.

In some cases unification of deities is conceived, as in *Trimūrti*[5] (i.e., Brahmā, Viṣṇu and Śiva). (Some families keep pictures of the Buddha and Christ beside those of their family deities, where photographs of the family *guru* or priest and the departed members of the family are also seen.)

Traditionally, a Hindu worships three types of deities: a personally chosen deity (*iṣṭa-devatā*), the family deity (*kula-devatā*), and the local/village deity (*grāma-devatā*); each may differ from the other. The chosen deity is worshipped in a private, meditative way. The family deity, placed in a niche or on a table, is worshipped daily with simple rituals. The local deity is regularly worshipped by a priest in the local temple. A pious Hindu may visit the temple daily, periodically or occasionally. The local deity is often a regional choice. Considering the vastness of India, one realizes why the choice of deities varies not only among families in a region but also between regions. In eastern India Kālī is a popular deity, in the south Śiva and Gaṇeśa/Gaṇapati, in the north Viṣṇu, and so on. In spite of this regionality, sects and sub-sects of Śaivas, Vaiṣṇavas and Śāktas (devotees of Śiva, Viṣṇu and Śakti/Kālī/Durgā respectively) are distributed all over India. Yet it can honestly be said that in a Vaiṣṇava ceremony, a devotional song about Śiva can be sung by a Śākta devotee and none of the attendants would find it strange. The Hindus see no contradiction in such complete tolerance because they believe that each group is praying to the same one and only Universal Spirit who is beyond all sectarian claims.

Codes of conduct associated with ritual worship: *Vidhi* (dos) and *Niṣedha* (don'ts)

In popular Hinduism there are a number of observances and avoidances concerning ritual worship. Bathing and fasting before and during worship, breaking fast with only *prasāda* (consecrated food), avoiding shoes (particularly leather ones), are just a few very commonly observed practices.

Some of these regulations are possibly dictated by the climate or by sanitary considerations. Hindu pollution laws against eating from another's plate or drinking from another's cup are examples of such considerations. Personal hygiene is strictly observed, and water plays an indispensable part in it. Bathing is not just for rituals but is a daily necessity. These daily (*nitya*) and occasional (*naimittika*) observances evolved into a series of treatises, collectively known as *Smṛti*s or *Dharmaśāstra*s, by the early Common Era. The most renowned of these treatises is *Manusmṛti*, attributed to an ancient sage called Manu. It embodies rules and regulations for civic living. 'These civic rules worked within the religious framework and sometimes even had religious sanction' (Sen, 1973: 61).

VIDHI (OBSERVANCES)

Snāna (bathing) cleanses the body and pacifies the mind before worship.

Upavāsa (fasting), Hindus believe, helps one to control emotions and passion. It strengthens one's willpower against indulging in greed or pleasure and is thus regarded as a penance. Fasting for ritual worship starts at daybreak and continues till the worship is over. It has two advantages: the first is purely physical or physiological and the second is psychological but is very much influenced by the first. The chief objective of fasting is to render the system clean, which in turn calms the mind.

Prasāda (literally, kindness/favour), the food that is offered to the deity during worship and thus consecrated, is taken at the end of worship to break the fast. It consists always of simple natural food available to all, e.g., various fruits, raisins and lumps of cane sugar. Even the feast that follows the religious ceremonies is almost always purely vegetarian. Vegetarianism became widespread in Hinduism through the influence of the *ahiṃsā* (non-violence) element of Buddhism and Jainism. In the tantric cult, on the other hand, meat of the sacrificial animal offered to the goddess Kālī is consumed by the worshippers as consecrated food.

NIṢEDHA (AVOIDANCES)

There seem to be several reasons for the prohibition of wearing shoes in any religious venue or even near the home shrine. The most obvious one is general cleanliness; shoes collect dust and dirt on a journey. This is why an Indian, on returning home, takes his or her shoes off outside the threshold and then enters the room barefoot. Secondly, taking shoes off is a sign of humility and respect for the shrine of God (cf.

Exodus 3:5). Thirdly, and most significantly, a non-violence (*ahiṃsā*) factor may be associated with the custom. The conscience of *ahiṃsā* rejects objects made of animal skin, like shoes, in a sacred place. Leather bags or cases are also objectionable. So when they go on pilgrimage, Hindus often choose rubber or canvas shoes for their long arduous journeys.

Prohibition against taking part in rituals during one's 'impure' state is strictly observed in Hinduism. For example, a woman during her menstruating period is not allowed to take part in a ritual. Similarly, in the event of a death, or even a birth, the immediate family is prohibited from taking part in religious rituals for a prescribed period. This period is regarded as impure (*aśaucha*). In the case of a death (*mṛt-āśaucha*), it is the period of mourning, and in that of a birth (*janmāśaucha*), it is the period of confinement. The length of such periods depends on one's caste: the lower the caste the longer the period.

Ritual worship

The procedure of a Hindu ritual act of worship, or *pūjā*, is so elaborate that the majority of Hindus often do not know the significance of the minute details. They are happy to leave it all to the priest who is a Brahman by caste, knows the scriptures, and is initiated and trained in the practicalities of all rituals.

Despite the multitude of deities, the basic format of Hindu ritual worship is fairly standard, with minor variations for individual deities. The actual ceremony is conducted during an auspicious period prescribed by the Hindu calendar, based on the constellations of stars. As a rule all rituals are governed by precise timings according to Hindu astronomy and astrological calculations.

PREPARATIONS

The fasting priest and the participating devotees bathe before engaging in any preparation.

The floor decorations (*rangoli*/*ālpanā*) are done in the ceremonial area. *Rangoli*, made by sprinkling powder colours in various formations and diagrams (see *yantra* above, p. 208), has mystic significance.

Ālpanā (or *ālimpana*), the floor painting of Bengal, is symbolic of good luck, fortune and fertility because it is made with rice paste. Strings of fresh flowers (e.g., marigolds) and mango leaves are hung to highlight the venue.

The image of the deity is adorned with patterns of sandalwood paste, dressed in silk of a specified colour (e.g., Viṣṇu – yellow, Sarasvatī – white) and garlanded with fresh flowers. Specific flowers and leaves are used in the worship of particular deities (e.g., red *javā*/hibiscus for Kālī, *tulasī*/*Ocymum sanctum* leaves for Viṣṇu). Flowers to be used in worship should not be smelt lest they become polluted and are no longer worthy of being offered to God.

A clay or brass pot (*ghaṭa*) filled with water from the holy river Ganges (Gaṅgā), with a bunch of five mango leaves (*āmra-pallava*), is placed at the foreground, often at the centre of the *rangoli*/*ālpanā* pattern. The full pot denotes the desired completeness of the ceremony. Finally, a green coconut marked with *svastikā*[6] or other auspicious (*māṅgalika*) symbols in red vermilion is placed on top.

The burning of camphor (*karpūra*) and incense (*dhūpa*) purifies the atmosphere, and the lighting of lamps (*dīpa*) welcomes the deity.

Offerings (*naivedya*) of fresh fruits, washed rice and grains, coconut and milk sweets are arranged on plates or banana leaves. At the end of worship, this consecrated food (*prasāda*) breaks the fast of the worshippers.

RITUAL

Recitation of appropriate *mantra*s by the priest (*purohita*/*pūjārī*), invoking the spirit (*prāṇa-pratiṣṭha*) of the deity into the inert image, transforms the image from an object to a person deserving obeisance.

The worship from then on progresses through the stages of welcome (*āvāhana*), chanting of hymns of praise (*stava-stuti*), and offering (*anjali* – literally, 'in cupped hands') of flowers. A sacrificial fire (*homa*/*havana*) is lit and oblations of clarified butter (*ghṛta*) are made to the deity Agni (fire). Devotees finally prostrate (*praṇāma*) in complete submission.

The waving of lamps (*ārati*) in front of the image is a special feature of a Hindu *pūjā*. During *ārati* devotees sing hymns together and bells and drums sound. After *ārati* devotees move their hands over the lamp for the warmth of the flame and purify themselves by touching their head. This sacredness of fire can be traced back to vedic worship.

The sounding of a conch-shell (*śaṅkha*), hand-held bell (*ghaṇṭā*) and drum (e.g., the *ḍhāk* of Bengal) is incorporated at specific stages of worship.

The sacrifice of animals (often goats) in Śākta worship (of Śakti/Kālī/Durgā) is a rarity now. Ceremonial sacrifice of vegetables (e.g., pumpkins) or fruits is made instead. The practice of animal sacrifice is symbolic of destroying the base qualities within human nature (namely, lust/*kāma*, anger/*krodha*, greed/*lobha*, attachment/*moha*, pride/*mada* and envy/*mātsarya*), and thus making the devotee a better person.

COMPLETION

The priest sprinkles the devotees with holy water (*śānti-jala*) from the ceremonial pot (*ghaṭa*) and chants the final *mantra* of peace (*śānti-vachana*) to mark the successful completion of the ritual.

At the end of festivals the casting off (*visarjana*) of the spirit of the deity from the image is performed with appropriate *mantras*. The gesture of *visarjana* demonstrates that Hindus do not practise idolatry in worshipping images. The image is a mere symbol of the deity, and the clay images (*pratimās*) from temporary public *pūjā* venues are taken in a procession to a river or lake to be ceremonially immersed.

Forms of worship

Since Hinduism has various modes of worship there is no single, structured, formal way for all to follow and hence no congregational worship. Though there are innumerable Hindu temples all over India, dedicated to individual deities, they are not places for congregational worship. Terms for a temple, such as *devālaya*, *devagṛha* and *mandira*, literally mean 'a residence/house of God'. Streams of people go there all through the day to have a glimpse (*darśana*) of the deity and offer their respect. They do not gather at a particular time or take their place in the temple in a particular fashion. As the priest goes about doing his own job of decorating the images, preparing for worship, etc., devotees stand or sit or prostrate themselves on the floor, praying as long as they like, irrespective of the priest's presence, and leave when they please. For the majority of Hindus, worship in temples is less important than their worship at home. Some Hindus go to a temple daily, some occasionally, and some seldom. The temples have their own trustees and priests who organize and conduct the daily worship of the diety with prayers and rituals. Devotees are content with the general worship that is done by the priest in the temple, but they know that their own particular commitment (worship) to their own personal God has to be met in their own way in their own time and place, usually at home.

Solo worship: Meditative worship is essentially solo. Often a rosary (*japa-mālā*) of 108 beads is used as a tool in *japa*, the repetitive murmuring of prayers or God's name.

Family worship: The members of a family get together to worship collectively, with the family *guru* or the head of the family conducting the ceremony for the well-being of the whole family. In urban situations it may well be the mother who offers *pūjā* early in the morning on behalf of her family.

***Kīrtana*:** The only form of worship that can be called semi-congregational is the worship of the *bhakti* groups in the form of singing *kīrtana*s (repetitive singing of a sacred phrase or God's name) or *bhajana*s (songs of praise). Even that has no structured format. Devotees get together and sing for hours; people come and join at any point in the continuous singing and leave when they need to.

Time for worship

Although Hindu religious ceremonies are numerous and vary from area to area and from community to community, reflecting the heterogeneity of Hinduism arising from many cultures, yet they may be classified according to their frequency and purpose. The following is Sen's classification (1973: 32).

Daily worship: To be performed twice a day during both the twilight hours: early morning and dusk. *Prātaḥ-kṛtya* (to be performed early in the morning) and *Sandhyā* (at dusk) are performed by the high-caste Hindu daily in his own home, where it is usual to have a family shrine with images or symbols of deities (e.g., a special *śālagrāma* stone for Viṣṇu or *liṅga* for Śiva). There is also daily worship in most temples conducted by the Brahman priest. This includes prayers and detailed rituals.

Weekly worship: Some Hindus follow weekly religious observances: for example, fasting on a particular day of the week and ending the fast with simple ritual worship. Often this is a Thursday (*Bṛhaspati-vāra*: *Bṛhaspati*/the name of the *guru* of the gods; *vāra*/day), when women fast and worship Lakṣmī for the general well-being of the family. Thursday, known also as *Guru-vāra* (the day of the *guru*), is considered an auspicious day in the Hindu week.

Fortnightly and monthly worship: Some prayers and fastings are observed according to the lunar calendar. The moon is believed to have a direct influence on the human body and mind as it has an influence on nature (e.g., the ebb and flow of the tide). Fasting is prescribed at the time of the full moon and the new moon to keep one's body fit and one's emotions under control. Fasting usually ends with worship of the family deity or the deity related to the occasion.

Annual religious festivals: These are mostly connected with the worship (*pūjā*) of various deities of the Hindu pantheon: e.g., *Lakṣmī-pūjā*, *Sarasvatī-pūjā*, *Durgā-pūjā*, *Kālī-pūjā*, *Śiva-rātri*, *Gaṇeśa-chaturthī*, and so on. These can be performed at home, in temples or in outdoor temple-like structures temporarily erected for the festival. Some of the annual religious ceremonies even celebrate mythical events like the birth of Rāma (e.g., *Rāma-navamī*) or Kṛṣṇa (e.g., *Janmāṣṭamī*), and the mythical personalities are worshipped on those occasions.

There are other annual occasions for praying to God for all sorts of reasons. For example, on *Bhrātṛdvitīyā* sisters put sandalwood marks on the foreheads of their brothers and wish them freedom from death. At *Navānna* (the new rice), the harvest festival, God is thanked for the agricultural, thus economic, success of the community. On all these occasions and many others there is ritual worship of God in various forms, depending upon the occasion itself.

Often the same festival may have different names in different regions. For example, what is known as the festival of *Navarātri* (nine nights) in Gujarat and other parts of India is in Bengal known as *Durgā-pūjā*, coinciding with the last three nights of *Navarātri*. The worship of the Mother for nine days and nights finishes with *Dasserā* or *Vijayā* or *Vijayā Daśamī* (the tenth day). Similarly, the harvest festival is called *Navānna* in Bengal, *Pongal* in Tamilnadu and *Onam* in Kerala. During *Dīvālī*, or *Dīpāvalī*, the festival of lights, most regions of India, especially in the north, commemorate the legendary hero Rāma's victory over Rāvaṇa and his homecoming with his wife Sītā, yet in Bengal *Dīpāvalī* is in celebration of *Kālī-pūjā*.

Incidental worship: Occasional worship, such as a *vrata* (votive worship), is primarily optional. *Vrata*s 'have little scriptural backing, are performed mainly by women, and are intended normally for the welfare of the family or the community. *Sāvitrī Vrata* is for the welfare of the husband, *Shashṭhi Vrata* for the well-being of the children, *Māghamaṇḍala Vrata* for sunshine in the winter months, *Pausha Vrata* for good harvests, and so on' (Sen, 1973: 33).

Astronomical occasions: On days of certain auspicious astronomical configurations and eclipses people often gather in temples or at river pilgrimage sites, such as river confluences, for prayer and bathing. For example, every twelve years, on the occasion of the auspicious *Kumbha* configuration, people from all over India gather at Allahabad, located at the confluence of the rivers Gaṅgā (the Ganges) and Yamunā. The gathering (*melā*) lasts for a month. At the height of the *melā*, on a single day about ten million worshippers take a dip in the water and greet the dawn with prayers. In that month a number of non-stop outdoor Hindu ecumenical congresses take place on the mudflats.

Sacraments: Each stage of a Hindu's life is sanctified formally with an act of worship, whether it is a ceremony of *nāmakaraṇa* (naming of a child), *annaprāśana* (a child's first rice-eating) or *vivāha* (marriage). Sixteen such sacraments (*saṃskāra*s) are observed throughout life from conception (*garbhādhāna*) to funeral (*antyeṣṭi*).

Places of worship

There is no specified place for worship in Hinduism. There are home shrines, roadside shrines, temples, places of pilgrimage or the seclusion of the woodlands and the mountains. However, the most common place of worship is one's own family shrine, be it a humble wooden shelf with images of deities on it, an elaborately ornate brass throne with a canopy over it, or a complete room set aside as a *mandir*.

For a *jñāna-yogī* (see p. 212 above) even a shrine with images is unnecessary. A quiet place is all he needs for contemplative meditation. Some prefer to leave the community for seclusion. The caves of the Himalayan foothills are renowned secluded spots.

All over India, humble roadside open-air shrines are found at the base of trees such as *vaṭa*s or *aśvattha*s (*Ficus religiosa*) that are considered sacred. A symbolic stone (e.g., the *Śālagrāma-śilā* of Viṣṇu) or a *Śiva-liṅga* is often installed there. Flowers or small sums of money are offered by the passers-by as homage to the deity. Thus an abode of a living God for the local communities comes into being.

Temples are the permanent 'residence' of a deity and daily worship is performed by the priest, but the majority of Hindus visit temples only on special occasions. Worship in temples is wholly optional for them.

On specific religious festivals, temporary temple-like structures are erected in open fields or parks where statues of the deities are placed and worshipped ceremonially. In Bengal, during festivals such as the grand *Durgā-pūjā*, *Kālī-pūjā* and *Sarasvatī-pūjā*, the temporary structures become as sacred as the temples.

Places of pilgrimage, associated with the lives of mythical heroes such as Rāma or Kṛṣṇa, or with the birth or enlightenment of a saint, attract pilgrims all the year round. The sites of river pilgrimages do the same on auspicious days (see above, p. 222).

Worship and the arts

Religion and the everyday life of the people are almost inseparable in Hinduism. Consequently, the creative activities of daily life are also inseparable from worship. A musician or an artist, for example, often humbly declares that his whole life is a long act of worship. Whatever he creates is an offering to his God. He considers himself a mere instrument. Through him God is creating beautiful things and no credit is due to him. The often-observed anonymity in Hindu art creation is due to this attitude among artists.

Artists in general are *karma-yogī*s (see p. 210 above) as they achieve enlightenment through their creative work (*karma*). They may join others in celebrating religious festivals without caring much for rituals. To them *pūjā* is dedication and not ritual worship. However, *Sarasvatī-pūjā* is the rare occasion when musicians, artists and artisans place the tools of their trade to be blessed at the feet of Sarasvatī, the goddess of the muses.

MUSIC

Hindu music is rooted in religious worship. It can be traced back to the age of the *Sāma-veda* (*c.* 1500 BCE) when hymns in praise of individual gods were sung around the sacrificial fire. For the desired result from a sacrifice, the pronunciation of hymns had to be accurate and the singing needed to be precise, with long–short durations of notes (*svara*s) and with prescribed high–low–medium tones. Three musical pitches or tones are mentioned in the Veda for the singing of the hymns: *udātta* (high), *anudātta* (not high, i.e., grave) and *svarita* (sounded, i.e., articulated). Over the ages, from these simple three-pitch plain songs grew a sophisticated system of seven pure (*śuddha*) notes (*svara*s) with their sharp (*tīvra*) and flat (*komala*) variations.

The earliest form of Hindu vocal music, with the complete gamut of musical notes, is known as *dhruvapada* (*dhrupada* for short) which means 'the constant (*dhruva*) syllable (*pada*)'. The themes of *dhrupada*s are always in praise of deities, often Śiva as the Lord of cosmic rhythm and dance (*Naṭarāja*).

Communal singing in praise of a deity is a special feature of the act of worship in some sects in Hinduism. The advent of the *bhakti* (devotion) movement in the eleventh and twelfth centuries generated the singing of *kīrtanas*/*bhajana*s (devotional songs) which became an integral part of a popular form of worship. The simple but passionate songs of great poet-saints like Jayadeva, Chandidasa and Mira won the hearts of millions in their day, and still stir up emotions in present day Hindus. Music is recognized as a powerful medium of spiritual communication, and *kīrtana*s are sung in groups in temple courtyards or in a procession, though mostly in family gatherings.

The *Bāul*s of Bengal are especially renowned for their simple songs with mystical or metaphysical content. They are the minstrels or bards whose lifestyle is free and not inhibited by any dogmas or social injunctions. They regard their own body as the temple of God, who resides in it in the disguise of their own soul. They ignore all rituals and worship their inner soul (*maner mānuṣ*), the God within, with spontaneous songs. The Nobel laureate poet-musician Rabindranath Tagore (1861–1941) was greatly influenced by the *Bāuls*' mystic philosophy and their simple moving tunes, and he composed several songs with similar simple tunes and spiritual lyrics.

DANCE

Hindu classical dance-forms, like Hindu music, are associated with worship. References to dance and music are found in the vedic literature, indicating that some form of ritual dancing constituted an integral part of the sacrificial rites. The graceful art is mentioned in the *Ṛg-veda*, and more frequently in the *Atharva-veda* and *Yajur-veda*. But the earliest specific detailed documentation on dancing is found in Bharata's *Nāṭya-śāstra* (*nāṭya*/dramaturgy, *śāstra*/manual – probably compiled between the fourth century BCE and the first century CE), where the arts of music and dancing are dealt with as essential components of the dramaturgy of the day. A divine origin is attributed to dramaturgy itself as a whole. According to the *Nāṭya-śāstra* (I. 11–17), at the request of the gods, Brahmā the creator composed *Nāṭya-veda*, taking the text from the *Ṛg-veda*, music from the *Sāma-veda*, gestures from the *Yajur-veda* and sentiments from the *Atharva-veda*. Śiva and his consort Pārvatī contributed to the dance. Śiva's cosmic dance of destruction constituted the rigorous masculine form – the *tāṇḍava* – and Pārvatī's dance constituted the enchanting feminine style – the *lāsya*. The sage Bharata was authorized to popularize the divine dance-forms in the world through his *Nāṭya-śāstra*.

At the outset of a recital, a classical dancer pays a ritual homage to Śiva as the Lord of the dance (*Naṭarāja*). This simple act of *pūjā* shows that dance is considered not merely as an art-form giving expression to physical and emotional exuberance but as an offering to God.

As the cult of Śiva expanded during the seventh to fourteenth centuries and hundreds of temples were built, dancing developed as one of the principal temple rituals. In South India the *Bharatanāṭyam* dance-form originated as the temple dance of the *devadāsī*s (handmaidens of God), dedicated for life to God's service. They were ceremonially married to the principal deity of the temple and offered their dance and song to the deity as oblation. They went through long and rigorous training and were accomplished in dancing and music and other allied arts.

The *Odissi*, the dance-form of Orissa in north-eastern India, also originated as a temple dance. The dancers were known as the *māhārīs*. During the eleventh and twelfth centuries the cult of Viṣṇu spread through this region. The Vaiṣṇava philosophy of Rāmānuja and Jayadeva's devotional poetry *Gīta-Govinda* influenced the arts tremendously. The worship of Jagannātha (Lord of the world, a form of Viṣṇu/Kṛṣṇa) became widespread. In the temple of Jagannātha in Puri several *māhārīs* were installed. The synthesis of the Śaiva and the Vaiṣṇava traditions is visible in the *Odissi* dance performance of today. Similarly, the *Kuchipudi* dance of Andhra Pradesh and the *Kathākali* dance of Kerala are also associated with the regional temple dances.

Thus the arts of Hindu dance and music were preserved over the centuries as temple culture, in spite of political upheavals in the country. Manuals (*śāstra*s) of the arts, including sculpture and architecture, were compiled and stored in temples. Temples became centres of learning. Though in northern India temples often fell victim to the Islamic invasion, in the south they survived and so did the great treasure-houses of Hindu culture, providing a remarkable degree of continuity to this day.

THE VISUAL ARTS

Similar to the performing arts, Hindu visual arts also evolved around religion and objects of worship. There is a close relationship between sculpture, painting, architecture and worship. Very often Hindu works of sculpture and painting are devoted to revealing the divine personality in the images, and those of architecture to increasing the dignity of temples. The images of deities are often not anatomically precise, but the aim is to emphasize the emotion or *bhāva* in expression. For expressing specific sentiments or *rasa*s,[7] the artists are guided by a number of manuals (*śāstra*s) on aesthetic procedure.

Hindu arts, therefore, developed through the ages not just as the execution of an artist's uncontrolled aesthetic inspiration, but were also moulded by the conventions on proportion, pose, gesture and even colour of the images. Because the devotees are also familiar with these conventions, they readily recognize the intended emotion portrayed in the image. The dancing form of Śiva (*Naṭarāja*) or the tri-flexed (*tribhaṅga*) posture of Kṛṣṇa evokes certain emotions in the mind of the worshipper. The prescribed colour of Viṣṇu, Kṛṣṇa, Rāma and Kālī is dark, whereas that of Śiva and Sarasvatī is white, and so on. The image installed in the sanctuary of a temple, to be worthy of worship, has to be perfect in proportion, pose and gesture in accordance with the strict scriptural canon. However, the artist has more freedom in making images that are not intended for worship, e.g., the numerous sculpted figures on the outer walls of Hindu temples. Even secular subjects, like a group of musicians or amorous couples, found their way into the temple art of the Hindus.

Alongside the classical tradition of prescribed, stylized visual art-forms there developed a branch of folk art, especially painting. Like any folk art, it reflects the spontaneity and vivid imagination of the artists at the grassroots. Such paintings are often done on scrolls, using the mythological stories of gods and goddesses. The illustrated scrolls are used by wandering bards as an aid to telling stories. In Bengal, religious paintings (*paṭas*) are done on clay plates that are hung on the wall. The colours used are typically vibrant red, blue, yellow, green, black, and so on.

This tradition of folk art, though still continuing today, has taken the new form of printed posters and calendar pictures. People frame these brightly coloured prints of Hindu deities and keep them in their family shrine or hang them on the wall. This mass-produced, easily affordable religious art-form has made the presence of the deities visible in all Hindu homes worldwide.

Worship as a natural response

The first sound that many Hindus utter when they wake up in the morning is the name of their God, repeated three times, e.g., *Om Rām Rām Rām* or *Om Durgā Durgā Durgā*. They believe that the utterance will see them safely through the day. Going out of the house they do the same, and again at the end of the day before going to sleep. Uttering God's name or praying to God has become so much a part of everyday life that a Hindu does not often stop and think what he or she has been doing. Worship has become second nature.

Notes

1 The four Vedas are the most revered scriptures of the Hindus, believed not to have been composed by humans (*apauruṣeya*) but revealed to the seers (*ṛṣis*). The word *veda* (from the root *vid* meaning 'to know') means knowledge. The *Ṛg-veda*, the earliest Veda, consists of hymns (*ṛcs*), metrical in form, in praise of deities. The *Sāma-veda*, the Veda of songs (*sāman*), consists mainly of Ṛg-vedic hymns selected to be sung aloud during sacred rites (cf. the Book of Psalms in the Bible). The *Yajur-veda* (*yajus* means 'worship') deals, mostly in prose, with the formulae of actual performance of rituals. The *Atharva-veda* deals with magical formulae for destruction of evils and sins, herbal cure of ailments and other fields of knowledge which may not relate to sacred rituals directly.

2 In a vedic *yajña* the priests of the four Vedas have their respective roles to play. *Hotā*, the Ṛg-vedic priest, recites the hymns from the *Ṛg-veda*; *Udgātā*, the Sāma-vedic priest, sings the hymns aloud from the *Sāma-veda*; *Adhvaryu*, the officiating priest of *Yajur-veda*, performs the actual detailed ritual; and Brahman, the priest of the *Atharva-veda*, supervises the conduct of the *yajña* as a whole.

3 The cult of *Tantra* stresses action rather than renunciation. It believes in overcoming desires and fears by thoroughly experiencing them because ultimate mastery is achieved by recognizing and accepting human limitations.

The central theme of *Tantra* is dualism in which two factors together create a single whole. Each creation is the result of interplay between two equally important principles: the passive experiencing consciousness is the masculine (*Śiva/puruṣa*) and the creative acting force the feminine (*Śakti/prakṛti*). Sexual *yoga* and rituals in tantric tradition are the result of acceptance of sexuality as the basis of all creation.

4 See Chapters 1 and 2 of this book for a more detailed discussion of the important Hindu concepts of *mukti* and *mokṣa*.

5 The *Trimūrti* (three manifestations) is a symbolic unification of the three essential elements of the divine, and is examined in Chapter 7 of this book.

6 *Svastika/kā* is an ancient symbol of good luck (*svasti* signifying well-being) found all over India on the walls, doorways and arches of Hindu temples. It can be traced back to the Indus Valley civilization (*c.* 2000 BCE) where bricks have been found stamped with the sign. It derives from the cross. From a central point the arms extend outwards in four directions signifying that diverse worlds, activities, faiths share a basic unity of spirit. It also implies the continual cyclical movement of time.

Svastika can face either way, showing two ways to the spirit: the (clockwise) right-hand path (*dakṣiṇāchāra*) of rituals and worship, and the (anti-clockwise) left-hand path (*vāmāchāra*) of esoteric techniques, e.g. *Tantra*.

7 Hindu aesthetics is based on the realization of *rasa*. Any art-form, whether performing, visual or literary, has to pass the test of *rasa*, a kind of emotional involvement or relish felt by its recipients. Eight main *rasa*s described in Bharata's *Nāṭya-śāstra* (VI.15) are based on pre-experienced human feelings (*bhāva*s). Thus *bhāva* is the root-cause (*janaka*) of *rasa*, the effect (*janya*). The experience of *rasa* is always pleasant. Even an unpleasant natural human feeling, like grief or fear, can give rise to a pleasurable feeling of pathos or suspense when *rasa* is achieved through art-forms.

Further reading

Appadurai, A., Korom, F. J. and Miles, M. A. (eds) (1991) *Gender, Genre and Power in South Asian Expressive Traditions*. Philadelphia: University of Pennsylvania Press.
Cavendish, R. (1980) *The Great Religions*. London: Weidenfeld & Nicolson for W. H. Smith.
Chaudhuri, N. C. (1979) *Hinduism: A Religion to Live By*. London: Chatto and Windus.
Fuller, C. (1992) *The Camphor Flame: Popular Hinduism and Society in India*. Princeton, NJ: Princeton University Press.
Heesterman, J. C. (1993) *The Broken World of Sacrifice: An Essay in Ancient Indian Ritual*. Chicago and London: University of Chicago Press.
Mookerjee, A. and Khanna, M. (1977) *The Tantric Way: Art Science Ritual*. London: Thames and Hudson.
Radhakrishnan, S. (1971) *The Hindu View of Life*. 16th edn; London: Unwin Books.
Rawson, P. (1988) *The Art of Tantra*. London: Thames and Hudson.
Sen, K. M. (1973) *Hinduism*. 8th edn; London: Penguin.
Swami Swarupananda (1982) *Srimad-Bhagavad-Gita*. Calcutta: Advaita Ashrama.
Swami Vivekananda (1963) *Hinduism*. Madras: Sri Ramakrishna Math.
Younger, P. (1995) *The House of the Dancing Śivan: The Traditions of the Hindu Temple in Citamparam*. Oxford: Oxford University Press.
Zaehner, R. C. (1972) *Hinduism*. 3rd edn; London: Oxford University Press.

9. Sacred place

Anuradha Roma Choudhury

As a religion Hinduism is heterogeneous in character. It is a synthesis of many different beliefs and practices, various sets of values and morals, culminating in a way of life. Strictly speaking, it is not a 'religion' in the accepted Western sense. Religious and non-religious matters are never truly distinguished in Hinduism. Each and every activity of life is thought to have some kind of divine purpose in it. The ordinary daily chores which are usually seen as 'secular' can be seen by an orthodox Hindu as having some divine potential. Accordingly, the topic of 'sacred place', as the Hindus see it, covers a very broad and varied arena indeed.

As sacredness has a religious connotation, places that are considered sacred are often closely associated with religious worship. In that context, for a Hindu, family shrines, temples, places of pilgrimage, all are considered sacred and will be discussed later. In addition, there are places of natural beauty such as awe-inspiring mountains, vast oceans, peaceful woodlands, which are not directly linked with religious worship but which are still held sacred by the Hindus for their serenity, magnificence and conduciveness to calm and a philosophical mood. Hence, sacred places are not necessarily confined to religious buildings alone, but can be discovered in the context of nature worship of the ancient Hindus.

Sacred natural environment

MOUNTAINS

Hindus of the past and present have always been attracted by the Himalayas (Himālaya = abode/*ālaya*, of snow/*hima*). Its snow-clad peaks, beckoning with undiscovered mysteries and overwhelmingly awe-inspiring height and grandeur, held the Hindu spellbound. The innate humility one experiences in front of such a massive phenomenon develops into the kind of veneration that Hindus feel for this mountain. Though there are other mountains (e.g., Vindhya, Nilagiri, etc.) in India picturesque enough to inspire Sanskrit poets (e.g. Bhavabhuti of the eighth century in *Uttara-Rāmacharita*), yet Himālaya enjoys a special reverence that others do not. It has been revered from ancient times as the abode of the gods of the Hindu pantheon. Durgā, the Universal Mother, also known as Pārvatī (lit. of the mountain/*parvata*), is the daughter of Himālaya according to Hindu mythology. Her consort Śiva lives in Kailāsa, a peak in the Himālaya, where he performs his long and arduous meditation. There are numerous references to sages (*ṛṣis*) and saints engaged in penances (*tapas*) in the Himālaya in the epics *Rāmāyaṇa* and *Mahābhārata* and in various mythological episodes in the *Purāṇas* (the ancient/*purā* narratives). The classical Sanskrit literature is full of praises for the Himālaya. Kalidasa, the most renowned Sanskrit poet, addresses Himālaya as *devatātmā* (the Divine Soul or the soul/*ātmā* of the gods/*devatā*) and elevates it to the status of divinity (*Kumārasambhava* I.1).

The symbolism of the mountains is evident even in the architecture of Hindu temples, which are modelled on the soaring peaks of natural mountains. The architectural terminology also makes this connection. The crown of a temple is called *śikhara*, a word which also means 'mountain peak' or 'crest'. That a temple can be identified with a mountain peak is seen from the name of Kailāsa Temple in Ellora. In the North Indian style of temple architecture, a conscious attempt to imitate the gradual ascending pattern of a complete mountain range is noticeable in the various levels of a temple complex. The fact that the Hindus chose to model their religious structures on the mountains indicates the sacredness they attach to them. After all, a grand mountain is not just a visual spectacle, but its soaring height symbolizes the spiritual height a Hindu hopes to achieve.

CAVES

In association with the mountains, the caves (*guhās*) are also often regarded as sacred places. As George Michell (1977: 69) points out:

> The cave is a most enduring image in Hinduism, functioning both as a place of retreat and as the occasional habitation of the gods. Caves must always have been felt to be places of great sanctity and they were sometimes enlarged to provide places of worship.

The rock-cut temples (e.g., in Elephanta caves), with their interior spaces skilfully hewn and decorated with sculpted images, indicate that the man-made grottoes were considered to be as sacred as their natural prototypes.

The sanctity of the caves is transposed to the innermost sanctuary of the temples, which is kept deliberately unadorned, small and dark, with no vent for natural light, strongly resembling a natural cave. On entering a temple, the symbolic mountain, a pilgrim gradually progresses towards the interior, the symbolic cave, where the image or symbol of the deity is housed. The progression from light into darkness, from large open foreground to the small confined sanctum, from elaborately ornate exterior to unadorned plain interior 'may be interpreted by the devotee as a progression of increasing sanctity culminating in the focal point of the temple, the cave' (Michell, 1977: 70).

SEA AND LAKES

Just as the grandeur of a mountain humbles the human mind, so does the vastness of a sea. The tranquillity of the sea gives it a meditative and hence a sacred connotation. Peninsular India is surrounded by sea on three sides and there is a tradition of shore temples built in this sacred environment. The famous temple of Jagannātha (a form of Viṣṇu) is situated in the seaside city of Puri, in Orissa, on the eastern seaboard of the Bay of Bengal. Further south, by the Bay of Bengal, are the most renowned shore temples of Mahābalīpuram and Rāmeśvaram temple; and at the confluence of the Bay of Bengal, the Indian Ocean and the Arabian Sea is the temple of Kanyākumārī. The western seaboard is also studded with temples of various dimensions and description, of which the cave temple of Elephanta is particularly eminent. In the epic *Mahābhārata* (III.118.4), the sea is described as *lokapuṇya*, which literally means 'where people acquire religious merits' (people/*loka*, religious merit/*puṇya*) or in other words, 'sacred/holy to people'. Also, mention is made (III.118.8) of places of pilgrimage by the sea (*tīrthāni cha sāgarasya*). Like many others in search of spiritual realization in the past, Swami Vivekananda, the Hindu monk of the late nineteenth and early twentieth centuries, chose a rock in the sea at the southernmost tip of India, near Kanyakumari, for his seat of mediation. It is now known as Vivekananda Rock and can be seen on the pilgrims' map.

Of the lakes in India, Puṣkara lake near Ajmer and Mānasa Sarovara near the Kailāsa peak of Himālaya in Tibet are considered specially holy by Hindus.

RIVERS

Rivers in general have very special significance in Hinduism for their life-sustaining and purifying qualities, and the Ganges (Gaṅgā) is regarded as the holiest of them all. To Hindus Gaṅgā is known as the Mother who 'bestows prosperity' (*sukhadā*) and 'secures salvation' (*mokṣadā*). In *Brahma-vaivarta Purāṇa* (*Kṛṣṇajanma Khaṇḍa* 34) it is said in praise of Gaṅgā:

> She is the source of redemption. ... As fire consumes fuel, so this stream consumes the sins of the wicked. ... If a man, at an auspicious hour of time, takes a dip in the holy river, he dwells cheerfully in Vishnu's heavenly world, *Vaikuṇṭha*.
>
> (Singh, 1989: 47)

The water of Gaṅgā and its banks are held in such high esteem by Hindus that it is believed that dying at its bank liberates one's soul from the cycle of rebirths. Not so long ago, devout Hindus used to express as their last wish that they should be taken to the bank of Gaṅgā in their final hours of life. This final journey is known as *Gaṅgā-yātrā* (journey/*yātrā* to *Gaṅgā*). Such conviction and faith in Gaṅgā elevates the river almost to divinity.

Mythologically, Gaṅgā, the river of heaven, originated from Viṣṇu's toe. It was brought down to the earth by King Bhagīratha through severe austerities and penances, to wash away the sins of his dead ancestors. Śiva, the great god (Mahādeva), agreed to hold the first thrust of the tumultuous river falling from heaven in his matted locks, thus softening its blow to the earth. Because Gaṅgā was led by Bhagīratha, one of its names is Bhāgīrathī. In reality, Gaṅgā originates from the Himalayas. At Hardwar (Haridvāra) it descends to the plains, and near Allahabad at Prayaga it meets the river Yamunā. The meeting point (*saṅgama*) of any two rivers is considered sacred; especially so is the confluence of Gaṅgā and Yamunā. Hindus gather from all over India to bathe there on auspicious days in order to acquire extra religious merit. All the places, cities and towns through which Gaṅgā flows are also considered to be sacred, e.g. Haridvāra, Varanasi (Banaras), Kalighat (Calcutta), etc.

WOODLANDS

Hindus have a long and ancient tradition of forest culture. Woodland is revered not only for its contemplative atmosphere, but also for the continuous process of renewal of life that goes on in nature. The vedic priests and poets worshipped the forest as Araṇyānī (*Ṛg-veda* X.146), the Goddess of the Forest. There is also a whole set of vedic texts called *Āraṇyaka*s (lit. related to *araṇya*/forest). They deal with life during *vānaprastha* (related to *vana*/woodland), the third phase (*āśrama*) of a Hindu's life, the period of retirement. The *tapovana*s (woodlands/*vana*, for religious austerities/*tapas*), frequently referred to in Sanskrit literature, are places where individual sages (*ṛṣis*/*munis*) have their hermitages (*āśrama*), and where the setting is ideal for the training of students in religious and philosophical pursuits. Thus, *tapovana*s and *āśrama*s, the seats of educational, intellectual and spiritual interactions, are considered by Hindus as places worthy of reverence. The epic *Rāmāyaṇa* has a whole chapter called *Araṇya-kāṇḍa* (*araṇya*/forest, *kāṇḍa*/chapter – *Rāmāyaṇa* III), where there are many descriptions of *tapovana*s and *āśrama*s of various sages, and references to how revered these places were. The same is true of the epic *Mahābhārata*, where a whole chapter (III), called *Āraṇyaka-parvan* (*āraṇyaka*/related to forest, *parvan*/chapter or episode), is dedicated to the life of the Pāṇḍavas, the five heroic brothers, in the forest. In later classical literature also there are ample examples of sacredness that people attach to such *tapovana*s or *āśrama*s. For example, in the play *Abhijñāna-Śakuntalam* by Kalidasa (Act I), Duṣyanta the hero says 'let us purify ourselves with a sight of the holy hermitage (*puṇyāśrama-darśanena tāvadātmānam punīmahe*)'.

Some individual types of trees and plants are also considered by Hindus as sacred; these attitudes are discussed in greater depth in Chapter 4 of this book.

Considering the reverence Hindus attach to their natural environment – mountains, rivers, woodlands, etc. – it is not unreasonable to infer that the sense of such sanctity originated from nature worship. Sacredness of a place, therefore, for a Hindu, is not necessarily confined to religious structures made by people.

Places of pilgrimage

Pilgrimage to holy places is not an obligatory duty for a Hindu as the pilgrimage to Makkah is for a Muslim. Yet Hindus undertake long arduous journeys to places considered as sacred. The most commonly believed purpose of this practice is to cleanse away one's past sins and acquire spiritual merit for one's future life after death. The more austere the journey, the more spiritual merit one gains.

The Sanskrit word for a place of pilgrimage is *tīrtha* (from the root *tṛ*/to cross over). It has several connotations such as a ford, passage, stairs for descent into a river, bathing place and so on, but all of them are connected with water. In fact, a significant number of the sacred places are located on the banks of bodies of water. This association of water with *tīrtha*s, or sacredness in general, may have continued from a very early period, following on from the vedic reverence for water or rivers. In the *Atharva-veda* (1.VI.2–4) water is upheld as the bestower of remedies and protection. At places of pilgrimage where there is no natural water supply, artificial ponds are cut, because physical cleansing of devotees prior to participation in rituals is important.

The term *tīrtha*, apart from having the primary meaning of crossing over water, also has a symbolic meaning. It symbolizes the location of the intersection of two realms, the mundane and the spiritual, the profane and the sacred. In that respect, the physical journey to the *tīrtha*s is instrumental in the spiritual progress of the pilgrims.

The practice of pilgrimage (*tīrtha-yātrā; yātrā*/journey) must have gained religious significance from very early times. It is given prominence in the *Mahābhārata* and the *Purāṇa*s, where many *tīrtha*s, their presiding deities, the glories and fruits to be gained by visiting, are celebrated at length. In the *Mahābhārata* a major section of the *Āraṇyaka-parvan* (Book of the Forest) is devoted to a grand tour of pilgrimage sites in India (*Tīrtha-yātrā-parvan*, III.80–93, 109, 114, 118–120, 129, 140–153). Several *Purāṇa*s glorify numerous shrines throughout India, as Morinis (1984: 50) points out (e.g., *Matsya Purāṇa* 13.103–112, 186–194; *Skanda Purāṇa* 2, called *Tīrtha Khaṇḍa*; *Vāyu Purāṇa* 105–112; *Kūrma Purāṇa* I.30). In later texts, especially in the *tantras*, more lists of sacred places and their characteristics appear. Although some of the *tīrthas* named in the above sources have disappeared and some new ones have arisen (e.g., Puttapurti in South India has become a *tīrtha* this century because of the presence of Satya Sai Baba, the saint of miracles), many of the ancient sacred places named are still regarded as important *tīrthas* for Hindus today (e.g., Varanasi/Kasi/Banaras).

HOW DOES A PLACE BECOME RECOGNIZED AS A *TĪRTHA*?

As mentioned earlier, in India sacred places are often associated with regions of natural serenity and grandeur, especially mountains and rivers. The Ganges (Gaṅgā) itself has multiple *tīrthas* along its banks. Yet not all scenic sites or miles of riverbank are revered as places of pilgrimage. There are several factors which contribute to the transformation of an ordinary site into a *tīrtha* – factors that initiate the development of some kind of religious activity. A *tīrtha* might be a place where an individual achieved recognized spiritual inspiration (e.g., Bodhgaya for the Buddha), or where realization came to a devotee about his or her deity (e.g., Dakshineshwar for Ramakrishna Paramahamsa, who had visions of the goddess Kālī there), or where an image of a deity was unearthed or miraculously appeared under unusual circumstances, or where the water of a pond or a river was believed to cure diseases, and so on. Some charismatic individuals, both historical (e.g., the Buddha, Chaitanya, Ramakrishna Paramahamsa) and legendary/mythical (e.g., Rāma, Kṛṣṇa), become prominent enough to be remembered with reverence, and therefore the places associated with their lives (places of birth, spiritual enlightenment, preaching, etc.) come to be recognized as sacred.

When a place is considered worth visiting for one reason or another, eventually a temple is built there, dedicated to the deity popular in that region or associated with the individual concerned. Often it is the ruling prince or a wealthy benefactor who endows the land or provides funds for the temple. The erection of a temple itself helps to glorify the site of devotion. It is the prior recognition of the sanctity of a place (*sthāna-māhātmya; sthāna*/place, *māhātmya*/glory) that prompts the building of a temple and not the other way round, but once the temple is there, it becomes the focal point of religious activities, a centre for spiritual discourses, a meeting place for devotees. In its turn the temple helps to attract pilgrims from far and wide, making the region into a thriving *tīrtha*.

VARIOUS TYPES OF HINDU *TĪRTHA*

Tīrtha-yātrā is an age-old tradition with Hindus from every part of India. Yet it is possible to identify a body of sacred places of overall importance visited by all Hindus as opposed to *tīrtha*s which are important to the sub-sects of Hinduism and sub-cultural regions. The *tīrtha*s that are mentioned in ancient and classical religious texts are the most revered by all Hindus, such as the famous group of seven *tīrtha*s designated as *mokṣapurī*s (holy cities/*purī* where one gains liberation/*mokṣa*), i.e., Ayodhya, Mathura, Kasi, Kanchi, Avantika, Puri and Dvaravati. Then there are *tīrtha*s visited mostly by the devotees of individual sects: the Śaivas or devotees of Śiva (e.g., Varanasi); the Śāktas or devotees of Śakti/Devī/Mother (e.g., Kamakhya) or the Vaiṣṇavas or devotees of Viṣṇu (e.g., Vrindavana). Even among the national *tīrtha*s, Kasi/Varanasi and Avantika/Ujjayini are more frequented by the Śaivas, as Śiva is the presiding deity of those two holy cities. Similarly, Ayodhya, Mathura and Puri are the most important *tīrtha*s for the Vaiṣṇavas, as these are the cities associated with either Rāma or Kṛṣṇa (incarnations of Viṣṇu). Other kinds of variations in *tīrtha*s are found on a regional sub-cultural basis. For example, in the Bengal region, which is a stronghold of Śāktas and Vaiṣṇavas alike, Tarapith (Śākta) and Navadvip (Vaiṣṇava) are the most important *tīrtha*s for Bengali Hindus, but may not be so for Hindus from other parts of India.

GROUPING OF *TĪRTHAS*

There is a tradition in India of grouping sacred places in various systems. The seven *mokṣapurī*s, the cities that bestow liberation on the pilgrims, have been mentioned earlier. Then there is the group of seven *tīrtha*s (*sapta-tīrtha*, using the primary meaning of water), referring to the seven holy rivers that wash away sins and purify a Hindu, i.e., the Ganges, Yamuna, Sarasvati, Narmada, Kaveri, Godavari and Sindhu. The group of four *dhāma*s (holy sites) comprising Badrinath, Kedarnath, Gangotri and Yamunotri combine together as the *tīrtha*s in the mountainous Garhwal region of the Himalayas. Another version of four *dhāma*s groups Badrinath, Dvaraka, Ramesvaram and

Jagannatha-puri together. In South India the tendency is to group together *tīrtha*s with shrines of a particular deity, to make a cluster of shrines. For example, the five *bhūta-liṅga*s dedicated to Śiva, the six centres of the deity Murukān, the six *tīrtha*s of Ayyapan (as quoted in Morinis, 1984: 46–7) and so on.

In North India, on the other hand, the practice of pilgrimage involves completing a holy circuit within the region of the main centre. For example, in visiting Gaya pilgrims can choose from several rounds consisting of five, eight, thirty-five or thirty-eight stations on the journey. In Banaras (or Varanasi/Kasi) pilgrims can choose from two routes of circumambulation of the city. One consists of five main stations (*pañcha-tīrtha*) and the other of a fifty-mile (*pañcha-kośī*) walk encircling the city, which is considered to be more meritorious than the former. Similarly, as Morinis states:

> A 600-mile course around the Himalayan sites above Rishikesh, including Gangotrī, Kedārnāth and Badrināth, is sacred for its inclusion of the sources of the three main branches of the Ganges: the Bhāgīrathī, Mandākinī and Alakanandā. The grandest circuit of all is that which covers the entire length of the Ganges, beginning on one bank at the source, travelling to the mouth, then returning up the other bank to the source again.
>
> (Morinis, 1984: 47)

Different systems of pilgrimage for different sects

THE ŚĀKTAS (DEVOTEES OF ŚAKTI/DEVĪ/MOTHER)

The idea of *Śakti*, on the one hand, is that of a supreme female deity representing the creative energy (*śakti*) of the universe, and on the other hand, she is the protective Mother or Devī. As is characteristic of all Hindu deities, *Śakti* has two aspects. As cosmic energy she is formless, boundless and beyond time, but as the Mother she has numerous forms and names (e.g., Kālī, Durgā, Umā, Satī, Pārvatī, Tārā, Chaṇḍī, Chāmuṇḍa, etc.) by which she is affectionately worshipped by the devotees.

The places of pilgrimage of the Śākta sect are known as *pīṭha*s (seats). A *pīṭha* is regarded as the sacred seat where the unmanifest goddess makes herself manifest. It is believed that *pīṭha*s are the places where she is in residence, where she can be approached personally.

Pīṭhas known as *siddha-pīṭhas* (*siddhi*/enlightenment) are considered particularly effective for acquiring spiritual power, wisdom and bliss (e.g. Tarapith in Bengal).

A myth that links most of the Śākta *pīṭhas* together and accounts for their sanctity is found in diverse Hindu texts, e.g., the *Mahābhārata* (XII.282–283), *Brahmā Purāṇa* (chapter 39) and several *tantra* texts. The myth is about Satī, who is the daughter of Dakṣa and the wife of Śiva. The narrative runs as follows.

Dakṣa, one of the sons of Brahmā, held a great sacrifice (*yajña*) to which he invited neither his daughter nor his son-in-law, due to some offence he had taken at Śiva's conduct. Satī was offended at this but nevertheless went to the sacrifice uninvited. She felt humiliated by her father who chose to insult Śiva in an open court and Satī took her own life in protest. On hearing this, Śiva charged the place of sacrifice, killed Dakṣa and retrieved the body of his wife. In inconsolable grief at the loss, Śiva placed Satī's body on his shoulder and began his dance of fury (*tāṇḍava*). The whole of creation was threatened by his wild dance. Viṣṇu was asked by the gods to appease Śiva and save the creation. To detach Satī from Śiva, Viṣṇu dismembered Satī's body with his discus (*chakra*). Without the body of Satī Śiva calmed down. The scattered parts of Satī's body fell to the earth and all the places where they landed became the sacred *pīthas*.

The list of these *pīṭhas* varies with different versions of the myth, but most commonly known are the fifty-one *pīṭhas*. Each *pīṭha* is identified by the part of Satī's body and the name and form of Devī in which she is worshipped there (e.g., in Varanasi-*pīṭha* where her ear-lobe fell, Śakti is worshipped in the name of Viśālākṣī). These *pīṭhas* are scattered geographically over a large region: Kanchipuram in the south, Hingula in Beluchistan in the west of Pakistan, Kashmir and Nepal in the north and Assam in the east. As Morinis (1984: 20) points out, the myth 'which unites the diverse and dispersed temples of the various goddesses strengthens the unity and organisation of the Śākta sect. The unity is expressed in the concept of each Śākta *pīṭha* sharing in the body of Satī.' The myth also helps to emphasize the sanctity of these *pīṭhas*, each having been energized by contact with the flesh of the goddess.

Not all the *pīṭhas* mentioned in ancient texts are active places of pilgrimage today and not all the present-day *tīrthas* are mentioned in the early texts. More recent well-visited Śākta temples are getting recognized as places of pilgrimage. For example, the Kālī Temple of

Dakshineshwar, near Calcutta, built in the nineteenth century, is now established as a place of Śākta pilgrimage, due to its association with the saint Ramakrishna Paramahamsa, for whom Kālī was a living deity.

The images or symbols of the goddess in the Śākta *pīṭhas* are not always in human-like forms. Sometimes they are rocks embedded in the floor of the temple (as at Labhpur, decorated with painted eyes and smeared with vermilion paste) or rough, uncarved stones (as in Tarapith, stored inside a hollow human image of the goddess).

The sect of Śakti is related to that of Śiva. Śiva and Śakti are conceived symbolically as a wedded couple. In every Śākta *pīṭha* Śiva is installed as a *liṅga* (phallic symbol) in a small shrine next to that of the goddess. There he is also visited by the pilgrims but holds a secondary status to that of the goddess.

THE ŚAIVAS (DEVOTEES OF ŚIVA)

Śiva, primarily the destroyer in the Hindu Trinity, is also revered as the supreme ascetic. The Śaiva sacred places are often busy refuges for wandering ascetics/*sādhus* and *yogīs*. In most places Śiva is worshipped in the form of a *liṅga*, a stylized phallic symbol. The *liṅga* worship may have originated from the pre-Aryan fertility cult which was absorbed by the Aryan Hindus into their cult of Rudra-Śiva in the post-vedic period. The *liṅga*, as the principal symbol of Śiva, represents his vast generative energy.

The places of Śaiva pilgrimage are known as *kṣetras* (fields). As in the Śākta tradition, the Śaiva tradition also recognizes a unity among its holy sites throughout India. The number of Śaiva *kṣetras* varies – five, twelve or sixty-eight. *Śiva Purāṇa* (XXXVIII.17–20) is the source of detailed accounts of Śaiva places of pilgrimage. It describes twelve *kṣetras* of sacred *liṅgas*, together with their names and the names by which Śiva is known there. For example, in Varanasi Śiva is *Viśveśvara* or *Viśvanātha*, in Ujjayini he is *Mahākāla*, in Saurasthra, *Somanātha* and so on.

In some Śaiva *kṣetras*, *liṅgas* are not installed by humans but are discovered as though they had risen up from the ground by themselves. These are considered to be the most sacred *liṅgas*, known as *svayambhū* (self-born) *liṅgas*. For example, in Amarnath, the Himalayan *tīrtha*, the natural *liṅga* made of ice melts away every summer and is naturally re-formed in winter.

THE VAIṢṆAVAS (DEVOTEES OF VIṢṆU/KṚṢṆA/RĀMA)

According to Hindu texts (e.g., *Daśāvatāra stotra*) Viṣṇu, the preserver of creation in the Hindu Trinity, is believed to have appeared in earthly forms through various incarnations (*avatāra*s) to save the creation from extinction. Rāma and Kṛṣṇa are both described as Viṣṇu's incarnations at different times. Rāma is the legendary hero of the epic *Rāmāyaṇa* and Kṛṣṇa plays an important role in the epic *Mahābhārata*. The sites that are associated with these legendary figures are revered by the Vaiṣṇavas as *tīrtha*s. Viṣṇu himself is said to have visited Gaya and left a two-foot long footprint (*Viṣṇu-pada*) there, which has led to Gaya's sacredness. It can be said that Vaiṣṇava *tīrtha*s are mostly associated with divine individuals.

The Vaiṣṇava sacred places are known as either *dhāma*s (abodes) or *līlā-bhūmi*s (*līlā*/play/sporting, *bhūmi*/ground). Places where Rāma led his life are marked as *dhāma*s, e.g., Ayodhya (birthplace), Chitrakuta, Nasik, Sitakunda, etc. But the most holy and most visited are the places of *līlā* (divine play) of Kṛṣṇa. Vrindavana, Gokula, Mathura and Dvaraka are the places in North India where Kṛṣṇa 'played' his role among humans as a youthful cowherd and later as a princely ruler. The historical personage, Gautama Buddha, is also regarded by Hindus as an incarnation of Viṣṇu and thus the sites of important events in his life are revered by the Vaiṣṇavas.

In the Vaiṣṇava pilgrimage tradition there is a second type of personage whose associations are no less important than those of the divinity. The well-known *bhakta*s (devotees) of Viṣṇu/Kṛṣṇa, the saintly individuals who led an exemplary life according to the ideals of Vaiṣṇavism, are held in high esteem, sometimes to the point of deification. Among such celebrated *bhakta*s, Sri Chaitanya (fifteenth century CE) is the foremost. His contribution to the Vaiṣṇava sect by rejuvenating the *bhakti* (devotion) tradition is so great that places associated with him have become Vaiṣṇava *tīrtha*s. Chaitanya was born in Navadvip in Bengal but spent much of his time visiting places of pilgrimage throughout India. The Jagannātha (a form of Viṣṇu) temple of Puri is rendered holy not only by the presence of the deity, but doubly so by its association with Chaitanya. Similarly, all the Vaiṣṇava sacred places that were visited by Chaitanya on his pilgrimage have become enhanced in importance and sacredness. Such places are marked either by a shrine or by an annual festival or fair (*melā*) that has developed there. Another Vaiṣṇava *bhakta* who is commemorated by an annual fair (in Kenduli in Birbhum) is Jayadeva, the poet who composed *Gīta-Govinda*, a marvel of Vaiṣṇava literature.

The dust (*dhūli*) from a sacred place has a special significance for a Vaiṣṇava. Gathering the dust off the feet (*pada-dhūli*) of a holy man is a symbol of humility. While visiting *tīrtha*s, the pilgrims rub the dust of the holy place on their forehead and body as a mark of humble devotion.

However, all three sects – the Śāktas, the Śaivas and the Vaiṣṇavas – share some common features in their attitudes to pilgrimage. All hold that visiting a sacred place, or living in one, is meritorious (acquiring spiritual merit/*puṇya*). Even dying in a *tīrtha* is desirable, as it is thought to liberate the soul. This explains why Hindu *tīrtha*s have a significant association with death. *Tīrtha*s like Varanasi, Gaya and Hardwar/Haridvarā are celebrated for death-related rituals and acts. As *tīrtha*s are regarded as the crossing points from the mundane to the spiritual world, as the meeting points of humans and the divinity, as places where divinity is in residence and accessible to devotees, all sects recommend pilgrimage to sacred places as a means to spiritual ends. But in reality, only a minority seek liberation (*mukti*/*mokṣa*). The majority seek more earthly rewards such as health, happiness, children, success, cure from diseases, etc.

To discourage people from making pilgrimage for material reasons, all three sects emphasize the purity of mind and intention rather than the actual physical journey itself. Pilgrimage as an act of devotion must result from a devotional frame of mind. *Devī-Bhāgavata* (VI.12.26 – quoted in Labye, 1973: 370), a Śākta text, states that 'purity of mind is the best Tīrtha, more holy than Gaṅgā and other sacred places'. It is probable that, because the Hindu tradition attaches paramount importance to the spiritual effect of pilgrimage, some thinkers strongly oppose mere observance of geographical pilgrimage. It is easier to venture on a physical journey than to achieve a spiritual discipline. If the soul of the pilgrim has not been led along the path of God, the pilgrimage is futile. The essence of this theme comes through again and again, not only in Hindu scriptural texts, but even in vividly worded folk songs of simple people close to the soil. The *Bāul*s (wandering bards) of Bengal are well known for their concept of God as *maner mānuṣ* (the person living within one's own mind) and the human body as the living temple of resident God.

Sacred buildings: the temples

As sacred buildings, Hindu temples present a vast variety of architecture, sculpture, size and location, depending upon the period, the region and the religious sect of the people building the temple. Nowadays, when the theme of Hindu sacred places is mentioned, non-Hindus immediately think of magnificently ornate temples. It may seem strange, then, to learn that 'not a single text of the revealed scriptures of the Hindus refers to images or temples, and even the epics do not' (Chaudhuri, 1979: 90). The early form of Hinduism was without image-worship and without temples. Vedic worship, with its sacrificial fire, was an open-air activity. Even during the compilation period of the two epics, temples do not seem to be around as there is no mention of people visiting temples. Yet there are numerous references to people praying to deities, practising meditation in the Himalayas or in woodland retreats (*tapovana*s), or visiting places of pilgrimage. As mentioned before, the *Mahābhārata* has a whole chapter on pilgrimage (*Tīrtha-yātrā-parvan*). It is most likely that image-worship was introduced by the cults of Śiva, Viṣṇu/Kṛṣṇa and Śakti/the Mother. By the time the cults took firm hold, possibly by the beginning of the Common Era, image-worship in temples was established. It is hard to imagine Hinduism now without the image-worship and temples with which it is identified by the non-Hindu world.

In the Indus Valley excavations, no specific structure was found that can be identified as a temple, though the archaeologists found many examples of female figurines (which, according to some, are examples of image-worship of a Mother cult). N. C. Chaudhuri (1979: 52) points out that the earliest structure which can be regarded as a temple was actually found in Afghanistan.[1] It has been dated as early as the second century CE. It is not certain whether it was a temple for a god or for some kind of imperial cult like that of the Roman emperors. Two other temples, both dedicated to Viṣṇu, thought to be the earliest specimens of temples in India, are in Deogarh and Bhitargaon. They are dated approximately between the fifth and seventh centuries CE. An important point of contrast to be remembered in this context is that, whereas South India is known for its profusion of temples that survived through the ages, there is a curious absence of particularly old temples in the Gangetic plains in the north. This is due to the historical fact that they were systematically destroyed by the Muslim conquerors, who very seldom invaded the south in the early days.

STATUS OF TEMPLES

Though worship of images in temples is a widely known and accepted practice, it is interesting to note that it is wholly optional. Most Hindus do not need to go to temples, because the worship could just as well be done at home. They visit temples only on special occasions. Moreover, Hindu theologians often maintain that real Hinduism lies in the pursuit of spiritual depth, and worship in temples is only for simple people for whom the highest expression of Hinduism is too abstract to comprehend.

However, the most important point about temples is that they are not, strictly speaking, places of worship, at least not in the same sense as a church is to a Christian on a Sunday. A temple is the 'residence' of a deity. The Hindu term for a temple is *mandira*, which literally means 'an abode', 'a dwelling'. In Hindu temples there is installed an image or symbol of a deity who is in residence there. It is the daily duty of the priest, symbolically speaking, to awaken the deity in the morning with musical chantings or songs of praise (*bhajana*s) and then to bathe and adorn the image. With ritual worship (*pūjā*) food is offered to the deity. In the afternoon the deity is put to rest and the activities quieten down. In the evening the deity is welcomed again with ceremonial prayer with lamps (*ārati*) and entertained with devotional music and dance. (Most classical forms of Indian dance originated from temple dance. Temples had dedicated female dancers who were married ceremonially to the deity of the temple.) As Chaudhuri (1979: 90) points out, the 'whole routine of daily worship in temples is only a replica of the daily life of the Hindu king'. A temple is, therefore, not a place where devotees congregate to worship at a particular time on a particular day, but a place where devotees come to pay their homage to the deity at his/her home at any time of the day they wish.

THE HOUSE OF GOD

Terms like *devagṛha* (*deva*/God/deity, *gṛha*/house) and *devālaya* (*ālaya*/house), denoting a temple, clearly point to the belief that, in the house of God, God makes himself/herself accessible to humans in the form imagined by the worshippers. The sacred image or symbol of the deity is housed within the temple in a small sanctuary called *garbha-gṛha* (womb-chamber), a term indicating that it contains the kernel and essence of the temple. The sacred images or symbols are not identified with the deities but considered as the temporary forms in which they manifest themselves after being invited into them by the priest or devotee. The image is not enlivened until the deity is welcomed into it by necessary rituals. Elaborate rituals of consecration of the image are performed before it is ceremonially enshrined. A temple is revered only because it houses the deity or deities. If the rituals are not performed and so the deities are not present, then 'the temple lies dormant as the deities are not "in residence"' (Michell, 1977: 62).

THE STRUCTURE OF A TEMPLE

The structure of a Hindu temple is guided by sets of instructions from ancient texts on temple architecture. The architectural rules are dictated by rigid rules of mathematics and symmetry. The shape and height of the temple, the location of the sanctuary in the temple, the direction in which the temple should face are all decided by the metaphysical considerations of ancient Hindu theologians in relation to the cosmos and its creation. The ground plan of a temple is a sacred geometric diagram known as *yantra* (further developed in Buddhism as *maṇḍala*) that symbolizes the essential structure of the universe. It is usually a square divided into a number of smaller squares by an intersecting grid of lines. The central square, dedicated to Brahmā or a prominent deity associated with creation, is the base of the sanctuary, which is the focal point of the temple. Around this square are the other squares, dedicated to the planetary divinities, including the sun and moon, guardians of the directions of space, all playing their roles in the universe. By constructing the temple as a miniature of the universe and placing the image of the deity at the focal point in the sanctuary, a symbolic representation is created of the creative energy emanating from the centre. The central square is, therefore, the most significant part of the plan, 'as it is here that the worshipper may experience transformation as he comes into direct contact with the cosmic order' (Michell, 1977: 72).

The outer appearance of a temple often resembles a mountain peak (see p. 231 above). Some temples with several tiered arrangements suggest the visual imitation of a mountain range. With the development of building techniques, the tendencies in temple-building to extend upwards seem to aspire also to represent the soaring heights of the mountains.

The tip of the temple, the summit of the symbolic mountain, is positioned precisely over the sanctuary or womb-chamber (*garbha-gṛha*). The highest point of the elevation of the temple is aligned with the most sacred part, the sanctuary that holds the image of the deity. The metaphysical significance of the link between the summit and the sacred centre along an axis is that the forces of energy radiating from the centre project upwards. This upward projection, in its turn, symbolizes the 'progression towards enlightenment, and the goal of this journey is identified with the crowning finial of the superstructure of the temple' (Michell, 1977: 70). The axis also symbolizes the supporting pillar between heaven and earth, and is known as *Meru*.[2]

The womb-chamber (*garbha-gṛha*) also, like the axis *Meru*, is a significant feature of temple architecture and probably plays the most important role in temple worship. It symbolizes a cave, which is regarded as a place of sanctity by Hindus (see above, p. 231). Generally, in Hindu temples the sanctuary, the holy of holies, strongly resembles a cave. It is 'small and dark as no natural light is permitted to enter, and the surfaces of the walls are unadorned and massive' (Michell, 1977: 69–70). The analogy of the sanctuary with a cave seems consistent with that of the temple with a mountain. However, later temples do not always follow this convention and in modern temples, particularly, the images of deities are placed in well-lit focal points.

While visiting a temple it is customary for a worshipper to go round the central structure of the temple on foot in a clockwise direction to complete the circle before gradually penetrating inwards. This circular journey is known as *pradakṣiṇa* (circumambulation). Because of the importance of this journey, many temples are furnished with ambulatory passageways, e.g., in the temple of Ramesvaram one has to walk through a series of enclosures which become increasingly sacred as the sanctuary is approached. Usually the approach to the sanctuary is along an east–west axis. As the direction of the approach is important for reasons of ritual, most temples face east. The worshipper enters the temple from the east, then walks along the ambulatory passage clockwise in the order, east, south, west, north and back to the east before approaching the interior.

In front of the doorway leading to the sanctuary there is often a pillared hall called *maṇḍapa*, serving as an assembly hall for the devotees. As Percy Brown (1942: 72) points out, some of the earlier temples indicate that the *maṇḍapa* was a detached building, isolated from the sanctuary by an open space (e.g., in the shore temples of Mahabalipuram – about 700 CE). Later on it became the custom to unite the two buildings.

According to the Hindu texts of temple architecture, to have the desired effect of energy emanating from the sanctuary, the whole structure of the temple has to be precisely measured and accurately symmetrical. That is why mathematics is considered to be a sacred subject by Hindu theologians. Mathematical schemes are often introduced by theologians and philosophers to describe the celestial or even the ethical world. According to them, if a temple is to function in harmony with the mathematical basis of the universe, it has to be constructed correctly according to a mathematical system. Thus, the welfare of the community and happiness of its members can result from the erection of a correctly proportioned temple that generates desired harmony.

However, measurement is not confined to temple architecture alone; the sacred images of the deities have to be carved according to the strict mathematical discipline of iconometry, the geometry of image-making. The face-length is used as the module (*tāla*) for the figures. The appropriate facial expressions (*bhāva*s, e.g., *raudra*/anger for *Kālī*), postures (*bhaṅgī*, e.g., *tribhaṅga*/tri-flexed for Kṛṣṇa), hand gestures (*mudrā*, e.g., *abhaya*/security for protection), colour (*varṇa*, e.g., *kṛṣṇa*/dark for Kālī and Kṛṣṇa), garments (*vasana*, e.g., *pīta*/ yellow garment for Kṛṣṇa) and even weapons (*āyudha*, e.g., *chakra*/ discus for Viṣṇu) of individual deities are all prescribed by strict iconographical texts. Only a correctly made image will be able to invite the deity to reside within it. Therefore the texts stress that the worship of an image not made according to prescribed rules is fruitless.

PROTECTION OF THE TEMPLE

To ensure the security of a temple and to avert accidents, each stage in the building process (e.g., selection of the site, drawing the plan on the ground, laying the foundation stone, etc.) is initiated with appropriate rituals. Once completed, the temple continues to need protection from negative forces. Much of the temple art, for example the motifs and symbols that decorate the doorways, provide such protection. Hindu temple art is full of minor deities, guardians and attendant figures (e.g., *yakṣīs/apsarās* or semi-divine creatures, tree nymphs and *dvārapālas*/door guardians) which surround the sacred image once it is installed, offering their protection. Images of secondary deities are placed in key positions in elaborately decorated niches, especially at the centres of the north, west and south walls of the sanctuary, facing outwards. Some occupy the four corners of the walls as well. Guardians of eight directions are often depicted as protecting the temple from all sides. Demonic mask motifs over doorways are also used for warding off evil forces.

Some temples in the south are protected by perimeter walls with tall gateways called *gopurams* (cow-gates). While the walls themselves have the appearance of a fortress with very little aesthetic value, the tall pylon-like monumental entrances or *gopurams* have considerable architectural character with rich sculptural embellishments. A typical *gopuram* is oblong in plan, rising up into a tapering tower often over 150 feet in height, with a doorway in the centre of its long side. The lower storeys are built of solid stone masonry providing stable foundation for a superstructure made of lighter materials like bricks and plaster. On the flat summit rests the distinctive barrel-vaulted uppermost storey with gable ends. Often the actual temples inside the perimeter walls are retained in their original humble forms, without any structural alterations, keeping their religious antiquity and sanctity undisturbed. The surrounding high walls emphasize their sanctity and ensure their security, while the imposing *gopurams* appear like watch-towers.

ART IN TEMPLES

Hindu temples, whether in India or in South-east Asia, are well known for their ornate stone carvings, especially on the outside. Intricate terracotta reliefs are also found in the few existing brick-built temples. As most Hindu art-forms have originated from religious roots, it is no wonder that religious buildings are profusely decorated with appropriate sculpture.

The most frequently used decorative motifs are often taken from nature, e.g., flowers (particularly lotuses), trees, creepers and birds. But the themes of the large-scale sculpture on the outside walls of temples are based on various deities, with their individual characteristics as described in Hindu mythology. These images of deities are not meant for worship but are purely artistic representations of popular mythological personages. Another favourite theme seems to be scenes from the epics *Rāmāyaṇa* and *Mahābhārata*, usually depicted in series of panels.

But not all the temple art themes are religious in nature. There are some temples where secular themes found their place as evidence of pure art. The most frequently mentioned temples of Khajuraho in Madhya Pradesh are of this kind. It is believed that at one time 85 temples existed in this region but only 20 have survived. These temples 'are known for their elegance, graceful contours and rich sculptural treatment' (Narain, 1982: 14), and also for their treatment of varied and sometimes unconventional themes. The themes depicted in stone are often secular, e.g., groups of dancers and musicians, sculptors at work, warriors marching, hunting parties, teachers and disciples, domestic scenes, etc. But the most talked about scenes are those of amorous couples and their sexual exhibitionism. The controversial sculpture of an erotic nature on temple walls has puzzled spectators as to how sex and religion co-exist in Hindu temple art. As Narain (1982: 7) explains, 'the large time gap between the building of the temples and our modern assessment of them, and the almost total change in cultural values has resulted in some misunderstanding' and bewilderment. Several explanations for the depiction of sexual motifs in religious buildings are available.

One commonly used explanation is that these erotic figures are a reminder of sexual desires that have to be conquered if one wishes to attain spiritual heights. In that context, the outside walls of a temple work as an aid to screening out people who are not yet spiritually ready to enter a sacred place and can easily be tempted away by sexual scenes. Devotees who are unperturbed by the erotic scenes of the exterior are worthy of entering the interior of the temple. Another explanation is that, because in most ancient societies the primary concern of religion was the conservation and generation of life, sexual activities gained a religious and mystical connotation. Particularly in Hinduism, where there is no concept of 'original sin', most of the deities are coupled with their consorts (e.g., Śiva–Durgā, Viṣṇu–Lakṣmī, etc.). Hindu mythology is full of the amorous play of gods and goddesses. As a temple is regarded as the personal dwelling place of a deity, living there in human fashion, all the normal occurrences of everyday human life, including sexual activity, find their way on to the temple walls.

Moreover, it is not only art in temples but also the classical literature of the Hindus that is full of the amorous sport of heroes and heroines, who are often the divine personalities from Hindu mythology. In addition, several treatises were written on sexual behaviour, *Kāma-sūtra* (well known in the West) being just one of them. All these factors indicate that social attitudes towards sexuality were in general fairly liberal.

Not only in Hindu temples but also in Buddhist religious monuments (e.g., at Sanchi and Bharhut in central India) there are numerous carvings of amorous couples in pilasters and panels. Mildly amorous depictions of male and female figures standing very close with arms around each other 'were considered auspicious and were used as *alankāras* (decorative elements). They are in no way connected with the Buddhist religion but are simply a reflection of the artistic tradition of the time' (Narain, 1982: 32).

It is a possibility that the sculptor artists used these temple walls as permanent museum galleries or exhibition spaces to show their intricate artistry in the popular art-form of the day, knowing that stonework would outlive every other medium. Although, with changed moral values, one might find it difficult to associate eroticism with religion, yet these magnificent pieces of sculpture demand appreciation in their own right as pure art. Nude figures and life-drawing have been accepted as an important theme in art all over the world, and Hindu art is no exception.

Whatever may be the reason for the co-existence of erotic art in Hindu religious buildings, one is reminded by these findings that in Hinduism religion is never compartmentalized as a separate activity. Religious and secular activities are intertwined, and often inseparable, in Hinduism, as every secular activity is somehow linked with the will of God.

Small shrines

WAYSIDE SHRINES

Compared with the magnificently ornate temples, considerably less spectacular in appearance and insignificant in size, but no less important in sacredness, are the wayside shrines that can be found in abundance in rural and urban India. It is often a symbolic stone or a lump of clay daubed with red vermilion paste, or a Śiva-*liṅga*, placed at the root of a tree (most commonly a *vaṭa* or *aśvattha*, known as sacred trees – see above, p. 98) that makes a basic shrine. Passers-by pay their homage to the deity of the shrine with a flower or a small amount of money. Though they may look insignificant, these roadside shrines are the nerve-centres of rural religious life and are intimately linked with local people's everyday life of vows and thanksgivings, births and deaths. Their deities may be regional deities who avert diseases prevalent in the area (e.g., the deity Śītalā in Bengal, for smallpox), yet their sanctity is no less than that of the temples of Viṣṇu or Kālī. People's simple faith makes them into living sacred places.

TULASĪ-ALTARS

Many Hindu families, especially in rural India, cherish in their courtyard an altar with a *tulasī* (*Ocymum sanctum*) plant in it. *Tulasī* is revered as a symbol of Viṣṇu, and it is watered regularly, and a lamp is lit in the evenings at its altar. This outdoor *tulasī*-altar is treated as a sacred place in a Hindu household.

FAMILY SHRINES

Hindus, generally speaking, have a home shrine placed in the midst of the family hubbub, connected with the daily chores of secular activities. It can be a whole room or a little corner in a room. It can be a big wooden or brass throne-shaped structure with a canopy on top, or just a wooden stool on which images or symbols of deities are placed. Whatever the size, however gorgeous or humble in decoration, this shrine is the most sacred place for a Hindu family. Nobody touches the shrine unbathed. Usually twice a day, morning and evening, a lamp is lit and incense burnt in reverence to deities who co-exist happily in Hindu households. Members of the family sing songs of praise (*bhajanas*) or chant from the scriptures, sitting on the floor in front of the shrine with faith in God's presence there. This is the most intimate sacred place for a Hindu.

No need for a sacred place

There are Hindus who regard no specific external space as sacred but believe only in internal sacredness. Such Hindus do not need even a family shrine, or a temple to go to, but feel that any place is sacred enough in which to meditate. Then there are others, for example the *Bāuls* (wandering bards) of Bengal, who maintain that the human body is the only sacred place, as it houses the God within.

Variable sacred places

The concept of a sacred place, therefore, is variable in Hinduism. To different people it brings different visions. A place is sacred if one feels sanctified within oneself by being there. Some feel sanctified by visiting distant places of pilgrimage, some by paying homage to the local temple, some by sitting quietly in front of the family shrine, and some just by possessing an invaluable human body that uniquely holds an immortal soul within.

Notes

1 'They were discovered at a place called Surkh Kotal in 1951 by Schlumberger, who was then the head of the French archaeological mission at Kabul' (Chaudhuri, 1979: 52).

2 The axis *Meru* is a significant concept in Hindu geology and even in human physiology. The earth's axis of rotation is known as the axis of *Meru* and, accordingly, the North Pole and South Pole are named as the north and south end of the axis *Meru*: *uttara*(north)-*meru* and *dakṣiṇa*(south)-*meru* respectively. The word *Meru* has the connotation of being the central position around which everything else revolves. Again, *Meru*, or *Sumeru*, is the mythical mountain at the centre of the earth, storehouse of gold and gems and hailed as the abode of gods.

The spine of a creature is called *meru-daṇḍa* (rod/support), which is vitally important for its physiology and consciousness. Especially in a human body, according to the tantric cults, *meru-daṇḍa* plays the role of a central channel along which the spiritual consciousness awakens and moves upward towards the experience of liberation or *mokṣa*.

Further reading

Brown, P. (1942) *Indian Architecture: Buddhist and Hindu Periods*. Bombay: D. B. Taraporevala Sons.

Cavendish, R. (1980) *The Great Religions*. London: George Weidenfeld and Nicolson for W. H. Smith.

Chaudhuri, N. C. (1979) *Hinduism: A Religion to Live By*. London: Chatto and Windus.

Eck, D. L. (1983) *Banaras: City of Light*. London: Routledge and Kegan Paul.

Hawley, J. S. (1981) *At Play with Kṛṣṇa: Pilgrimage Dramas from Brindaban*. Princeton, NJ: Princeton University Press.

Labye, P. G. (1973) *Studies in Devī-Bhāgavata*. Bombay: Popular Prakashan.

Michell, G. (1977) *The Hindu Temple: An Introduction to Its Meaning and Forms*. London: Elek Books.

Morinis, E. A. (1984) *Pilgrimage in the Hindu Tradition: A Case Study of West Bengal*. Delhi: Oxford University Press.

Narain, L. A. (1982) *Khajuraho: Ecstasy in Indian Sculpture*. New Delhi: Roli Books International.

Parry, J. P. (1994) *Death in Banaras*. Cambridge: Cambridge University Press.

Singh, K. (1989) *Pārāśarapraśna*. Amritsar: Guru Nanak Dev University, Department of Guru Nanak Studies.

10. Rites of passage

Gavin Flood

Recent scholarly debates about the nature of ritual have tended to regard it either as primarily expressive of symbolic systems, concerned with communication between ritual actors, or as primarily functional or pragmatic, concerned with the bringing about of specific goals.[1] That is, ritual has been regarded either as a way in which humans 'speak' with each other within a community and through the generations, and with putative transhuman entities as well, or as a kind of magical technology which brings about effects desired by an individual or group. Because of the variety of ritual theories, particularly within anthropology, perhaps the most fruitful way of arriving at an understanding of Hindu rites of passage is to begin with an indigenous Hindu classification of its own ritual systems. Hinduism has understood ritual in terms of both communication and pragmatism, and even, by some ritualists, as action for its own sake with no other purpose. As Piatigorsky has observed, in examining Indian religion we are examining something which has already examined itself and developed terms for its own self-description.[2] Such indigenous systems of classification are of vital importance in understanding Hindu rites of passage.

The authoritative sources for Hindu rites of passage are the secondary revelation, or *smṛti* texts. These, based on the primary revelation of the Veda (*Manu* 2.6–7), are the group of writings subsumed under the general category of *Kalpa sūtra*s or ritual manuals. These texts, composed about the sixth century BCE, comprise three categories: the *Śrauta sūtra*s, concerned with explaining the sacrificial procedures of the older *Brāhmaṇa*s; the *Dharma sūtra*s, concerned with correct human conduct; and the *Gṛhya sūtra*s, concerned with domestic religious observances. It is this last category of texts which is mainly concerned with the performance of rites of passage, though the *Dharma sūtra*s and *śāstra*s (authoritative treatises) also contain accounts of these rites. In the *Gṛhya sūtra*s and in *Manu* we find the rites of passage classed as a 'bodily rite' (*śarīra-saṃskāra*), in contrast to daily and seasonal rites, a distinction which is maintained in the *Dharma śāstra*s. These texts are not, however, the only source, there being regional oral traditions (*laukika*) which have contributed to the development of rites of passage. Thus, high-caste rites of passage in any particular region of India will be a fusion of śāstric and folk elements.

The *smṛti* literature divides ritual into three classes: obligatory, daily rites (*nitya-karman*), occasional rites (*naimittika-karman*) and rites for a desired object or purpose (*kāmya-karman*) (ritual in the pragmatic sense mentioned above). Rites of passage fall within the second category of rituals 'occasioned by a special occurrence' (*Āpastamba Gṛhya-sūtra* 1.1.11). They are of central importance in constructing 'Hindu' identity within the overriding brahmanical culture which has moulded Hindu traditions and maintained the continuity of those traditions.

Saṃskāra and *dharma*

A fundamental distinction can be made within Indian religions between soteriology and worldly life.[3] This distinction is explicit in philosophical traditions such as Advaita Vedānta, which distinguished between liberating knowledge of the absolute and ritual action, and in the social institutions of the world-renouncer and the householder. While the renouncer's final goal is liberation (*mokṣa*), the householder is concerned with daily ritual activity. Rites of passage are entirely within the realm of the householder's life and are nothing to do with the Hindu soteriology of freedom from the cycle of reincarnation which the renouncer is seeking (except in so far as only twice-born males in orthodox Hinduism can generally become renouncers). Hindu rites of passage are concerned with the transition between different phases in the life of the householder and do not include the rite of renunciation or the various sectarian initiations which may be regarded as liberating (see below). Although Manu says that the performance of *dharma*, which would include rites of passage, does lead to happiness after death (*Manu* 2.9), this is not salvation, which is beyond social laws and cannot be attained through rites concerned with social transformation.

The Sanskrit term used for rites of passage is *saṃskāra*, implying something which is 'put together' or 'constructed' (from *saṃ*, 'together' plus *kāra* from the root *kṛ*, 'to make'). The term is appropriate and reflects the early Hindu perception that rites of passage, or transformative rites, moulded or helped construct social identities. The importance of the *saṃskāra*s in this process cannot be overestimated. They are the link between the higher-order laws of the transpersonal *dharma*, and the personal reality of the high-caste householder, moulding his or her life to the culture and community to which he or she belongs. Through the *saṃskāra*s people's social role and even, to some extent, ontological status are defined, and through the *saṃskāra* they are given access to resources within the tradition which were previously closed to them. Through the *saṃskāra* the initiate enters into a new field of activity and awareness, a new realm or state.

The *saṃskāra*s are transformative processes linking different states. The distinction between 'state' and 'process' indicates that 'society' (identified with 'state') is a hierarchical structure of relations, while the rite of passage is an interstructural situation between social positions; it is a 'period of margin or liminality'. The liminal condition characteristic of rites of passage functions to reinforce social institutions: liminality is legitimized by the society and in turn legitimizes the social structure. Hence, rather than 'rites of passage', Bourdieu refers to them as 'rites of institution'.[4] The Hindu *saṃskāra*s are thus rites of institution in that they serve to maintain social order.

Hindu society has developed as a hierarchy which, for any one person, has been experienced as a series of 'states' connected by liminal periods or processes. This society has developed over the centuries as a complex structure in which social relations have been delineated in terms of purity (*śuddha*) and impurity (*aśuddha*), auspiciousness (*śubha*) and inauspiciousness (*aśubha*).[5] Concern for the network of social relations has been one of the main features, if not the main feature, of *dharma*, a complex term which encompasses social duties and responsibilities. In the *saṃskāra*s we can see the practical application of *dharma*, specifically of the *varṇāśrama dharma*, duty with regard to one's class/caste (*varṇa*) and stage of life (*āśrama*).

For the Hindu householder (the majority of Hindus), the maintaining of *dharma* ensures a morally upright life. Madan cites the example of the Kashmiri Brahmans or Pandits, whose life is governed by *dharma*, which they understand as *bhaṭṭil*: the Bhaṭṭa's or Kashmiri Brahman's lifestyle, largely concerned with domesticity and the householder's purposes of life (*artha*). This is so central to their world-view and their lives that it alone is sufficient reason for doing anything in a particular way. Madan writes: 'When children ... and even curious adults ask of those who might know why something should be done in a particular way, or done at all, the Pandit answer usually is: "it is *bhaṭṭil*, it is our way of life" ' (Madan, 1987: 30).

Rites of passage are *dharma* or *bhaṭṭil* in action. They are the expression of *dharma* in time; the way in which *dharma* works through a person's life, marking the exit from one dharmically determined social state and the entry to another. Rites of passage are therefore connected with ethics in so far as the actors in a ritual, in R. A. Rappaport's words, 'accept, and indicate to themselves and to others that they accept, the order encoded in that ritual'.[6] Morality is, as Rappaport points out, 'intrinsic to ritual' in that through accepting the constraints of the ritual a participant is accepting the moral constraints of the tradition. In performing the *saṃskāra*s Hindus are subjecting themselves to the higher power of *dharma* and allowing themselves to be moulded by that higher force.

The power of *dharma* is expressed through ritual in the body. Rites of passage are focused on the body and its transformations over time, leading through the process of maturation to eventual death. In being centred on the body, the Hindu rites of passage are an expression in the human, material world of the transpersonal, cosmic *dharma* which itself is eternal (*sanātana*). They are the way in which *dharma* orders the nature-given human body, which itself becomes an expression of *dharma* and a way of patterning or ordering human behaviour. In rites of passage the body becomes a vehicle for the expression of tradition. The body, subject to genetic controls and the process of ageing, is constrained in ways determined by the tradition by means of the *saṃskāra*s, constraints which are, in fact, perceived to facilitate a person's growth or development through time. The general point about tradition's control of the body has been emphasized by D. M. Levin:

> Religion is a tradition of rituals which bind and fasten the body: it binds us

> to the performance of special tasks, special postures, gestures and movements; it dedicates the body to the incarnation of a spiritual life, promising that the body's careful adherence to such strict regulations will not be experienced, in the end, as its restriction, but rather, on the contrary, as its dream of health, well-being and liberation.[7]

While not liberating in the specific Hindu technical sense, the general idea of Levin's statement pertains to the *saṃskāra*s. While the body is certainly in many cases undergoing various inevitable, biological changes – at birth, puberty and death – these are defined and delineated by tradition through the *saṃskāra*s which use the body, and through the body, determine a person's 'state'. There are of course gender issues here, in that male and female bodies are constrained by *saṃskāra*s in different ways or by different, gender-specific, rites. The *Dharma śāstra*s deal only with male rites of passage, but throughout India, women have undergone rites of passage based on oral or folk (*laukika*) traditions, as V. K. Duvvury has shown with regard to South Indian Brahman women (Duvvury, 1991: 102).

The *saṃskāra*s

For the high-caste or 'twice-born' Hindu male, the theoretical model maintains that there are four stages of life through which he can pass: the student stage (*brahmacārya*), the householder stage (*gṛhastha*), the forest-dweller stage (*vānaprastha*) and the renouncer stage (*saṃnyāsa*). The first two stages are concerned with worldly life, the third with a life retired from household duties, and the last with world transcendence and salvation. This scheme is, however, a theoretical model and most Hindus do not, and perhaps have never, passed through it in an ordered sequence; most remain as householders, while some become renouncers without ever having been householders.

Each of these stages or *āśrama*s is a 'state': a stable social condition which lasts for a significant period of time within a person's life, which defines the kind of person one is, and defines the social and religious possibilities which are open to one. The term 'state' is wider, however, than the Sanskrit *āśrama*, in that it incorporates all stages of human development, whereas *āśrama* refers only to states of being after initiation in childhood. Moreover the last *āśrama* is not technically accessed by a rite of passage, for the *saṃskāra*s are concerned purely with social life and not with liberation.

The junctures between states from birth, or before, until after death, are marked by rites of passage. At each of these junctures, the Hindu undergoes a ritual process of purification and is made ready for the next stage in his life. As R. Pandey says, the *saṃskāra*s are 'for sanctifying the body, mind and intellect of an individual, so that he may become a full-fledged member of the community' (Pandey, 1969: 16). They are the processes between states, marking off the major transition points in a person's biography at birth, during youth (perhaps at puberty but not necessarily so), marriage and death. The *saṃskāra*s also mark out less significant transition points within childhood which do not indicate any radical, ontological shifts. For example, the ritual of the child's first outing is lower in significance than the rite of becoming a member of high-caste society.

The system of *saṃskāra*s is a 'liturgical order' in Rappaport's sense of the term,[8] in that it is an invariant sequence making up a complete cycle and controlling the unfolding householder's biography. The performance of a *saṃskāra* entails the implicit acceptance of the other rites, of *dharma* and of the Hindu orthoprax value system. The actual number of *saṃskāra*s varies in different *Dharma śāstra*s, but the important point is that, although there are specific variations, the totality of the *saṃskāra*s is a ritual sequence or complete system which expresses *dharma*. Up to forty are recorded in the *Gautama-dharma-śāstra*, though the standard number in the *Gṛhya sūtra*s is between twelve and eighteen (Pandey, 1969: 17–24). The *Manusmṛti* (2.16; 26; 29; 3.1–4) mentions thirteen, though sixteen is the standard number, a number which itself has magical connotations.[9] Access to these *saṃskāra*s is dependent upon class and gender, and only Brahman males can perform all of them.

The significance of Hindu rites of passage is that their performance entails a brahmanical value system and acceptance of brahmanical distinctions between those who can perform the rites and those who cannot. The *saṃskāra*s underline, implicitly if not explicitly, differences in gender roles and social classes or castes. Indeed, it has been argued that the primary function of rites of passage is not so much to ensure the temporal transition between states, for example from childhood to adulthood, but to ensure the separation of social groups; to ensure the separation between 'those who have undergone it, not from those who have not yet undergone it, but from those who will not undergo it in any sense, and thereby instituting a lasting difference between those to whom the rite pertains and those to whom it does not pertain'.[10] The high-caste boy who undergoes the vedic initiation or *upanayana* ceremony is separated not only from his younger contemporaries who have not yet undergone the rite, but also, and for life, from those castes and from women, who are not eligible to undergo the rite.

The standard list of sixteen *saṃskāra*s implies these distinctions and exclusions. We shall here list the standard sixteen *saṃskāra*s before going on to discuss some in more detail, and more general issues.

The first three are prenatal rites, followed by birth, childhood and educational rites, then marriage and lastly death rites. (1) *Garbhādhāna*, the rite of the 'conception of the embryo', or the 'infusion of semen' performed at the time of conception. (2) *Puṃsavana*, the rite of 'bringing forth a boy', performed with a pregnant woman to ensure the birth of a male child. (3) *Sīmantonnayana*, the rite of 'parting the hair' of the pregnant woman during the fourth, sixth or eighth month of her pregnancy in order to ensure her well-being and to protect her from inauspicious spirits. (4) *Jātakarman*, the birth rite for the safe delivery of the child. (5) *Nāmakaraṇa*, the name-giving rite on the tenth to twelfth day after birth. (6) *Niṣkramana*, the child's first outing on an auspicious day. (7) *Annaprāśana*, the rite of first feeding the child solid food. (8) *Chūḍākaraṇa*, the rite of tonsure during the first or third year. (9) *Karṇavedha*, the ear-piercing ceremony between three and five. (10) *Vidyārambha*, the learning of the alphabet when the child is between five and seven. (11) *Upanayana*, the rite of initiation and investiture of the sacred thread from about eight up to about twenty-four. (12) *Vedārambha*, the rite of beginning vedic study. (13) *Keśānta*, the first shaving of the beard. (14) *Samāvartana*, the formal end to student life. (15) *Vivāha*, the marriage rite. And finally, (16) *Antyeṣṭi*, the funeral rites.

Of these the most important transition points for the high-caste Hindu, apart from birth, have been the initiation ceremony (*upanayana*), which marks out the transition from childhood to high-caste society, the marriage ceremony (*vivāha*), marking out the beginning of the householder's life, and the funeral rites (*antyeṣṭi*), which mark the end of the householder's life and the beginning of a new existence. In contemporary Hinduism, very often the *upanayana* and marriage ceremonies are conflated for reasons of economy, particularly in urban areas. We shall here examine four of these processes: the birth, youth, marriage and funeral *saṃskāra*s.

THE BIRTH RITES

In contrast to death, which is inauspicious (*aśubha*), birth for a Hindu is a joyous and auspicious (*śubha*) occasion. The bringing forth of a child, especially a boy, is a sacred duty incumbent upon all married couples, yet, like death, it is associated with danger and impurity (*aśuddhi*). All products of the body, such as hair, nails, blood and semen, are impure for the Hindu, and the process of birth is therefore polluting (Madan, 1987: 56). As Louis Dumont notes, 'impurity corresponds with the organic aspect of man' (Dumont, 1980: 50) and those who service impurity, the washer castes who wash the soiled linen after a birth, live in a constant state of impurity which the high-caste householder enters only briefly. The biological process of birth needs to be contained and controlled within a ritual structure in order to limit and even negate the effects of pollution. Indeed, Manu says that the performance of the birth rite of passage counteracts the birth pollution caused through conception (the mixing of semen and blood) (*Manu* 2.27).

Hindu rites of passage can be seen to follow the pattern of separation from the previous state, margin or transition, and aggregation or reintegration into the new state. With a first pregnancy a woman generally leaves the marriage home and goes to the home of her parents after the *sīmantonnayana*, the rite of parting the hair, thereby physically separating herself from her previous condition. Although preparation preceded the birth by a month or so, the actual performance of the birth ceremony (*jātakarman*) was begun, according to Manu, before the severing of the umbilical cord (*Manu* 1.29). The actual ceremony comprises a number of rites to ensure the production of intelligence or wisdom in the child, long life and strength (Pandey, 1969: 75–7). According to the *Āśvalāyana Gṛhya-sūtra*, the first is achieved by the father muttering in the child's ear invocations to the deities Sāvitrī, Sarasvatī and the Āśvins; long life by feeding the child honey and clarified butter on a golden spoon; and strength by touching the baby's shoulders and reciting a vedic verse (*Āśvalāyana Gṛhya-sūtra* 1.15.1–3). After the baby's birth a woman might remain at her parents' home for some months before being reincorporated into her marriage home again with the new, higher status of mother, especially higher if she is the mother of a male child.

Because of the pollution of birth, which lasts for a period of about ten days, both mother and child are in danger from evil spirits (*grāha*) and ceremonies are performed to protect them. To mark the end of this period of impurity – the liminal period when the mother is truly outside 'ordinary' human transactions – a Brahman priest might sprinkle the house with a sprig of mango from a pot containing holy water (Duvvury, 1991: 184ff.) This is followed by the naming ceremony (*nāmakaraṇa*) on about the eleventh day.

Undoubtedly, throughout Indian history and in contemporary India, the birth of a boy, particularly a first child, is regarded as more auspicious than the birth of a girl, though this is not to say that the birth of a girl is regarded as inauspicious. When a man sees his son he has repaid his debt to the ancestors (*Manu* 9.106). Duvvury gives a good example of the importance of a son among the Aiyars, the Tamil-speaking orthodox or Smārta Brahmans, among whom it is believed that with the birth of a son, the first of three generations of ancestors passes over from the intermediate realm of the ancestors (*pitṛloka*) into the world of heaven (*svargaloka*). She writes that upon the birth of a son the father 'feels relieved that he has at last done his duty to the manes of his forefathers and has enabled his line to attain immortality' (Duvvury, 1991: 182). Indeed, the *Āśvalāyana Gṛhya-sūtra* (1.6.1) even says that the birth of a son brings purification to twelve descendants as well as twelve ancestors on both the husband's and wife's sides. Such a son will grow and pass through the various childhood rites of naming, first outing, tonsure and so on, until he reaches the time for initiation into caste society, a very important rite of passage.

THE HIGH-CASTE INITIATION (*UPANAYANA*)

This is of great significance for the high-caste male in that it marks his entry into caste society and makes him a *dvija*, 'twice-born'. According to the ritual literature, the *upanayana* rite was performed between the ages of eight and twenty-four, depending upon class. The *Āśvalāyana Gṛhya-sūtra* states that a Brahman boy should be between eight and sixteen, a *kṣatriya* between eleven and twenty-two and a *vaiśya* between twelve and twenty-four (1.19.1–7; cf. *Manu* 2.36). The text even says that it is not possible to initiate youths beyond these ages and such a person would be cut off from the community, having lost his right to learn the vedic *mantras* (1.19.8). In contemporary India, attitudes are less strict, and many take initiation just before their marriage when they may be older than the textually prescribed age limits. Indeed, holding the *upanayana* on the day before the wedding is common practice. It is therefore not appropriate to call the *upanayana* ritual a 'puberty' rite, as it may occur well before puberty or long after, though its significance of formal entry into the community may well be akin to puberty rites in other cultures. The ceremony might also accompany the marriage of a female relative, partly on economic grounds to avoid too many long journeys for relatives who live at a distance. This is especially important in Britain, where relatives might travel from India for an *upanayana* or wedding.

That the *upanayana* rite separates the boy from childhood and brings him into closer proximity to adulthood is also significant in that it excludes him from other spheres of social life and activity. Through undergoing the *upanayana*, the high-caste boy is being separated from the world of women, who are excluded from undergoing the rite, and the sphere of the mother, legitimizing gender distinctions and roles. Indeed, this rite implies a Hindu cosmological symbolism which legitimizes social structure and gender roles: male is to female as sun is to moon, Śiva to Śakti, and spirit (*puruṣa*) to matter (*prakṛti*), a hierarchical symbolism in which the former term is always higher than the latter.[11]

Through the high-caste boy's distinction being highlighted, there is a large group of people, the non-twice-born castes, whose exclusion is thereby underlined. The rite excludes a vast body of low-caste Hindus from the higher echelons of Hindu culture. In performing the *upanayana*, the high-caste boy is acceding to the brahmanical value system which entails the exclusion of the impure castes. Again, the rite taps into a cosmological symbolism in which the lower class emerges from the feet of the giant male person at the beginning of the world, while the higher classes emerge from his thighs, shoulders and mouth. But to return to the rite itself.

The *upanayana* ceremony usually takes a whole day, during which time the initiate sits with the officiating priest before the sacred fire, before a sacred tree, and before a large pot, symbol of the Goddess. Although ritual details vary in classical texts as well as regionally, the general pattern is that the boy's head is shaved except for the tuft on the crown, he is then bathed and given a *kaupīna* or loin cloth, and the boy's father brings him into the presence of the priest and the fire pit or metal container in which the sacred fire is kindled. Oblations are offered to the fire and a girdle or cord is tied around the boy's waist.

For a Brahman this was traditionally made of *muñja* grass, for a *kṣatriya*, a bow-string, and for a *vaiśya*, it was made of wool. He also traditionally wears an antelope skin over his shoulders or clothing of various colours depending on caste, and holds a sacred staff, the symbol of the vedic student. These rites are accompanied by the recitation of vedic *mantras* by the officiating Brahman.

The boy takes a vow of celibacy, and then follows the most important part of the *upanayana*: the investiture of the sacred thread, the symbol of twice-born (*dvija*) status, worn over the right shoulder and renewed each year during the month of *Śravan* (August) until either death or renunciation (*saṃnyāsa*). After the investiture of the thread, which comprises a number of strands, usually three or five, joined by a single knot, the boy is taught the famous 'root *mantra*' (*mūla-mantra*), the Gāyatrī, which thenceforth is recited daily at dawn by Brahmans,[12] and he receives a secret name. He will also learn the procedures for making offerings into the sacred fire (*homa*). At the end of the ceremony, the 'departure' for Kāśī (i.e., Varanasi) is the symbolic gesture of leaving for the religious centre of Hinduism in order to study. The boy, however, is 'persuaded', sometimes with some mirth, by his maternal uncles not to go, but rather to remain and be tempted by the promise of a bride. This is then followed by a feast in contemporary Hindu households, and the giving of gifts to the boy.

An elaborate and rich symbolism is entailed in these rites, each ritual object having layers of symbolic resonance. The strands of the sacred thread, for example, are said to represent the three qualities (*guṇa*) of nature (*prakṛti*), namely lightness (*sattva*), darkness (*tamas*) and passion (*rajas*), or the three debts owed by a Hindu to the ancestors, the gods and the seers. An elaborate colour symbolism is involved in these rites. For example, the colour of the upper garment worn by the boy traditionally reflected different classes. The law books state that reddish clothing should be worn by a Brahman, a different shade of red (dyed with madder) should be worn by a *kṣatriya* and yellow should be worn by a *vaiśya* (*Āpasthamba Gṛhya-sūtra* 1.19.10).

Traditionally, the *upanayana* marked the entry into the celibate, student stage of life (*brahmacārya*) and, according to Pandey, originally meant no more than going to a teacher and asking to be admitted as his student (Pandey, 1969: 114), though its later significance is undoubtedly that the young man becomes a high-caste member. As a student, he repays his innate debt of vedic study to the seers (*ṛṣi*) and a further rite is performed, usually the day following his initiation, of 'beginning vedic study' (*vedārambha*). According to the traditional model, the end of vedic study is marked by the *samāvartana saṃskāra*, during which the *guru* is paid a fee (*dakṣinā*). The young man takes a bath, thereby becoming a *snātaka*, 'one who has bathed', and becomes eligible for marriage (*Manu* 2.245–246; 3.4). He is not practically a complete member of his caste until his marriage, though after his initiation he is empowered to learn and hear the Veda, and, once married, to perform the vedic daily and occasional rituals. Indeed, there are solemn obligations attached to the wearing of the sacred thread invested during this time, namely, the obligation to perform one's ritual duty (*dharma*) according to one's caste and stage of life, and the obligation to avoid pollution. The high-caste Hindu will adhere strictly to caste rules of endogamy and commensality.

The *upanayana* gives a high-caste boy access to resources within the tradition which allow him to develop into a full member of his society and to experience its richness. After initiation he can, and indeed must, learn the Veda, the sacred revelation, and perform its ritual injunctions, such as, after marriage, maintaining the sacred household fires, which he must do for the rest of his householder's life. Manu (2.170–171) says that 'the sun-god is spoken of as his mother and the teacher as his father. The teacher is spoken of as the father due to his giving of the Veda, ritual action (*karman*) is not performed without the investiture of the sacred thread.'

While the *upanayana* is strictly for high-caste boys, according to the *śāstras*, women were and are not excluded from membership of high-caste communities. According to Manu, marriage is a woman's *upanayana*, and serving her husband is the equivalent of living with the vedic teacher, while housework is the woman's equivalent of the man's obligatory fire rituals (*Manu* 2.67)! But there are rites of passage for girls in Hindu communities at puberty, though these are not based on the Sanskrit textual tradition of the *śāstras*, but on oral or folk traditions (*laukika*). It is important, as Julia Leslie has pointed out, not to see women in a South Asian context 'merely as the passive victims of an oppressive ideology but also (perhaps primarily) as the active agents of their own positive constructs'.[13]

In a recent study Duvvury has shown how Aiyar women have their own rites of passage, including an apparent equivalent of the *upanayana*. During their first menstruation, girls undergo an initiation (*tirandukuli*) which separates them from childhood. The initiation involves the girl being separated and isolated in a darkened room for three days (though with her friends for company, in the case cited by Duvvury, 1991: 117), and lewd songs being sung by the older women of the community who have high status (*sumaṅgali*). On the fourth day the girl takes a ceremonial bath and a feast is held. She is also taken by her mother to the temple and to visit other households where the older women perform ceremonies (*arati*) for the young girl (Duvvury, 1991: 120–32). The Aiyar girl is then in a 'liminal period' between childhood and motherhood, when she achieves a higher status and becomes 'auspicious' (*sumaṅgali*).

Such women's rites have probably long been a part of the Indian religious scene, but have largely gone unrecorded because of their 'folk' or *laukika* origins. Through these distinct rites of passage, women, says Duvvury, have been able to express their concerns and ambitions, though these are always within the context of a male-dominant social world. Women's concerns have almost always been on the leash of brahmanical orthopraxy. It must be remembered that in the dominant brahmanical ideology, the folk tradition is of lesser significance than the sacred Sanskrit, textual tradition. We have here a number of hierarchical distinctions implied between male/female, Sanskrit tradition (*śāstra*)/folk tradition (*laukika*), Sanskrit language/vernacular languages, and universal law/human convention. Indeed, Duvvury claims that in expressing their concerns and hopes, women are ironically 'reinforcing man-made ideals of women in society', a society which 'continues to define women largely in terms of their functions as mothers and wives' (Duvvury, 1991: 229).

MARRIAGE

Unless a person becomes a renunciate, which may mean joining a monastic order, marriage (*vivāha*) has been the expected norm in Hindu communities. With the marriage *saṃskāra* the high-caste young man enters fully into the householder's life and he can here pursue the human purposes (*puruṣārtha*) of duty (*dharma*), gaining wealth and worldly success (*artha*), and pursuing pleasure, particularly sexual pleasure (*kāma*). For a young Hindu woman, marriage marks an end of her life with her parents and her childhood friends and the beginning of a completely new life with her husband and his family, taking up the duties and expectations of a married woman and, ideally, giving birth to a son, perhaps the primary purpose of a Hindu marriage. Often a marriage ceremony, because of this rift with the past, is emotionally traumatic for a young girl who, indeed, is culturally expected to display some signs of sorrow at leaving her old way of life. Most Hindu girls will desire marriage, as a necessary transition into complete womanhood, but are nevertheless sad to leave their old life and home. Concerning the importance of marriage for the Hindu woman, Duvvury writes:

> For a woman, marriage is a journey to a new locality, status, role, group affiliation and set of relationships, and, above all, it is the only means to motherhood and integration into the world of women as well as into society as a whole. It is also an essential rite through which a woman can reach heaven.
>
> (Duvvury, 1991: 138)

Marriage in Hinduism has a supreme social and religious significance. It theoretically unites families and provides the context in which to rear children, adhering to the religious and social norms appropriate to the particular caste. It also symbolizes basic Hindu concepts such as the union of Śiva and Śakti, the male and female poles of the cosmos (Duvvury, 1991: 139), and expresses at an interpersonal level the Hindu's transpersonal reality.

Marriage has been, and continues to be in the majority of Hindu homes, an arrangement between two families. The overriding concern, expressed in the law books, is not the emotional state of the young couple – whether or not they love each other – but their social status and educational and economic compatibility. Indeed, I have heard it said that a Hindu youth does not marry the girl he loves, but loves the girl he marries. Marriage based on choice due to an affective bond, 'love-marriages' as they are called in India, is still the exception to the rule, even in cities in which there is much Western influence. Such 'love-marriages' are regarded with a certain amount of humour and curiosity, though they are not without precedent in Indian society. There may have been a tradition of noble girls choosing their own husbands in a ritual gathering (*svayamvara*), the most famous instance of which is Damayantī's choice of Nala in the Nala episode in the *Mahābhārata*. Manu, too, in his list of eight kinds of marriage, lists the *gandharva* marriage, in which a couple have sex due to mutual desire (*Manu* 3.32).[14]

Compatibility in terms of caste is the most important factor to be considered in a marriage, though other factors are taken into account such as wealth, occupation and the respective horoscopes of the boy and girl. Manu specifies that families should check the health of the potential bride's family, ensuring that there is no disease, that they do not have hairy bodies(!), and have not abandoned the vedic rites (*Manu* 3.7). Marriage is not taken lightly in Hindu communities, and the families involved are generally eager to ensure a good match, which primarily means the families' social compatibility.

Within caste (*jāti*), marriage is mostly endogamous, yet generally exogamous with regard to kin-group (*gotra*), usually within one village. That is, in rural India, while marrying within a caste, a person will marry outside their village. Manu says that a twice-born man should marry a girl of the same class (*varṇa*) who has the appropriate characteristics (*lakṣana*), by which he means is a virgin and, while being within the caste, is outside of the kin-group or family lineage (*gotra*) (*Manu* 3.4–5).

The social realities of marriage among Hindus are, however, more complex than Manu's prescriptions, and there are many regional differences within India of the relation between marriage and kinship. For example, cross-cousin marriage is desirable in the south among the people who speak Dravidian languages, but is undesirable in the north among the speakers of Indo-Aryan languages (see Dumont, 1980: 111). Another notable exception to caste endogamy is among the Nambuthiri Brahmans of Kerala. Here the oldest son in a family marries a Nambuthiri woman, but the remaining sons maintain alliances with the low-caste Nayar women. The children from these alliances belong to the Nayar caste, living in the house of their mother and mother's brother. Their Brahman father might visit the house, though he would, of course, bring his own food and utensils, for to eat with non-Brahmans, even his 'family', would be polluting (Dumont, 1980: 119).

The marriage *saṃskāra* is the most important rite in a Hindu's life and is an elaborate occasion. The marriage of a daughter, involving as it does the giving of gifts to the bridegroom's family, is an occasion involving great expense and, according to Dumont, is the main cause of debt in rural India, 'so imperative are the dictates of prestige, even for the poor' (Dumont, 1980: 110). A marriage ceremony is an opportunity to display a family's wealth, and it expresses the hierarchical relations between groups, not only between castes, but also between families. In this social hierarchy the bride's family usually have a lower status than the bridegroom's, who, it is almost expected, will criticize the proceedings organized by the bride's father.

The actual process of the marriage *saṃskāra* will vary in different regions to some extent, for marriage ceremonies are a mixture of both vedic and folk elements, though the essentials, such as the couple circumambulating the sacred fire, remain constant. The marriage ceremony itself is quite simple, though the entire wedding may take several days of festivities. The rite takes place in a booth constructed traditionally of banana and mango leaves, and begins with the formal giving away of the bride by her father to the groom and his father. As Duvvury says, in Hindu perception, 'one of the greatest gifts a man can bestow on another is the gift of a virgin daughter in marriage', for which he will obtain good *karman* or merit (*puṇya*) (Duvvury, 1991: 137). Singing songs of blessing follows this ceremony, which in turn is followed by oblations being offered to the sacred fire before which the couple sit. The bride's wrist is tied with a thread and she places her foot three times on the groom's family grinding stone, a gesture which represents fidelity. The couple then take seven steps (*saptapadi*) around the fire, the bride following the groom. The *homa* or making offerings to the sacred fire, which the groom learned at his *upanayana*, is then performed by the groom with his bride. If the ceremony is in the evening, the couple might go out to see the pole star, Dhruva, and the bride will vow to be constant like the pole star. The wedding feast then continues.

Eventually when the proceedings are over, the bride will return to her husband's home to take on her new role in the extended family as wife, daughter-in-law and, probably within a short time, as mother. The birth of a son will give the couple, particularly the woman, high status and they will have truly embarked on the state of the householder, the *gṛhasthāśrama*.

FUNERAL RITES

If a householder does not become a renouncer, then when he dies his body will undergo a funeral. Death, as in most cultures, is inauspicious in Hinduism and a death in the family, as L. A. Babb observes, brings the twofold danger of pollution and a potentially malevolent ghost (Babb, 1975: 90). The last *saṃskāra* attempts to neutralize this pollution and danger by reintegrating the family back into the social context from which they have been momentarily separated, and allowing the spirit of the dead to travel on its way, leaving the family in peace.

While the concerns of bereavement, the neutralizing of death-pollution and the freeing of the spirit from worldly attachments are pan-Hindu concerns, the actual funerary rites vary to some extent in different regions of India and in different castes. Cremation is usual, though among lower castes inhumation takes place and children and holy men are generally not cremated but buried. Indeed, a holy man, having previously undergone his own symbolic funeral at renunciation, might be simply immersed in a river, having transcended his social identity.

A dying person, having received the gift of holy water (preferably from the Ganges), is taken outside the house to die under the open sky. A general pattern of funerary rites is for the corpse to be washed and cremated on the same day as the death. The corpse is bathed, anointed with sandalwood paste, traditionally shaved if male, dressed or wrapped in a cloth, and carried to the cremation ground by male friends and relatives who, in contrast to Western funeral processions, move as quickly as possible, chanting the name of God (e.g., 'Rām'). On the funeral pyre, often by a river in which the ashes may later be immersed, the corpse's feet are directed to the realm of Yama, the god of death, to the south, and the head to the realm of Kubera, Lord of riches, in the north. A pot may be broken by the body's head, symbolizing the release of the soul. According to the law books, from three to five fires, which were the householder's sacred fires, kindle the bier, and the destiny of the deceased can be predicted from which of the fires reaches the body first (*Āśvalāyana Gṛhya-sūtra* 4.4.1–5). The remains of the body are gathered up between three to ten days after the funeral and either buried or immersed in a river, preferably the holy Ganges (Babb, 1975: 93ff.; Pandey, 1969: 234–63).

In the days immediately following a death, the family are polluted. This pollution lasts for a varying period of time during which *śraddha* ceremonies are performed. These are offerings of rice balls to the deceased in order to construct and feed its body in the afterlife. This body is complete ten days later and the family are released from the most dangerous death-pollution. Between thirteen days and a year after death, the final offering of rice balls (*piṇḍa*) is made at the *sapiṇḍikaraṇa* rite. Significantly, ten days elapse between death and the final formation of the *preta* body, which, Knipe observes, recapitulates the ten lunar months of the embryo's gestation.[15] The final *sapiṇḍikaraṇa* rite at the end of the life-cycle rituals can therefore be seen to be homologous with the birth rite at the beginning of life. Once the *sapiṇḍikaraṇa* is completed, the deceased is released from the intermediate world of the 'ghosts' (*pretaloka*) to the realm of the ancestors (*pitṛloka*).[16] The cycle of rites of passage is thus completed.

Sanskritization and the *saṃskāra*s

The *saṃskāra*s have performed, and continue to perform, a number of functions within Hindu society. They not only mark off critical transition points in a human biography, which may correspond to times of biological and psychological crisis and change (at birth, puberty and death, for example), but they also reflect Hindu systems of symbolic classification and so are about establishing Hindu value systems and a system of social acceptance and exclusion. Through the *saṃskāra*s a person becomes familiar with the social status of different actors, his or her own place in the community, and the regulation of gender roles.

Although there are regional variations, the *saṃskāra*s reflect the extraordinary success of the dominant brahmanical ideology, which permeates nearly all levels of social life. This process whereby the brahmanical ideology of *dharma* becomes the central guiding force in many people's lives is known as Sanskritization: the process whereby rituals, deities and ideas contained in orthodox Sanskrit treatises become assimilated by local, folk traditions. The *saṃskāra*s are derived from this literature and reflect brahmanical values which are implicitly accepted by the Hindu through participating in these rites, particularly in so far as they distinguish between purity and impurity. For example, the birth *saṃskāra*, through highlighting the distinction between purity and impurity, conveys a message about hierarchical gender relations and status. The ideal child is male and the father performs rites upon his wife; that is, although she gives birth, she has a minimal ritual function. The *saṃskāra*s also establish brahmanical values through the exclusion of lower castes (the non-twice-born), who are too impure to perform them, except for the marriage *saṃskāra* which is open to all. Through marriage, the entrance to the householder's life, even the lower castes are brought within the sphere of brahmanical influence and implicit acceptance of its value system. Indeed, to perform one *saṃskāra* is to adhere implicitly to the total ritual cycle, even though one might be excluded from particular rites because of caste or gender.

The Hindu rites of passage therefore contain implicit ideas about the nature of human life, social structure and destiny as represented in the ideal of *dharma*, with its double focus of performing one's correct caste duty and adhering to behaviour appropriate to one's stage of life. They underline social difference and emphasize the distinction of some groups from others, of the dominant groups from the subordinate ones.

With the funeral *saṃskāra* the cycle of Hindu rites of passage is at an end. Although the system of *saṃskāra*s is total and complete in itself, there are nevertheless other occasional rituals which a Hindu might perform. These are the ritual of renunciation (*saṃnyāsa*), the last stage of life, and optional sectarian initiations (*dīkṣā*) as a householder or renouncer.

As we have seen, there is a distinction within Hinduism between, on the one hand, liberation and, on the other, the householder's life in the world. The *saṃskāra*s are concerned exclusively with the latter. They are not conducive to liberation and are of social and dharmic significance only. By contrast, renunciation and sectarian initiation are generally for the purpose of eventual liberation.

Sectarian initiation

Rites of passage are not concerned with liberation. As we noted at the beginning of this chapter, the worlds of salvation and social transaction are clearly distinct. As a householder, the Hindu is concerned mainly with the maintenance of caste boundaries, the maintaining of the sacred fires and the performance of the *saṃskāra*s. Unlike the renouncer, he is not generally concerned with the path to salvation. However, should the householder aspire towards liberation, there are sectarian initiations which claim to lead to that goal. Sectarian initiations are open both to the householder and to the renouncer. Such initiations are not part of the normative Hindu rites of passage but can function in a similar way, giving a person access to traditions and teachings which were previously closed to him. An example can be given from Śaivism.

In Śaiva Siddhānta, a Hindu tradition flourishing particularly in South India, centred on the worship of the deity Śiva in his form as

Sadāśiva, there are essentially two initiations: into the tradition and into liberation. The initiation into the tradition, the *samaya-dīkṣā*, gives access to the cult of Śiva, bestowing on the initiate, who becomes a 'son of Śiva' or *putraka*, the right to hear certain texts, and requiring him to perform certain daily obligatory rituals. This initiation might at some time be followed by the *nirvāṇa-dīkṣā* which gives access to liberation. After this rite the initiate will perform obligatory daily rituals until death, when he will be liberated by the grace of Śiva.

Renunciation

Not technically a rite of passage, renunciation, the last of the Hindu stages of life (*āśrama*), is such an important institution within Hinduism that it needs to be mentioned here. The ritual of renunciation is undoubtedly a 'process' between two distinct 'states', which marks the boundary between the condition of caste member with legal and moral obligations, and the condition of castelessness, traditionally beyond legal obligations. The renouncer is in some ways therefore akin to the non-twice-born Hindu, for renunciation entails going beyond caste and renouncing social obligation in order to achieve, eventually, salvation or freedom (*mokṣa*). The householder is clearly a social being, with defined duties and responsibilities, while the renouncer is not a social being in the same sense, having no obligations to family and caste, though he nevertheless depends upon the community for his livelihood, gives teachings and perhaps lives in a monastic community.

As has been noted by a number of scholars (e.g., Dumont, 1980), there is a tension between the ideals of renunciation in which the ascetic feels disgust for the world and cultivates detachment, and those of the householder who cultivates the goals (*artha*) of duty, worldly success and pleasure. Rites of passage in the sense of the *saṃskāra*s might therefore be seen as essentially life-affirming, while the rite and institution of renunciation is essentially life-denying. This can be seen in texts on renunciation which describe the ritual act, such as the *Treatise on World Renunciation* which even advocates suicide by, among other means, starvation in order to be free from the suffering of the world.[17] This text describes how the renouncer should deposit the sacrificial fires, which he has kept all his life as a householder, within himself, discard or burn the sacrificial thread, shave his head and take up the minimal possessions of the renunciate.

What is of interest here is that the ritual of renunciation, the liminal phase between two socially defined states, is almost the reverse of the *upanayana* ceremony. The renouncer is, as it were, undoing the adult caste identity imposed upon him through that rite as a boy or young man. The ritual of renunciation can be contrasted therefore with the *saṃskāras* as a whole and the *upanayana* in particular. As the *upanayana* excludes certain groups of people and makes a statement about identity within a hierarchical social structure, so the rite of renunciation draws a clear line between those within the dharmic realm, and so within the realm of *saṃskāra*, and those who are, symbolically at least, beyond that world on their way to liberation. The Hindu rites of passage say as much about human nature and destiny by what is excluded from them as by what is included. Their primary concern is the world of human transaction, the relation between social groups and genders, and providing the expression of an ethical resource for Hindu householders. The realm of salvation is not their concern, though that realm, the realm of the world-renouncer, derives its meaning only because of those worldly concerns. The *saṃskāras* are as important for what they say by excluding certain groups and ideas, as for what they include. Yet ultimately the *saṃskāras* and what they represent must, in the dominant Hindu ideology, be eventually left behind. In the householder/renouncer distinction, the renouncer is ultimately superior to the householder, because he is indifferent to the phenomenal universe and is fulfilling life's highest purpose, its transcendence. Yet the householder's world-affirmation through the system of the *saṃskāras* is the social foundation of this ideology which is its own negation: the 'inner conflict' of the tradition[18] which has produced such creative tension within Hinduism and throughout the history of South Asia.

Notes

1 C. Bell (1992) *Ritual Theory, Ritual Practice*. New York: Oxford University Press, pp. 69–71.

2 A. Piatigorsky (1985) 'Some phenomenological observations on the study of Indian religions' in R. Burghardt and A. Cantille (eds) *Indian Religion*. London: Curzon Press, pp. 215–17.

3 See R. Gombrich (1988) *Theravada Buddhism*. London and New York: Routledge and Kegan Paul, pp. 25–7.

4 P. Bourdieu (1992) *Language and Symbolic Power*. Cambridge: Polity Press, ch. 4.
5 See J. B. Carman and F. A. Marglin (eds) (1985) *Purity and Auspiciousness in Indian Society*. Leiden: Brill.
6 R. A. Rappaport (1992) 'Ritual, time and eternity', *Zygon* 27(1), p. 7.
7 D. M. Levin (1985) *The Body's Recollection of Being*. London: Routledge, pp. 180ff.
8 Rappaport, op. cit., p. 7.
9 See J. Gonda (1985) 'The number sixteen' in *Change and Continuity in Indian Religion*. Delhi: Munshiram Manoharlal.
10 See Bourdieu, op. cit., p. 117.
11 Ibid., p. 118.
12 The Gāyatrī mantra, named after its metre, the *gāyatrī*, from the *Ṛg-veda* (3.62.10), is:

Om. bhūr, bhuva, sva,
tat savitur varenyam
bhargo devasya dhīmahi
Dhiyo yo naḥ pracodayāt.

(Om, earth, atmosphere, sky. May we contemplate the desirable light of the god Savitṛ. May he inspire our thoughts.)

13 J. Leslie (1991) *Roles and Rituals for Hindu Women*. London: Pinter Publishers, p. 1.
14 Manu gives accounts of eight kinds of marriage and the various punishments for marrying outside of class prescriptions, yet at the same time allows for some variation and human weakness. For example, the text says both that a Brahman can marry a *śūdra* and that a Brahman cannot marry a *śūdra* (3.13–16). The ideal is the high-caste arranged marriage, but there are some circumstances in which different kinds of 'marriage' are appropriate, while some kinds of marriage are always to be condemned. The eight kinds of marriage are named after Brahmā, the gods (*daiva*), the sages (*ṛṣayaḥ*), the Lord of Creatures, the demons (*asurāḥ*), the heavenly musicians (*gandharvāḥ*), ogres (*rākṣasāḥ*), and the ghouls (*paiśācāḥ*). Of these, the first six pertain to the Brahman, the last four to the ruler and the last three to the commoner (*Manu* 3.21–23). The first four describe different ways of the father giving away his daughter as a bride, the demonic law refers to a man who wants a girl out of desire and gives much wealth to her relatives, the *gandharva* marriage is simply a girl and her lover uniting out of desire for each other, and the ghoulish marriage is a man having sex with a girl who is asleep, drunk or mad (*Manu* 3.27–34).
15 D. Knipe (1977) 'Sapiṇḍikaraṇa: the Hindu rite of entry into heaven' in E.

Reynolds and F. E. Waugh, *Religious Encounters with Death*. University Park: Pennsylvania State University Press.

16 J. Bowker (1991) *The Meanings of Death*. Cambridge: Cambridge University Press, pp. 149–51. The idea of the deceased going to the realm of the ancestors after death seems at one level to contradict the idea of reincarnation. Although there seems to be no cognitive dissonance experienced by Hindus in this matter (some say that a soul is reborn from the realm of the ancestors), it perhaps indicates the autonomy of the ancient ritual realm, in contrast to a comparatively more recent ideology of reincarnation. See Wendy O'Flaherty (ed.) (1980) *Karma and Rebirth in Classical Indian Traditions*. Berkeley: University of California Press, pp. xviii–xx, 3–37.

17 P. Olivelle (1977) *Vāsudevāśrama Yatidharmaprakāśa: A Treatise on World Renunciation*. 2 vols; Vienna: Publications of the De Nobili Research Library, pp. 96–8.

18 See P. Olivelle (1992) *The Saṃnyāsa Upaniṣads*. Oxford: Oxford University Press, pp. 19–23; J. C. Heesterman (1985) *The Inner Conflict of Tradition: Essays in Indian Ritual, Kingship and Tradition*. Chicago: Chicago University Press.

Further reading

Babb, L. A. (1975) *The Divine Hierarchy*. New York and Oxford: Columbia University Press.

Buhler, G. (1987) *The Sacred Laws of the Aryans*. Delhi: AVF Books.

Dumont, L. (1980) *Homo Hierarchicus*. Chicago: University of Chicago Press.

Duvvury, V. K. (1991) *Play, Symbolism and Ritual: A Study of Tamil Brahmin Women's Rites of Passage*. New York: Peter Lang.

Fuller, C. (1992) *The Camphor Flame: Popular Hinduism and Society in India*. Princeton, NJ: Princeton University Press.

Guha, R. and Spivak, G. (1988) *Selected Subaltern Studies*. New York and Oxford: Oxford University Press.

Madan, T. N. (1987) *Non-Renunciation*. Delhi: Oxford University Press.

O'Flaherty, W. (1991) *The Laws of Manu*. Harmondsworth: Penguin.

Pandey, R. (1969) *Hindu Saṃskāras*. Delhi: MLBD.

Stevenson, S. (1920) *The Rites of the Twice Born*. London: Oxford University Press.

Index

17127203R00153

Made in the USA
Lexington, KY
27 August 2012